Weaving and Dyeing in Highland Ecuador

Weaving and Dyeing in Highland Ecuador

ANN POLLARD ROWE, LAURA M. MILLER,
AND LYNN A. MEISCH
EDITED BY ANN POLLARD ROWE

University of Texas Press ⟡ *Austin*

First edition, 2007

Requests for permission to reproduce material from this work should be sent to:
Permissions
University of Texas Press
P.O. Box 7819
Austin, TX 78713-7819
www.utexas.edu/utpress/about/bpermission.html

♾ The paper used in this book meets the minimum requirements of
ANSI/NISO Z39.48-1992 (R1997) (Permanence of Paper).

Library of Congress Cataloging-in-Publication Data

Rowe, Ann P.
Weaving and dyeing in highland Ecuador / Ann Pollard Rowe, Laura M. Miller,
and Lynn A. Meisch ; edited by Ann Pollard Rowe. — 1st ed.
   p.   cm.
Includes bibliographical references and index.
ISBN-13: 978-0-292-71468-7 (cloth : alk. paper)
ISBN-10: 0-292-71468-8 (cloth : alk. paper)
1. Indian textile fabrics — Ecuador.   2. Dyes and dyeing — Textile fibers.
3. Handweaving — Ecuador — Patterns.   4. Dye plants — Ecuador.   5. Ecuador —
Social life and customs.   I. Miller, Laura M., 1961–   II. Meisch, Lynn, 1945–
III. Title.
F3721.3.T47R69 2007
986.6 — dc22
2006017297

To the weavers of Ecuador, past and present

Contents

Preface

This book describes the local hand-weaving and dyeing technology used to produce the clothing worn by indigenous people in highland Ecuador, as recorded in the late 1970s and the 1980s. Although some indigenous clothing was by then factory made, hand weaving was still used to produce at least some items, especially belts and ponchos. The focus is primarily on weaving on the backstrap loom, which is a major pre-Hispanic technology, although some information on treadle-loom weaving, which is of Spanish colonial origin, is also included. In the natural dye technologies, indigenous and European elements have been inextricably blended, but the indigenous elements are significant. In most cases, the work is done by the indigenous people themselves, but in others it is done by people who do not identify as indigenous.

In Euro-American culture, textile technology has become so industrialized that it is all but invisible and consequently tends to be taken for granted. Moreover, textile handwork has become marginalized because it is associated mainly with women's hobbies. It therefore needs to be emphasized that hand textile technology is far from being either taken for granted or marginalized in other cultures. If we wish to genuinely understand other cultures, it is necessary to take notice of the things that are important within those cultures' own context. Indeed, although we naturally do not wish to denigrate women's work, it is true that weaving is predominantly men's work in highland Ecuador, and, rather than being a hobby, it is a subsistence or a commercial activity. It also represents a significant indigenous body of knowledge and creative outlet, as well as providing a prominent ethnic marker that still has value among indigenous people. As such, it can offer a key to the understanding of many other aspects of such a culture.

Additionally, hand textile technology is subject to an enormous number of variables and is therefore highly sensitive to cultural influences of all kinds. It enables us to see not only the present but also the past. Distinguishing indigenous and Spanish techniques is only the beginning. We can also identify Inca and provincial Inca influences (Chapter 7), as well as amalgams of indigenous and Spanish concepts that are reflected in the social structure (Chapters 2 and 3). It appears that words from some of the long-vanished indigenous languages may survive in some of the local technical terms (Chapter 1). Tracing such terms and other technical features can also reveal pre-Inca ethnic boundaries or later migrations. Although European hand textile technology is, of course, understood in general terms, the variations characteristic of rural Spain during the period of its empire are poorly documented, so these Ecuadorian techniques shed some light on this subject too.

While painting, sculpture, and architecture have been the most prestigious media for visual artistic expression in recent times in the European tradition, these media have tended to be less developed in the Andes, where the highest technical and iconographic development instead took place in the media of textiles and ceramics. Textiles have been a major art form among Andean peoples from remote prehistory up to the present time. Just as the more one understands about the structure of music the more one can appreciate the works of Mozart, it is true that the more one understands about Andean textile technology, the better one can appreciate the great works of art it has produced. Although the people who produced the textiles of the pre-Hispanic period are gone, their modern descendants have preserved many of their technologies and habits of mind. Thus, by studying the surviving technologies we can come closer to understanding not only the present-day works of art but also how the great textiles of the past were created. Even if relatively few of the Ecuadorian textiles are themselves artistic masterworks, we not only can gain insight into ancient techniques but also can watch technical innovation happening.

This volume is part of a larger project that documents the indigenous costume of highland Ecuador. A companion book, *Costume and Identity in Highland Ecuador,* was published by The Textile Museum and the University of Washington Press in 1998. For purely economic reasons, information on additional hand textile technologies, including spinning, processing of leaf fibers, embroidery, felt and plaited ("Panama") hat making, and coastal shellfish dyeing, was published in *The Textile Museum Journal* in 2005. A third volume, on the historical development of the costumes, is still in manuscript form. While I have tried to keep the contents of these volumes as distinct as possible, a small amount of introductory information is repeated so that each can be read independently. Readers familiar with the earlier book may therefore wish to skip the Introduction here.

The text, although detailed enough, in many cases, to enable a reader to reproduce the processes, nevertheless does not presuppose any previous knowledge of textiles. All specialized terms are carefully explained and illustrated on first use. A glossary, primarily of the English terms that are used more than once in the text, is also provided.

As mentioned, most of the field data reported here were gathered during the late 1970s and the 1980s. The precise dates are given in the text and notes to each section. Change has been occurring very rapidly. As recently as the 1960s, most indigenous clothing was still handwoven, but by the time of our fieldwork that was no longer the case. Some of the techniques we recorded were clearly in the process of dying out. Therefore, in cases where we have only partial information, we include it anyway, both to make it available to others and to highlight the need for further work. This book has had a long gestation, and, unfortunately, we are unable to provide updates on current conditions except as specifically noted. The descriptions of weaving and dyeing nevertheless remain in the present tense, which still seems appropriate for field-recorded processes.

Although there is no single self-referential term used uniformly by all of Ecuador's indigenous groups, *indígena* (Spanish for "indigenous person") is currently the most common and accepted designation. It is employed by the national indigenous federation CONAIE (Confederación de Nacionalidades Indígenas del Ecuador), so we will follow their lead. Since our text is in English, however, we usually translate the term as "indigenous person." Although the term *Indian* is often used in North America, *indio* has acquired insulting connotations in South America. Since it is, in any case, a misnomer, we prefer to avoid it.

Orthography

Many highland indigenous people speak the Inca language, called Quichua in Ecuador and known to indigenous people as *runa shimi*, the people's language, or *Inka shimi*. What orthography to use in transcribing local terms is a difficult question because writing is recent, and there are three dialects with different pronunciations in Ecuador alone. Pronunciation in Ecuador also differs from that in the Cuzco area of Peru in having softer consonants and no sounds from the back of the throat. In this book, we have used different orthographic systems depending on the type of word in question. Thus, in order to make them as familiar as possible to residents of and travelers in Ecuador, we have spelled most place names as they appear on the maps of the Instituto Geográfico Militar, even though these maps are not consistent. Our informants' names are spelled as they prefer whenever possible.

In order to make the text as clear as possible, we describe all processes and tools using English textile terms. The local terms are interesting, however, and so are given parenthetically. Since the local terms are highly variable from one place to another, any given local term should be understood to have been recorded in the place under discussion and only to be valid for that particular place. The terms are a mixture of Spanish, Quichua, and pre-Inca words. We use the abbreviations Q. for Quichua and S. for Spanish to identify word derivations. In those cases where we could not determine the origin of the term, which may therefore reflect derivation from an otherwise lost indigenous language, no abbreviation is used. Even Spanish terms may not be in the form in which they appear in the dictionary and may be variable from place to place. In some cases, a Quichua word is used with a Spanish suffix, or a Spanish word with Quichua pronunciation or suffix. The terms are given only in the singular, even when the sentence uses an English or Spanish plural. (The Quichua plural is -*kuna*.) These terms are not included in the glossary, since they are always cited with their English equivalent.

The modern Quichua terms have been spelled according to the system suggested by linguist Regina Harrison (1989: xvi), which she arrived at in consultation with the late Lawrence Carpenter. Unlike her, however, we are not trying to present a composite of the different Ecuadorian dialects, but rather to represent the regional differences as best we can, despite not being linguists ourselves. For example, we differentiate between *ñajcha* (comb) in Imbabura province and in the Saraguro area, and *ñakcha* in Tungurahua province (Quero) and Chimborazo province (Cacha). The Spanish-language sound written "ll," and pronounced as "y," as in "yes," in southern Ecuador and in other Spanish-speaking countries is pronounced "zh" (like a French *j*) in northern and central highland Ecuador. The same sound change occurs in Quichua. For Spanish words, we write it as "ll" regardless, in order to make them familiar to Spanish-speaking readers. The Quichua words are also spelled "ll," in order to clarify the relationship, but the actual pronunciation is usually also given.

Maps and Photographs

We have attempted to include on the maps as many as possible of the places mentioned in the text. Some communities could not be located on any of the maps currently available to us, however, and in most cases we have omitted them rather than insert them in only an approximate location. We have tried to provide a general description of the location of such places in the text. In other cases, neighboring communities would not all fit on the scale of the maps used. Again, the approximate location is indicated in the text.

When the photograph credit reads, "Photo by . . . ," the photograph was produced from a black-and-white negative. When it reads, "Slide by . . . ," the photograph was produced by converting a color slide to black and white.

Acknowledgments

In any project of this kind, we researchers are wholly dependent on the hospitality of the people whose lifeways we want to record. In this regard, we wish to express our great appreciation to all those who explained their costume and dyeing, spinning, and weaving traditions to us, shared meals, and otherwise made us welcome. Those who provided data presented in this book are mentioned by name in the appropriate places, but here we would like to say thank you to everyone involved in this monumental project.

Lynn Meisch's initial work in southern Ecuador in 1977–1979 was funded by Fulbright-Hays, with a grant toward film expenses from the Institute for Intercultural Studies. She also worked under the United States Agency for International Development as a textile consultant in Otavalo from September 1985 to July 1986 in a project requested by local weavers. From October 1992 through January 1995, she conducted dissertation fieldwork in Ecuador on transnational contacts and indigenous ethnic identity, some of which overlapped with work on this book. Her dissertation research funds were provided by Stanford University's Institute for International Studies, the Wenner-Gren Foundation for Anthropological Research (Predoctoral Grant No. 5483), and the National Science Foundation (Doctoral Dissertation Grant No. NSF DBS-9216489).

Laura Miller's initial work in Ecuador in 1984–1986 was also supported by a Fulbright Fellowship. Meisch and Miller also received assistance in the summer of 1988 from the Bead Society of Los Angeles. Ann Rowe's first visit to Ecuador, in 1986, was supported by a grant from the Organization of American States.

When this project was in the planning stages, Margaret McLean, then-director of the Center for Field Research (the field research arm of Earthwatch), suggested to Meisch and Miller that the project was suitable for

Earthwatch funding. We thank her for her suggestion and support, which re-sulted in our fielding a total of six Earthwatch teams in Ecuador during the summers of 1988 and 1989.

The money used in Earthwatch projects comes from volunteers who also provide their labor to assist in the work. Volunteers who recorded data that appear in this book are credited in the notes and photograph captions, but this list acknowledges the financial support of all team members.

The volunteers in team 1 in 1988, based in Latacunga, Cotopaxi province, were Stephanie M. Burns, George W. Crockett, Patricia Grooms, Ellen R. Hanley, Carol J. Holmes, William H. Holmes, Constance Kenney, Marjorie Klockars, Sara Laas, Pamela Y. Lipscomb, Bonnie O'Connor, and Darby C. Raiser.

Volunteers in team 2 in 1988, based in Ambato, Tungurahua province, were Helen Daly, Betty L. Davenport, CJ Elfont, Edna A. Elfont, Dayna M. Elfont, Helen Evelev, Leonard Evelev, Marjorie Hirschkind, Carol Mitz, Sheila F. Morris, Maritza Mosquera, Norma Jean Nelson, Adelle M. P. Pol-lock, and Roberta Siegel.

Volunteers in team 3 in 1988, based in Riobamba, Chimborazo prov-ince, were Dianne B. Barske, Barbara U. Buech, Jean V. Fuley, Jean L. Hay-den, Edward Healy, Helen Healy, Judith A. Kelly, Renate Kempf, Kath-leen A. Jahnke, Emily M. Marsland, Ellen T. McQueary, Lorraine S. O'Neal, Robyn J. Potter, and Louise Taylor.

Volunteers in team 1 in 1989, which worked mainly in the eastern Imbabura area, consisted of Monique Andre, Gayle Bauer, Barbara Johnson Borders, Bettye Dennison, Elizabeth S. Drey, Nancy A. Fleming, Iris Garrelfs, Leslie Grace, Eileen Hallman, Patricia (Patt) C. Hill, Jennifer Lantz, Joy Mullett, and Linda L. Ruby. Leslie Grace had visited Lynn Meisch in Ecuador in 1978, and first suggested to Meisch the idea of studying and collecting complete costume.

Volunteers for team 2 in 1989, which was based in Riobamba, were Jean Dayton, Jack M. DeLong, Mary Ewing, C. Robert Foss, Celia S. Foss, Bee Henisey, Ken Henisey, Sandra Lewis, Kevin G. O'Brien, Suzanne Powell, Naeda B. Robinson, Carol Siegel, and AlJean D. Thompson.

Volunteers for team 3 in 1989, also based in Riobamba, were Sandra Baker, M. Catherine (Kate) Beamer, Lari Drendell, Jacquelyn Engle, Cynthia M. Ferguson, Louise Hainline, Kirby T. Hall, Margaret E. Jacobs, William I. Mead, Patricia L. Meloy, Mary C. Shook, and Nancy C. Tucker.

Earthwatch also provided funds to cover the expenses and honoraria for local assistants. Our assistant for teams 1 and 2 for both summers was Bree-nan Conterón, an Otavalo woman from Ilumán, who made a particularly significant contribution to our work. Chuck Kleymeyer of the Inter-American Foundation in Arlington, Virginia, put us in touch with Carlos Moreno of COMUNIDEC in Quito. Carlos's background as an adult-literacy instructor in Chimborazo province opened innumerable doors for us. In addition, his sons became valuable research assistants to our Earthwatch teams: Fernando Moreno Arteaga for team 3 in 1988, and Carlos Moreno Arteaga for teams 2 and 3 in 1989. Julio Chérrez S. also provided assistance to team 3 in 1989.

Several other people also participated in the Earthwatch research. Mrill Ingram, then of the Earthwatch staff, joined team 1 in 1988 to cover the project for the Earthwatch magazine but she also participated in our research. Her airfare was donated by Ecuatoriana Airlines. María Aguí, a filmmaker, joined team 2 in 1988. Dr. Lawrence K. Carpenter, a linguist at the University of North Florida in Jacksonville, was a visiting scientist for teams 2 and 3 in 1988 and team 2 in 1989. Although he contributed to the team research reports in 1988, his untimely death in 1990 prevented his further contribution to the project. Ann Rowe participated in team 2 and part of the duration of team 3 in 1988, as well as team 1 in 1989.

Other people in Ecuador were very helpful during the Earthwatch research. The late Olaf Holm, director of the Museo Antropológico del Banco Central in Guayaquil, wrote to the Instituto Nacional del Patrimonio Cultural in Quito on behalf of the project. We are also grateful to Gail Felzein, a Peace Corps volunteer based in Ambato, who in 1988 introduced us to invaluable contacts throughout Tungurahua province. Among these, Gonzalo Hallo, adult-literacy instructor with the Dirección Provincial de Educación, helped us with introductions to the Chibuleo community. Sylvia Forman, an anthropologist with the University of Massachusetts in Amherst, helped us by giving us the names of her friends in Majipamba and by her enthusiasm for the project. She generously bequeathed her Ecuadorian textiles to The Textile Museum on her untimely death in 1992. In Chimborazo province, Sra. Marta Borja of the Hacienda Gustús Grande was also helpful.

People in Quito who provided particularly valuable assistance were Costanza Di Capua, Ernesto Salazar, Myriam Salazar, Jill Ortman, and John Ortman of La Bodega Artesanías and Centro Artesanal. We would also like to thank the staff of the Fulbright Commission, especially the director, Gonzalo Cartagenova, and Helena Saona, Jenny de Castillo, María Mogollón, and María Eugenia Freile, as well as the late Presley Norton of the Programa para Antropología en el Ecuador.

Since 1977 many staff members of CIDAP (Centro Interamericano de Artesanías y Artes Populares) in Cuenca have gone out of their way to help our research, including the director, Claudio Malo González, and librarian Betti

Sojos, as well as Diana Sojos de Peña, Ana Francisca Ugalde, René Cardoso, and Blanca Inguíñez.

In Otavalo, Margaret (Peg) Goodhart and Frank Kiefer, former restaurant owners and then proprietors of the Hotel Ali Shungu, and Guillermo Cobos and Lala Gallegos of the Residencial El Rocío, fed our Earthwatch teams and were helpful in innumerable ways. Staff members of the Instituto Otavaleño de Antropología went out of their way to be helpful to us, especially Edwin Narváez Rivadeneira, the general director, and Hernán Jaramillo Cisneros, investigator and director of the journal *Sarance*. We would also like to thank Mariana Long, Matt Long, and Shannon Waits-Escobar, who hand carried film and manuscript chapters between Ecuador and the United States.

At The Textile Museum, the support of the Latin American Research Fund, a generous gift of the late Marion Stirling Pugh and the late Maj. Gen. John Ramsey Pugh, was critical. The fund supported the acquisition of the museum's collection of Ecuadorian textiles, some of which is illustrated here, paid Ann Rowe's travel expenses in 1988 and 1989, and made possible several aspects of the preparation of this book.

Photography of The Textile Museum's Ecuadorian collection was funded by a grant from the National Endowment for the Arts. This work was ably coordinated by Christine Norling of The Textile Museum staff, and the excellent photographs were taken by Franko Khoury. Additional photographic sessions and processing were coordinated by Christine's helpful successors, Amy Ward and Anne Weigant. The maps, based on my pencil sketches, were drawn on computer by Laurie McCarriar. I also greatly appreciate the help of Vuka Roussakis at the American Museum of Natural History, Kaye Spilker at the Los Angeles County Museum of Art, and Lucy Fowler Williams at the University of Pennsylvania Museum for making objects in their care available to me and assisting with obtaining the photographs and permissions.

I am also grateful for the support of Ursula E. McCracken, director of The Textile Museum until 2004, even when the project took far longer than planned. I would like to extend my thanks also to the Board of Trustees and the staff of The Textile Museum for their encouragement throughout. Their support was practical as well as verbal, since many staff members took on extra projects, particularly exhibitions, in order to free my time for writing and editing. I also thank interim director Carma Fauntleroy and incoming director Daniel Walker for their continuing support of the project.

Considerable editing of many of the sections in this book proved necessary in order to create a coherent volume, and I appreciate the authors' willingness to adapt to this situation. Additionally, I am grateful to the late Ed Franquemont for reading an earlier version of the manuscript and making many helpful suggestions for copyediting and condensing it. Frank Salomon provided very helpful last-minute assistance with the orthography but should not be held responsible for any remaining errors. It is a pleasure also to thank Theresa May, assistant director and editor-in-chief at the University of Texas Press, as well as the two reviewers, for their enthusiastic support of the manuscript.

Ann P. Rowe
Washington, DC
July 2005

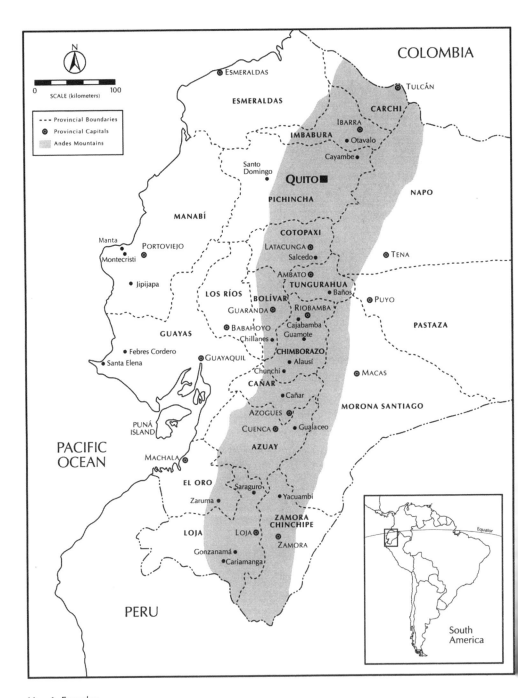

Map 1. Ecuador.

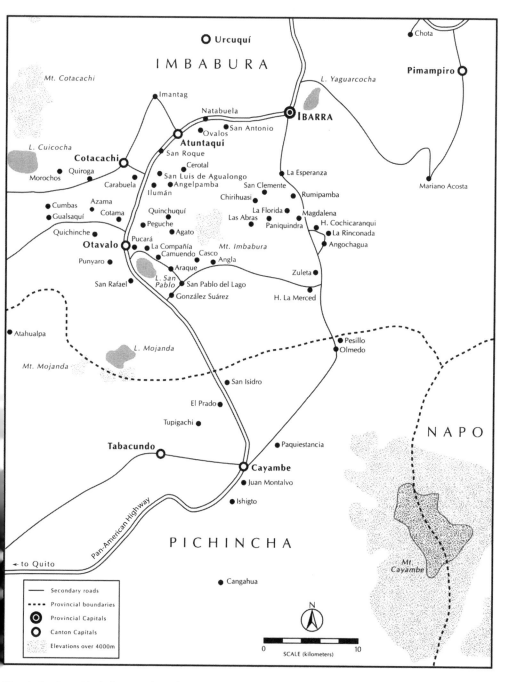

Map 2. Southeast Imbabura and northeast Pichincha provinces.

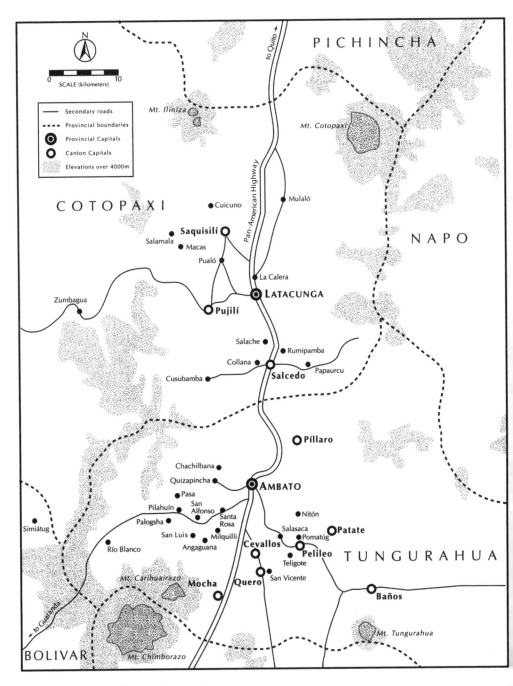

Map 3. Cotopaxi and Tungurahua provinces.

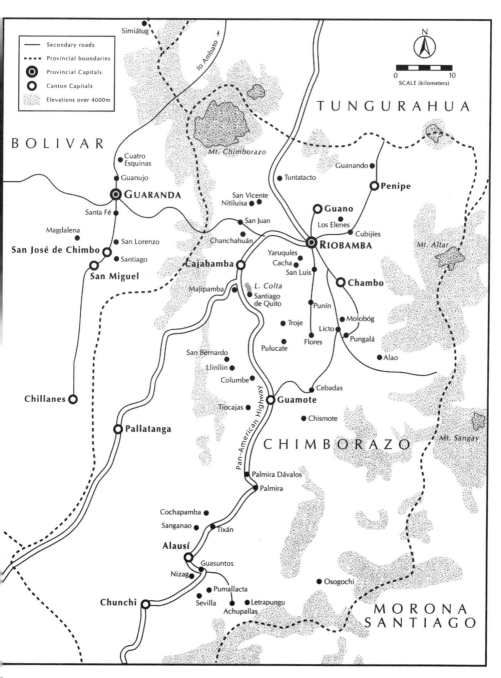

Map 4. Chimborazo and Bolivar provinces.

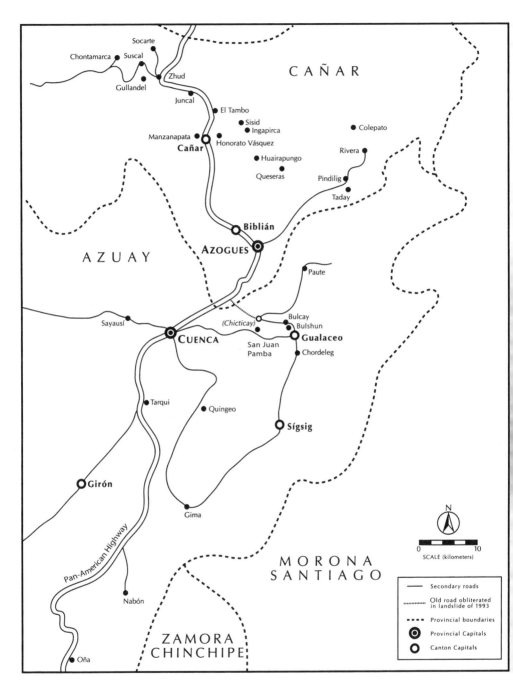

Map 5. Cañar and Azuay provinces.

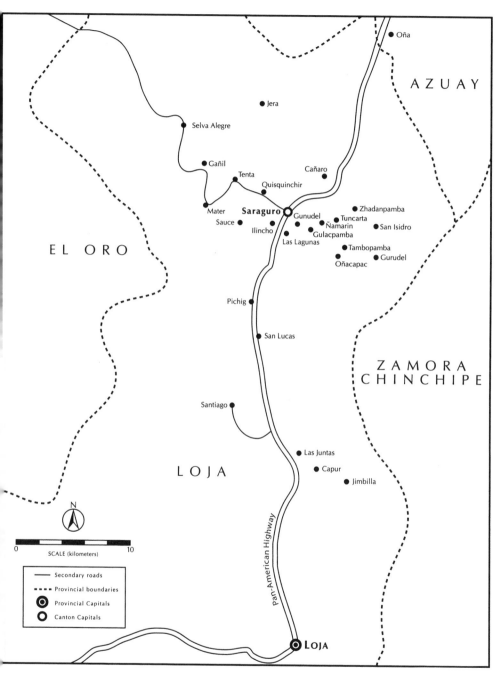

Map 6. Northern Loja province.

Weaving and Dyeing in Highland Ecuador

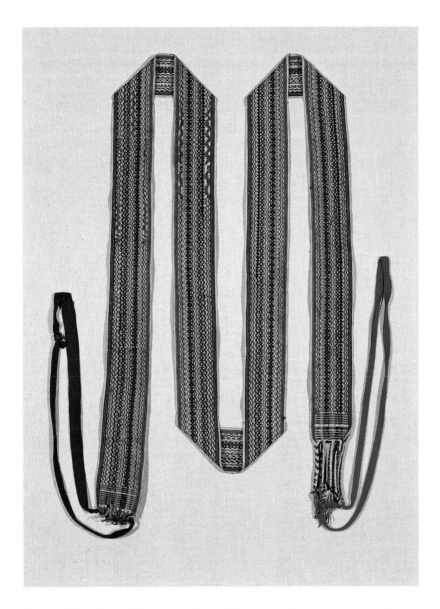

Plate 1. Belt of the *frutilla* style in cotton plain weave, with acrylic supplementary-warp patterning. Salasaca, Tungurahua province. 2.48 x .06 meters (8 feet 1 1/2 inches x 2 3/8 inches), excluding ties. The Textile Museum 1988.19.82, Latin American Research Fund.

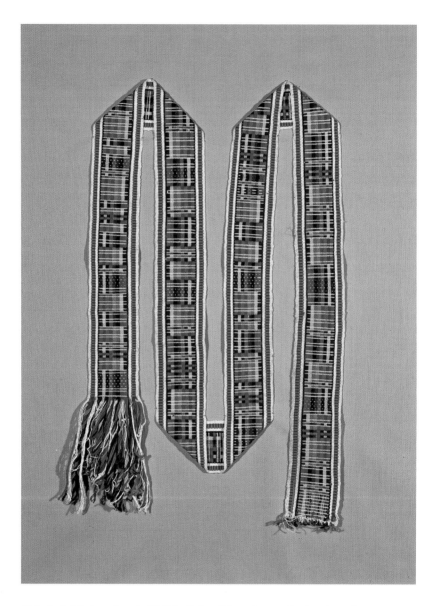

Plate 2. Belt in turn-banded 2/1 twill, in white cotton and colored acrylic yarns. Woven by Santiago Sula Sisa, Nitiluisa, central Chimborazo province. 2.64 x .078 meters (8 feet 8 inches x 3 inches). The Textile Museum 1989.22.80, Latin American Research Fund.

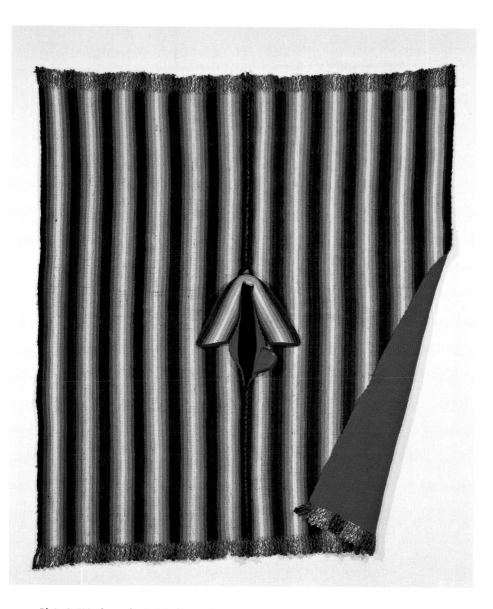

Plate 3. Wool poncho in 2/1 herringbone complementary-warp weave and different colors on the two sides. Probably woven in Carabuela; bought in the Otavalo market, Imbabura province. 1.51 x 1.33 meters (59 1/2 x 52 3/8 inches), including fringe. The Textile Museum, 1988.19.37, Latin American Research Fund.

Plate 4. Details of two wool *kawiña* belts, Chimborazo province, and two acrylic *banderilla* belts, eastern Imbabura province, in 3/1 alternating complementary-warp weave with 2/2 horizontal color change. Widths: 4–7.5 centimeters (1 1/2–3 inches). The Textile Museum 1988.19.108, 1987.20.3, 1989.22.19, 1989.22.30, Latin American Research Fund.

Plate 5. Detail of a Peruvian textile, possibly a small poncho, probably from the south highlands, period of the Inca empire (1460–1532). Stripes in warp-faced plain weave and in 3/1 alternating complementary-warp weave with 2/2 horizontal color change, of camelid hair. Los Angeles County Museum of Art M.75.50.15, Costume Council Fund. Photograph ©2005 Museum Associates/LACMA.

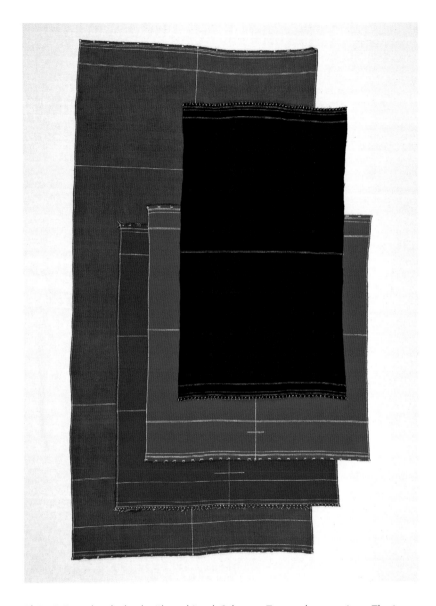

Plate 6. Four shawls dyed with cochineal. Salasaca, Tungurahua province. The top shawl was spun, woven, and dyed by Margarita Masaquiza Chango. Plain-weave wool with white cotton stripes and embroidered end finishes. Back to front: 2.09 x 1.02 meters (82 1/4 x 44 inches), *rebozo*; 1.16 x .95 meters (45 3/4 x 37 1/2 inches), *bayeta*; 1.025 x .94 meters (40 3/8 x 37 inches), *bayeta*; 1.26 x .71 meters (49 1/2 x 28 inches), *vara y media*. The Textile Museum 1988.19.86, 1988.19.138, 1987.9.10, and 1988.19.87, Latin American Research Fund.

Plate 7. Wool poncho in plain weave with bound-warp-resist patterning. Dyed and woven by Abel Rodas, Chordeleg, Azuay province. 1.90 x 1.48 meters (74 3/4 x 58 1/4 inches), including fringe. The Textile Museum 1988.22.19, Latin American Research Fund.

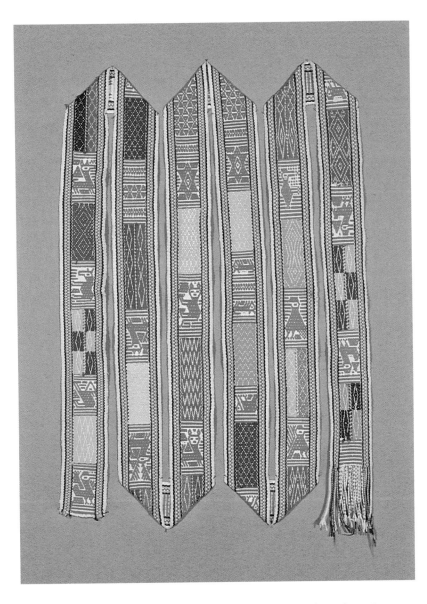

Plate 8. Belt in plain weave with both supplementary-warp and supplementary-weft patterning in white cotton and colored acrylic yarns. Woven by José Miguel Limaico, Ovalos (Natabuela area), Imbabura province. 2.935 x .05 meters (115 1/2 x 2 inches). The Textile Museum 1989.22.12, Latin American Research Fund.

Introduction: The Land and the People

ANN P. ROWE AND LYNN A. MEISCH

The Geographic Setting

Ecuador, a country the size of Oregon or Colorado, has ecological zones ranging from mangrove swamps and dense tropical rain forests to temperate valleys and snow-capped mountains. There are three main geographic divisions (see Map 1): the Pacific coastal lowlands; the Andes mountains, forming a north-south spine through the country; and the lowland Amazon basin rain forests to the east, usually referred to in Ecuador as the Oriente (East). The coastal lowlands are broader and the Andean highlands narrower than in Peru, Ecuador's southern neighbor.

The Coast

The coastal zone of Ecuador also forms a marked ecological contrast with that of Peru. The Peruvian coast is one of the driest deserts in the world, which is the chief factor in the preservation of so many archaeological textiles in that area. Off the coast of Ecuador, however, the cold Humboldt Current, which flows northward along the Peruvian coast, turns out to sea, and warm waters flow southward from Central America, causing a wetter climate. There is a rainy season from mid-December to mid-May, though with regional variations.

On the peninsula between Guayaquil and Manta (northwest of Portoviejo), rainfall is unreliable, and people subsist on fishing and raising cattle. To the north and east it is much wetter, supporting tropical-forest vegetation and tropical crops such as cotton, papaya, pineapples, and, by the 1980s, sugarcane, coffee, bananas, and bamboo. The most heavily populated region is the

Guayas basin, lying inland from the drier coastal area. The western slopes of the Andes, covered with tropical vegetation, rise precipitously.

The Highlands

The Andes mountains form two parallel chains, referred to as the western and eastern cordilleras, with a fertile valley between them where most people live and which in Ecuador ranges from 2,200 to 2,800 meters (6,750–9,000 feet) in elevation. The mountain chains include a series of spectacular snow-covered active volcanoes, and the area is also prone to earthquakes. The central valley is further divided, like a ladder, by other mountainous or desert areas into smaller basins, which also tend to coincide with indigenous ethnic divisions. There are ten basins of sufficient importance to be represented in our work.[1] Rain is frequent in this area, ranging between 1 and 2 meters annually (39–79 inches), though it is drier between June and October. Annual average temperatures range from 12 to 18 degrees Celsius (54–66 degrees Fahrenheit) on the valley floor. The different basins vary in fertility and climate, but, in general, the weather is pleasant due to proximity to the equator, which is only 13 kilometers (8 miles) north of Quito.

In early pre-Hispanic times, the lower elevations of the central valley were forested, up to an elevation between 3,000 and 3,500 meters (9,840–11,480 feet), but the land is now used for either agriculture or grazing. Above this altitude there is an area of colder grasslands, called the *páramo*, which is frequently overcast and rainy.

There is a narrowing of the high valley near the southern border with Peru, causing a natural geographic break. The extent of the cultural distinctions is unclear archaeologically, but in modern times the type of loom changes at about the same latitude. Other features, such as spinning methods (see Meisch, Miller, and Rowe 2005), continue across the border, and trading has certainly occurred.

The border with modern Colombia has a less-pronounced geographic break, and differentiation has depended primarily on politics. The border area was culturally unified in the pre-Inca and Spanish colonial periods, but the northern border of the Inca empire was in the same place as that between the modern republics. The loom style changes again in Carchi, the northernmost province of Ecuador (not at the border), although certain other cultural features continue into the southern part of Colombia. For example, animal fibers are found in southern Colombia, though, farther north, only cotton is used. While this feature appears to predate the Inca conquest, it is likely that some elements of costume and the supplementary-warp belt-weaving technique spread northward during the period of Spanish domination (Cardale Schrimpff 1977: 46).

In the central valley, maize is the most important indigenous crop at lower elevations, often intercropped with beans, lupine, or quinoa. At higher elevations, crops include barley and fava (broad) beans, introduced by the Spanish, as well as a variety of indigenous tubers. Sometimes, the lower elevations of the *páramo* may also be cultivated, while the higher elevations are used mainly for grazing. We saw mostly sheep and cattle, though there were a few llamas in the central provinces. Many indigenous households raise guinea pigs, an Andean domesticate, for festival feasts, and some also raise chickens or rabbits.

The Oriente

The Oriente includes the eastern slopes of the Andes and gradually flattens out to the east. It has very heavy rainfall, with tropical-rainforest vegetation. Climatically and culturally, it is similar to the eastern tropical areas of Peru and Colombia. Ecuador's claim to Amazonian territory was reduced by half as a result of an invasion by Peru in 1941 and a settlement to define the border in which Peru was supported by the United States. This settlement was not fully accepted in Ecuador until a further treaty was negotiated in 1998.

Historical Background

At the time of the Inca conquest, the territory that is now Ecuador was divided into many small and often antagonistic political units, which were smaller than the known linguistic units. At least six languages were spoken in the highlands. From north to south, these languages were Pasto (in what is now Carchi province), Cayambi (Imbabura and northern Pichincha), Panzaleo or Lata (southern Pichincha, Cotopaxi, and Tungurahua), Puruhuay or Puruhá (Chimborazo and Bolívar), Cañar (Cañar and Azuay), and Palta (Loja) (J. Rowe Ms).

Cotton (*Gossypium barbadense*) is indigenous to the western coast of South America and was domesticated probably in the third millennium BC. It appears to have been extensively used in the highlands in pre-Hispanic times as well, although it had to be acquired from lowland areas by trade. Around the beginning of the Christian era, camelid hair, probably from llamas, became available in the southern highlands of Ecuador (Bruhns 1990), but it supplemented and did not replace the use of cotton fiber. Fiber from the leaves of an agave family plant, *Furcraea andina,* which grows in highland areas, was also used (see Miller et al. 2005). Spinning was done using a simple handheld spindle (see Meisch et al. 2005). The two possible directions of twist are described as either S or Z, corresponding to the slant of the central portions of these letters, viewed with the yarn vertical.

The Inca Empire

The Inca empire originated in Cuzco in what is now the southern highlands of Peru. It conquered the highlands of what is now Ecuador as far north as Quito in the late 1460s.[2] The Inca army also campaigned in what are now Guayas and Manabí provinces on the coast, but it does not appear that this area was as thoroughly incorporated into the empire as was the highlands. In the early sixteenth century the Inca army marched as far north as the valley of Atres in what is now southern Colombia, but the territory actually incorporated into the empire ended at the current border between Ecuador and Colombia.

The Incas divided the territory of highland Ecuador into two provinces, one governed from Quito and the other from Tumi Pampa (modern Cuenca). The Incas introduced their language and ordered their subjects to learn it, and this process was well under way by the time the Spanish arrived. The Spanish found it convenient to continue this policy, with the result that the indigenous Ecuadorian languages all died out in the colonial period.

The Incas also had a regular policy of moving people from previously conquered areas to newly conquered ones, often on a large scale, as part of the pacification process. Many people were moved from one part of Ecuador to another as well as from Peru and even Bolivia into Ecuador. These resettled people were called *mitma* or *mitmaq* in the Inca language; the Spanish wrote this word as *mitima*.

Following the death of the Inca emperor Huayna Capac in 1528, there was a civil war between two of his sons: Huascar, who was Huayna Capac's choice in Cuzco; and Atau Huallpa (Atahualpa), who was the governor of Quito. The key event in terms of Ecuador was a battle at Ambato in 1531 in which Atau Huallpa defeated Huascar and subsequently massacred large numbers of Cañar men and boys for having fought on Huascar's side. Subsequently, Atau Huallpa succeeded in having Huascar and his family captured and killed.

The Spanish Empire

The Spanish under Francisco Pizarro arrived on the Ecuadorian coast in 1531, but first proceeded to Peru, where they captured Atau Huallpa in 1532 and put him to death the following year. A Spanish force under Sebastián de Benalcázar conquered Ecuador in 1534, with assistance from the Cañares, who were happy to fight against the supporters of Atau Huallpa.

The Spanish administration was very oppressive for Ecuador's indigenous people. Populations declined dramatically because of the introduction of European diseases. Spanish officials took much of the best land for themselves, relocating indigenous communities. Large tribute quotas were demanded in both labor and goods, including textiles. The Spanish forced some indigenous people to move long distances to provide labor for their mines or armies. Other people, hoping to avoid the tribute and labor demands, left their ancestral homes. Indeed, over half of the indigenous population was living on other than their original lands by the end of the seventeenth century (Alchon 1991: 82–85).

The Spanish introduced widespread sheep raising and treadle-loom weaving (see Chapter 8) almost immediately and in very large numbers. The use of the European spinning wheel does not appear to have been significant, however, and it is now known only in the Otavalo area. A simple spindle wheel is used, large enough in size that the spinner works standing—backing away as the yarn lengthens and walking forward to wind the yarn on the spindle, hence the term *walking wheel.* The indigenous camelids were greatly reduced until only a few llamas were left at the highest altitudes. The Spanish also introduced a Mexican maguey, *Agave americana,* which supplemented but did not displace the similar indigenous *Furcraea andina.* The fiber from both plants is used for binding warp resist (Chapters 2 and 3) and for looped bags (Miller et al. 2005). There are many local terms for these fibers, but in our English text the *Agave* fiber will be referred to as maguey fiber and the *Furcraea* fiber as *chawar,* its Quichua (Inca) name.

Because Ecuador lacked any appreciable mineral wealth, the economy was centered on agriculture and on textile production in factories (*obrajes* S.) using Spanish equipment (see, e.g., Cushner 1982). The fabrics produced were plain-weave and twill-weave yardage of cotton and wool in various grades, which were mostly exported to other parts of the Spanish empire. Some *obraje* cloth also seems to have been used for indigenous-style garments.

Working conditions in these factories were notoriously bad, and the pay amounted to little or nothing. By the eighteenth century, Ecuadorian *obrajes* were suffering from competition from fabrics made in Peru and Europe, and the economy stagnated (Tyrer 1976). Lowered *obraje* income caused the Spanish to raise tribute levels, sparking numerous localized armed rebellions (Moreno Yánez 1985).

The Republic of Ecuador

Spanish policies to raise money in the empire's South American lands also alienated the local elites of Spanish descent. They responded by initiating an independence movement, which succeeded in 1822. The modern state of Ecuador was founded in 1830. Nevertheless, the new republic continued to treat its indigenous population in much the same way as had the Spanish crown. The predominant (though not exclusive) pattern was that much of the agricultural land was owned by a small number of whites, who ruthlessly exploited indigenous labor to operate these estates (called haciendas).

It is only since about 1960 that this pattern has begun to break. Pressure from the Alliance for Progress of the Organization of American States and the fear of a Cuban-style Communist revolution spurred the 1964 agrarian reform law. In many cases, however, the land granted to indigenous families was still insufficient for economic survival, or rapidly became so due to population increases, and many people have migrated to the cities, coastal industries, or the Oriente to become wage laborers. Also, wealthy individuals still own large estates that include the best lands, so indigenous people have organized to pressure the government for further land reforms. Some improvements in the educational system have also been made, including increased access to it and more culturally sensitive books and teaching materials.

Modern Indigenous Peoples of Ecuador

Some 49 percent of the population lives in the coastal area and is a mixture of indigenous, Spanish, and African peoples. The indigenous population is, for the most part, not readily distinguishable as such. Nevertheless, remnants of indigenous weaving and metalworking traditions have been documented in some fishing villages on the coast (Klumpp 1983; Hagino and Stothert 1984; Stothert and Parker 1984; Álvarez 1987; Stothert 1997; Stothert and Freire 1997; Stothert 2005). The traditional loom in this area is vertical, with a continuously circling warp, and lacks the dovetailed join found in highland looms.

In addition, there are two small indigenous groups living in the northern tropical-forest areas near the western slopes of the Andes who have maintained a significant amount of their traditional culture. The Chachis (called Cayapa in the earlier literature), in the northern province of Esmeraldas, and the Tsachila (called Colorado [Red] in the earlier literature, because of their extensive use of red body paint), in the vicinity of Santo Domingo in Pichincha province, have a tradition of vertical looms similar to those of the coastal fishing villages. While Barrett (1925) carefully documented Chachis textile technology, there is an urgent need to do the same for the Tsachila before it is too late.

Some 48 percent of Ecuador's population lives in the highland valleys, and most are indigenous descendants of the pre-Hispanic peoples of the area. There is no census count of the indigenous highland population, but out of a total population of approximately 13,730,000 for the country in 2005, some 20 to 40 percent is indigenous; the vast majority live in the highlands. Their lifeways include a broad and varied mixture of pre-Inca, Inca, Spanish, and modern elements. For the most part, indigenous people are rural agriculturalists and/or artisans, but an increasing number are living in towns and cities, working as wage laborers or selling goods.

The Oriente is much more sparsely inhabited than either the highlands or the coast and, until the 1964 land reform and the discovery of oil in 1967, was of little interest to colonizing groups. The various indigenous peoples have thus preserved many of their pre-Hispanic cultural features. Although they make such items as baskets and hammocks, most of these peoples do not do much weaving, and their culture does not relate to highland traditions. The Shuar and Achuar (called Jívaro in earlier literature), living in the southern part of this area, while of predominantly tropical-forest culture, had a weaving tradition that seems to bear some relationship to that of adjacent highland areas (Bianchi 1982). Another group, the rainforest Quichua (called Canelos Quichua in earlier literature), has been heavily influenced by highland traditions, including language and costume.

Beginning in the 1960s, population pressures in the highlands have caused colonizing activity in the Oriente, deposits of oil have been found and exploited, and missionary activity has increased, causing depredation of both the natural environment and indigenous cultural traditions (see, e.g., Kane 1996).

Ethnicity in Ecuador is complex and subtle. There are differences between how people identify themselves and how they are identified by others, as well as differences in the categories used in different areas. In highland Ecuador, from the indigenous perspective, the fundamental distinction is between *blancos* (whites) and *indígenas*. The term *mestizo* (meaning mixed European and indigenous ancestry) is sometimes used by people to identify themselves or others and is sometimes hyphenated with the term *blanco*, as in *blancos-mestizos* (whites-mestizos), to indicate the nonindigenous population. The one exception to this dichotomy occurs in the Azuay valley, where there is a group of people referred to as *cholos* who wear a distinctive costume and consider themselves to be a class between indigenous and white.

There are many Ecuadorians of mixed descent, some of whom consider themselves white, others of whom consider themselves indigenous. These distinctions are not racial but social. Many people who call themselves *blancos* or *mestizos* have darker hair, skin, and eyes than do people who call themselves *indígenas*. The most important visible or public determinant of indigenous versus white identity in highland Ecuador today is the wearing of identifiably indigenous dress, although language (Quichua instead of or in addition to Spanish) is also a factor.

Among indigenous peoples living in the highlands, some identify with a particular ethnic group, composed of people living in several adjacent communities, while others identify only with their own community, although there may be other nearby culturally similar communities. People in Carchi province (Map 1), whose weaving is distinctive from that farther south, identify mainly with their communities.

Probably the best known ethnic group in Ecuador is the Otavalos, living in many villages around the town of Otavalo in Imbabura province (Map 2), as well as in the town itself. They are famous for their merchant activities, in particular making textiles for sale, which they have done since pre-Hispanic times. Natabuela and its vicinity, on the northern edge of the Otavalo area, have a distinctive costume and weaving substyle. East of Mount Imbabura and extending down into the northeastern part of Pichincha province (Map 2) is another group that wears a different costume. During the period of our fieldwork they did not use an ethnic group name, but since the late 1990s they have readopted their pre-Hispanic name of Cayambe (since the early 2000s also spelled Kayambi). Our weaving data for this group are from Paniquindra in eastern Imbabura province.

In Cotopaxi province, and in parts of Tungurahua province (Map 3), people simply identify with their community, but two distinctive ethnic groups also exist in Tungurahua province. One of these is the Salasacas, who live in dispersed settlements in and around the town of Salasaca, east of the provincial capital of Ambato. The other includes the Chibuleos, Pilahuins, and Angawanas, who live in several communities west of Ambato. The costumes of these latter groups are similar and they intermarry, despite the three ethnic group names. Our weaving data are from the community of San Luis, which is Chibuleo.

Chimborazo province is large and diverse, and most people there and in neighboring Bolívar province simply identify with their community (Map 4). We identified several different costume areas. In northern Chimborazo province, no distinctive costume is worn, but some weaving is still done, mostly on treadle looms using *chawar*. In central Chimborazo province, the indigenous costumes are similar with only subtle variations. We obtained weaving data from Nitiluisa in the San Juan area, which is north and west of the provincial capital of Riobamba, from several of the sixteen Cacha communities, which are not far south of Riobamba, and from towns in the Colta area, surrounding Lake Colta. There is a separate costume style area in eastern Chimborazo province and also in the southern part of the province, south of Guamote, where costume starts to look like that in Cañar province to the south.

The main ethnic group in Cañar province is the Cañaris (since the early 2000s also spelled Kañaris), living in many small communities centering on the town of Cañar (Map 5). In the southern part of the province, however, people have more cultural similarity to those in Azuay province. In Azuay, indigenous people identify mainly by community, as do the *cholos*. In the southernmost province of Loja, the main distinctive ethnic group is the Saraguros, who live in many small communities centered on the town of Saraguro in the northern part of the province (Map 6). Other indigenous people in the province identify mainly by community.

Indigenous Costume of Highland Ecuador

Indigenous costume in highland Ecuador combines elements from pre-Inca, Inca, Spanish colonial, and modern times. It varies regionally, but many elements occur in several areas. For a full discussion of the regional variations, see A. Rowe (ed.) 1998.

In most areas north of a line in southern Chimborazo, women wear a dark blue or black wrapped skirt based on pre-Hispanic antecedents. In the Otavalo area and in central Chimborazo, where the wrapped skirt occurs in a relatively long and narrow form, it has replaced a wrapped full-length dress, similar to Inca examples, commonly worn in Chimborazo as recently as the 1960s, but in Otavalo only in more remote communities and by older women. In other areas, the wrapped skirt is worn shorter and with tucks at the waist. In either case, it is usually called by an Inca term, *anaku*. Although sometimes woven on the indigenous style of loom, these skirts are more often of treadle-loom woven or increasingly of machine-made cloth.

The skirts are held in place by a patterned belt, usually called by its Inca name, *chumbi,* and woven on the indigenous style of loom. These belts boast the most elaborate patterning and hence the most complex weaving techniques in the Ecuadorian repertoire. Three decorative woven structures are used (see Chapters 4, 5, and 7). The belts are long and wrap multiple times around the woman's waist, with the ends usually secured by tucking them under other wrappings of the belt. Women's hair is often gathered at the nape of the neck and wrapped with a narrow woven band, sometimes decorated in a manner similar to belts. This indigenous hairstyle is not Inca.

In southern Ecuador and in the eastern Imbabura–northeast Pichincha area, women wear a Spanish-style skirt (usually called *pollera* or *centro*) tucked into a waistband. The tailored, embroidered blouses worn in many areas are also of Spanish origin (see Nason 2005 for a description of the techniques used). The fabrics used for these garments were formerly woven on Spanish-style treadle looms, although by the 1980s they were usually machine made. A belt is not needed with this costume, but in some areas one is worn anyway.

Throughout highland Ecuador, many indigenous women wear a rectangular shawl without fringe that is of pre-Hispanic origin. The shawls are called by a variety of Quichua and Spanish names (e.g., *lliglla*, *bayeta*). They are sometimes woven on the indigenous style of loom but more often on the Spanish treadle loom, or, by the 1980s, were of machine-made material. The shawls are sometimes secured on the chest in the Inca fashion with a straight pin called by its Inca name, *tupu*, or a safety pin, but sometimes the ends are simply knotted together. In some areas, the shawl may be worn under one arm, but otherwise it is worn over both arms, as in the Inca style. In some areas, various styles of machine-made shawls may also be worn.

Another textile used as a carrying cloth in central Ecuador and as a shawl by *cholos* in Azuay has bound-warp-resist dyed decoration and a fringe at both ends (see Chapter 3). It is woven on the backstrap loom, but knotting the warp fringe is a European introduction. The origin of this hybrid form is unclear but seems to date to the colonial period.

Felt hats were worn only by indigenous men through the mid-nineteenth century, but since 1900 have been worn by both men and women. The felting method with which they are made is based on the properties of sheep's wool and was introduced early in the colonial period. Although machine-made felt hats have become increasingly common, some hand felting of hats was still done in the late 1980s, especially in the barrio of Pomatúg, near Pelileo in Tungurahua province (A. Rowe and Conterón 2005). Plaited hats (the misnamed "Panama" hats), made in Azuay and southern Cañar province, are worn in the south highlands (A. Rowe and Meisch 2005).

In men's costumes, tailored shirts and pants were a Spanish introduction, although pre-Hispanic style tunics (called *kushma* in Ecuador) were still worn in some areas at the time of our fieldwork. In northern Ecuador, the pants were normally made of cotton, while in southern Ecuador they were of wool. The tunics were usually woven on indigenous looms, but shirts and pants were made of treadle-loom woven cloth. By the 1980s machine-made garments were common except in a few of the more conservative areas. Men generally do not wear a handwoven belt except in Cañar province, where it holds an unseamed *kushma* in place.

The preeminent indigenous item in the man's wardrobe is the poncho, or *ruana* (S.), as it is often called in the Ecuadorian and Colombian Andes. In function, it takes the place of the man's mantle, not of the tunic. It clearly derives from native technologies, usually being woven on the backstrap loom and made of two uncut panels sewn together.

The poncho's development into its current form, however, and its widespread use, occurred in the colonial period. The earliest evidence for it is among the Mapuche (called Araucanians in earlier literature) of Chile in the early seventeenth century (Montell 1929: 239). Its use gradually spread northward during the following century. Since ponchos in several scattered areas, including parts of Bolivia, Peru, and Ecuador, have stepped-diamond designs in bound-warp resist dyeing, similar to Mapuche ponchos, it may be that the association of this technique with poncho weaving is also Mapuche in origin (A. Rowe 1977: 19–22). Ponchos with these designs are woven in Cacha (in Chimborazo province; see Chapter 3), and in Cañar. The pulled-warp chevron patterning found in some other places, such as Azuay, may have a different source (see Chapter 2).

Context of Textile Production

Some of these costume items are made by people for their own use or for someone in their family, while others are commissioned from specialists, a process referred to as *pedido* (S., request) or *obra* (S., work). If the item is to be woven, the person commissioning the work supplies the yarn and consequently specifies the colors to be used. The weaver may or may not also ply or dye the yarn for the customer. This is a common arrangement for weaving in the whole Andean area. A more Europeanized system, in which weaving is done on speculation for sale to unknown customers in the market, is also occasionally found, but more often for belts or treadle-loom woven fabrics than for larger backstrap-loom woven items.

Although some people weave full time, especially in the Otavalo area, many people make textiles in the interstices of the agricultural calendar or whenever nothing more pressing is going on. In these cases, weaving is a supplement to the household economy, not the sole means of support. This system lends itself well to weaving for domestic use, since one can spend as much time as one likes, with a correspondingly beautiful result, on a textile for someone known and loved. It can also work adequately with barter within a society where values are shared. It is, however, open to exploitation in situations where a small cash income is a supplement to subsistence living, when the cash remuneration is often not proportional to the amount of time that the work takes.

Hand textile processes are inherently slow, especially using indigenous methods, a fact that may be difficult for those of us removed from these processes to appreciate. But it is no accident that the Industrial Revolution in Europe began with spinning. Once cash income becomes the predominant goal, the amount of time spent on the process becomes critical, and technical and artistic compromises naturally follow. Although there are exceptions, the belts of Cañar and Salasaca, which are made mostly for domestic use, are generally finer than the belts in Otavalo and Chimborazo, which are made for sale.

Another level of compromise is involved when the textile is made for sale to someone outside the community, who usually has different tastes and needs and is unaccustomed to paying for the time it takes to produce a textile by hand. In Ecuador the textiles woven for whites, local or tourist, are often totally distinct, in technique, in design, and in function, from those made for local use (as, for example, in Otavalo). This process is entirely logical. Indeed, the Otavalos understand this better than do most development workers. Thus, this book focuses primarily on textiles made for indigenous use.

CHAPTER 1

Plain Weave on the Backstrap Loom

Introduction

ANN P. ROWE   The backstrap loom is of pre-Hispanic origin and, at the time of our fieldwork, was still used throughout much of highland Ecuador to produce the most beautiful and distinctive garments. A vertical loom is used in the northern province of Carchi, a tradition that continues into highland Colombia, and belts are woven on a vertical loom in the Natabuela area of northern Imbabura province. The Carchi loom is described at the end of this chapter, while the Natabuela belt loom is described in Chapter 4. The following text describes general methods of backstrap-loom weaving in the rest of highland Ecuador, followed by a case study of a poncho-weaving workshop in Pualó, Cotopaxi province (Map 3).[1] The type of vertical loom used on the Ecuadorian coast has been described elsewhere (Barrett 1925; Klumpp 1983; Hagino and Stothert 1984) and is not considered here.

Ponchos are the most common wider textiles woven on the backstrap loom. We also recorded blanket weaving in Tungurahua, Chimborazo, and Azuay provinces (Chapter 2), and double bags (*alforja*) in Azuay and Loja. The cotton warp-resist dyed shawls are also backstrap-loom woven (Chapter 3). The pleated skirt (*anaku*), man's tunic (*kushma*), chaps (*zamarros* S.), and sometimes the woman's shawl (*lliglla*) are woven on the backstrap loom in Saraguro, while in Cañar the *kushma* and sometimes the *lliglla* are backstrap-loom woven. Elsewhere, the larger costume items (aside from ponchos) are usually made of treadle-loom woven or machine-made fabric. The wool used in these backstrap-loom woven garments is often handspun, adding significantly to the final aesthetic effect.

Belts are usually woven on the backstrap loom (Chapters 4, 5, 7). Although many are patterned, plain-weave examples with only warp stripes are also made. Machine-spun yarns are commonly used.

Weaving is predominantly men's work in the highlands, although women weave on the coast and in Carchi province in the north. In the highlands, some women weave belts in many areas, and it is not considered odd, but few weave the wider textiles on either backstrap or European treadle looms (Chapter 8). An exception was the area around Chicticay in Azuay province (Map 5) before the Josephina landslide of March 1993, where it was common for women and men to weave even large fabrics on the backstrap loom. In other areas, such as Bulcay, also in Azuay province, a few women weave wider fabrics but are considered strange for doing so.

The type of backstrap loom used in Ecuador differs in some respects from those found elsewhere in the Americas. The general information included here is drawn from observation of looms for undecorated textiles, as well as from the basic functions of looms for patterned textiles. The patterning techniques themselves are discussed separately in subsequent chapters. Actually, although patterning techniques are remarkably varied, the methods of producing plain weave are relatively consistent.

Producing Plain Weave

A woven cloth consists of a longitudinal set of elements called the *warp*, perpendicular to a transverse set called the *weft*. Functionally, the warp is put on the loom before the actual weaving process can begin, while the weft is inserted over and under the warp yarns during the weaving process. The complete process consists, first, of winding the warp (called *warping*); second, of attaching the loom parts or putting the warp on the loom; third, of inserting the weft (weaving); and, fourth, of removing the loom parts or taking the cloth off the loom.

In a plain weave, each weft yarn interlaces over one and under one warp yarn (Fig. 1.1), so the weaver needs to be able to separate the even- and odd-numbered warp yarns. He or she first raises the evens above the odds and passes the weft and then raises the odds above the evens to pass the weft again. The basic interchange of the odd-numbered and even-numbered warp yarns is called the *warp cross*, most clearly visible in a side view of the weaving (Figs. 1.2–1.4). The opening between the odd- and even-numbered warp yarns is called the *shed*.

In indigenous Andean weaving, the warp is made the exact size wanted for the finished piece. The size of the various loom parts more or less conforms

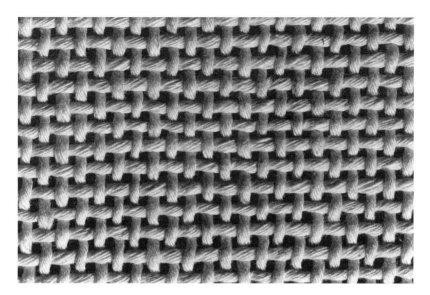

1.1 Balanced plain weave. From Emery 1980, fig. 85.

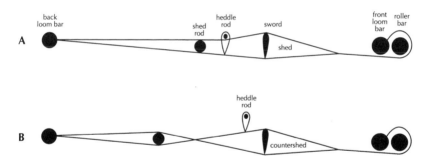

1.2 Profile diagrams of the Peruvian-style backstrap loom, with the warp in a single plane bound to the loom bars on both ends. Shown with the sword holding the shed open, ready to insert the weft. A: Shed rod shed open. B: Heddle rod lifted, showing the warp cross. Drawings by Laurie McCarriar based on drawings by Ann P. Rowe.

to the size of the warp, so a weaver uses different loom sticks for belts and for ponchos. This technology contrasts with the European tradition of weaving a very long warp that is then cut up into smaller pieces for use (see Chapter 8).

In most Andean weaving the warp yarns turn at each end of the fabric without being cut and are attached to the loom by various clever methods.

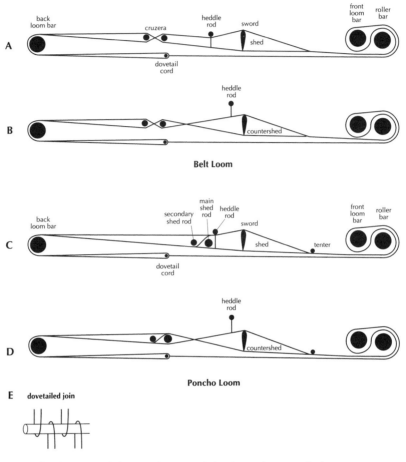

1.3 Profile diagrams of the Ecuadorian-style backstrap loom, with the warp passing around both loom bars and the ends dovetailed around a cord. Shown with the sword holding the shed open, ready to insert the weft. A: Belt loom with the *cruzera* shed open. B: Belt loom with the heddle rod lifted. C: Poncho loom with the shed rod shed open. D: Poncho loom with the heddle rod lifted. E: Detail of dovetailed join. Drawings by Laurie McCarriar based on drawings by Ann P. Rowe.

Thus, each fabric has not only the two finished side edges (selvedges) found on European-style yardage but also finished end selvedges. Therefore, traditional Andean garments are made of completely uncut square and rectangular fabrics. The edges of the rectangles are sometimes decorated, and two smaller rectangles may be sewn together, but there is no cutting and tailoring such as one finds in the European tradition.

Peruvian backstrap looms have the warp stretched flat, with warp loops at each end bound to a loom bar (Fig. 1.2). In Ecuador, on the other hand, the warp encircles the loom bars, so that the loom length is half the length of the actual warp (Fig. 1.3). In order to create a flat textile, the end warp loops pass around a cord (the dovetail cord) in alternating directions (Fig. 1.3E). In winding the warp, a stick is used to hold the dovetailing yarns and is usually replaced by a cord before weaving begins. After weaving, the dovetail cord is removed, separating the end selvedges.

Since the warp is not tied to the loom bars in Ecuador, other devices secure it. For example, many belt looms have a curved back loom bar to prevent the warp from slipping from one end of the loom bar to the other (see Fig. 4.45). This curved loom bar is usually wood, but in Cacha, Chimborazo province (Map 4), it may be deer antler.

At the front of the loom near the weaver, a separate roller bar, the same size and shape as the front loom bar, is placed on top of the warp (Figs. 1.4–

1.4 Belt loom showing the *cruzera* and the method of tying the loom to a house post. The heddle rod shed is open for weft insertion, though the heddle rod itself is flopped over. Cacha Machángara, Chimborazo province. Photo by Lynn A. Meisch, 1988.

1.5 Poncho loom showing foot bracing, use of tenter (to maintain the width of the fabric), and use of two shed rods. The weaver is putting the weft through the heddle rod shed. The cloth is almost finished; the dovetailed join is visible just above the shed rods. Segundo Mena, Pualó, Cotopaxi province. Slide by William H. Holmes, 1988.

1.5). The warp may be shortened by winding it one or more turns clockwise around both sticks. The loops of the backstrap are put around the ends of the further bar and under the closer one in order to prevent the warp from unrolling (Fig. 1.5). The roller bar is used both before and after there is any length of cloth on the loom, since its main function is to secure the warp to the loom bar. To adjust the position of the working area of the warp once some of the cloth has been woven, the weaver unwinds the warp from the roller bar and the front loom bar, slips the entire warp around the loom bars toward him, and rerolls the warp around the two bars.

The two sheds for plain weave are opened in different ways. A stick called the *shed rod* has alternate warp yarns above and below it so the warp yarns above are lifted when this stick is moved forward (Fig. 1.3C). In many Ecuadorian wide looms, this shed rod is supplemented by a secondary shed rod, which further divides the warp yarns over the main shed rod (Figs. 1.3C, D). Moving these two shed rods past each other helps open the shed. The weaver may also strum the warp yarns with a pointed stick called a *pick* to help open the shed.

In Ecuadorian belt looms, the stick that functions as the shed rod is often tied at both ends in front of a second stick that holds the opposite shed, so a cross appears between them (Figs. 1.3A and B, 1.4). These two sticks are usually called the *cruzera*, from the Spanish word for cross, *cruz*. The English term *cross sticks* (or *lease rods*) does not usually refer to something that functions as a shed rod, however. Since the form and function of these sticks appear to be particular to Ecuadorian belt looms, the Spanish term will be used here. Sometimes the back *cruzera* stick is grooved, to guide the spacing of the warp yarns. Three-stick *cruzeras* are found in some looms with a mechanism for warp patterning (Chapters 4, 5, 7). Of course, the grooves and ties on the *cruzera* also help secure the warp yarns in the loom.

A stick called the *heddle rod* is used to lift the warp yarns passing underneath the shed rod (Fig. 1.3). It is usually thinner and placed in front of the shed rod, resting on top of the warp. Loops of thread called *heddles* pass between the warp yarns above the shed rod and encircle each warp yarn below it. These loops must be approximately as long as the diameter of the shed rod, long enough to make a workable shed. In indigenous South American looms, the heddles are usually made of a single continuous yarn, but there are many possible methods to form and bind the heddles to the heddle rod. In Ecuador a different method is used in belt looms and wide looms (see below). In order to open the shed controlled by the heddles (often called the *countershed*), the heddle rod is lifted with the left hand while the shed rod is pressed down with the right.

To make sure the shed is clear and to bring the cross evenly against the woven edge, the weaver uses a hardwood stick called a *sword*. It has a profile like an airplane wing with one sharp and one rounded edge. The sword is inserted into the shed and pressed down against the woven edge, then turned on edge in the warp to hold the shed open for the insertion of the weft, carried on a narrow stick called a *shuttle* (Figs. 1.3–1.5). After passing the shuttle, the weaver turns the sword flat again to beat the weft into place. For wide looms, the sword is pointed on both ends, but for belt looms in Ecuador, it usually has a handle on one end, giving it a knife shape (Fig. 1.4).

Parts for wider looms are often very heavy, and considerable strength is needed to weave. The sword alone may weigh two or three kilos (five or six pounds).

It is essential to maintain warp tension in order to be able to separate the warp into sheds and to beat in weft. Through most of highland Ecuador, body tension serves this purpose. That is, the end of the loom nearest the weaver is affixed by ropes to a strong, broad strap that passes behind the weaver's waist or hips. The weaver leans back to increase tension on the warp—for example, when beating in the weft—and forward to decrease the tension—for example, to make it easier to lift the heddle rod. The variability in tension makes the warp yarns tend to draw together, so that most fabrics woven this way are either warp-predominant in count (in which the weft shows a little) or warp faced (in which the weft is completely hidden), meaning that the warp yarns are closer together than the weft yarns.

For wider looms, the support for the back loom bar usually consists of two stout posts driven into the ground, or built into the house in a convenient place, inside or on a porch (Fig. 1.5). These posts may be short or floor to ceiling. Usually, they are wood, but in Paniquindra, in eastern Imbabura province (Map 2), we saw short loom posts of stone (see Figs. 2.14–2.15). Belt looms sometimes use a similar built-in back loom bar, but the curved style of back loom bar is simply tied by a rope to a vertical support, usually a house post (Fig. 1.4).

To summarize the complete weaving sequence for plain weave on a back-strap loom:

1. Open the shed rod shed by moving the shed rod forward close to the heddle loops and strumming the warp crosswise with a pick or the tip of the sword above and/or below the shed rod while holding the warp tension firm (Fig. 1.6).
2. Insert the sword into the shed in front of the heddle rod (Fig. 1.7) and beat against the woven edge (Fig. 1.8).
3. Release tension enough to turn the sword on edge and pass the shuttle through the open shed (Fig. 1.9).
4. Increase the warp tension, turn the sword flat, and beat sharply against the woven edge, afterward removing it from the shed.
5. Open the heddle rod shed by lifting the heddle rod with the left hand. To facilitate this process, lean forward slightly to release tension on the warp, place the sword on top of the shed rod with the right hand, and press the shed rod down and back (Fig. 1.10).
6. While holding the heddle rod up, insert the sword into the shed formed (Fig. 1.11).
7. Release the heddle rod and bring the sword forward against the woven edge of the fabric, first gently, then sharply, simultaneously leaning back to increase warp tension.
8. Release the tension enough to turn the sword on edge to hold the shed open and pass the shuttle through the shed (Fig. 1.5).
9. Increase tension, turn the sword flat again, and beat it again against the woven edge. Begin again at step 1.

1.6 Poncho loom with two shed rods, demonstrating the basic weaving sequence for plain weave. The weaver is opening the shed rod shed by strumming the warp with a wooden pick. José Elias Pupiales, Paniquindra, eastern Imbabura province. Photo by Barbara Borders, 1989.

1.7 Inserting the sword into the shed rod shed. The right end of the tenter stick also shows clearly in this photograph. There is a second warp tied to the loom posts behind the warp that is currently being woven. José Elias Pupiales, Paniquindra, eastern Imbabura province. Photo by Barbara Borders, 1989.

1.8 Beating the shed rod shed with the sword. José Elias Pupiales, Paniquindra, eastern Imbabura province. Photo by Barbara Borders, 1989.

1.9 Inserting the weft into the shed rod shed. José Elias Pupiales, Paniquindra, eastern Imbabura province. Photo by Barbara Borders, 1989.

1.10 Opening the heddle rod shed. José Elias Pupiales, Paniquindra, eastern Imbabura province. Photo by Barbara Borders, 1989.

1.11 Inserting the sword into the heddle rod shed. José Elias Pupiales, Paniquindra, eastern Imbabura province. Photo by Barbara Borders, 1989.

The Quichua word for "slow" is the same as that for "good," *ali* in Otavalo (Meisch 1987: 128), *ayllilla* in Saraguro, a combination of meanings that is particularly appropriate for weaving on the backstrap loom.

Warping

A warper may plan color combinations by laying balls of yarn side by side or refer to a finished textile as a guide. In Quero, Tungurahua province (Map 3), we encountered Eliva Villacruz Vinueza, who had a series of sticks wrapped with yarn in different arrangements of stripes as a reference for customers to choose color combinations (Fig. 1.12). She did spinning and warping, but not weaving.[2] A few other cases we encountered where different people did warping and weaving were usually for commercial production, but sometimes it was done for tricky warping, as for pattern weaves. More often, however, the weaver warps.

Yarn for warping is usually wound into a ball (A. Rowe [ed.] 1998: 96, fig. 82, shows a man winding yarn from a spindle into a ball). The ball may be left to unroll next to the weaver's legs (Figs. 1.13–1.14), or protected from dirt and wandering in a container such as a basket, enamel bowl, or plastic bucket. Occasionally in the Otavalo area, the yarn may be left on the spindle for warping. The weaver in Figure 1.15 holds the spindle between his toes.

Warping is done on a set of vertical stakes mounted on a wooden base, or warping board (Figs. 1.13–1.15) or simply pounded into the ground. Wider textiles such as shawls and ponchos (and sometimes belts) require a horizontal bar held between slight notches or flattened areas at the tops of the end stakes. This bar keeps the end posts parallel to each other, to produce a rectangular rather than a trapezoidal textile. If the warping stakes are pounded into the ground, the horizontal bar may also function as a measuring device (as in Salasaca).

Since the warp is wound with the ends dovetailed, the configuration of the stakes is as follows (Fig. 1.16). There are two end stakes (labeled A and D), set at approximately half the length of the warp apart (a warp-faced fabric will be slightly shorter than the unwoven warp). The dovetail stake (labeled B), used to form the dovetail join, is set between the end stakes, usually slightly in front of the plane of the end stakes. In addition, there are one or more cross stakes (labeled C) used to separate the yarns of the cross, so that they do not need to be separated manually when the loom is set up. The cross stakes are usually set to the right of the dovetail stake, although occasionally to the left. For plain weave, only one cross stake is strictly necessary (Figs. 1.13–1.14) but two are sometimes used (Fig. 1.15). While it is essential that the end stakes and dovetail stake be firmly fixed and vertical, the cross stakes are often loose.

Warping begins at the dovetail stake (B) and usually proceeds toward the warper's right. The yarn is led past the cross stake (C), around the right end stake (D) from front to back, then left toward the other end stake (A), and around that end stake from back to front, then right again toward the dovetail stake, and around the dovetail stake (Fig. 1.16). This pass creates one warp yarn and will be referred to as a *half round*. The round is completed by reversing the direction. The thread is carried from the dovetail stake left toward the left end stake, around the end stake from front to back, then right toward the right end stake, and around the right end stake from back to front, then left past the cross stake, toward the dovetail stake again. If the yarn is carried from

1.12 Sticks wrapped with yarns as samples of stripe patterning. Eliva Villacruz Vinueza, Quero, Tungurahua province. Slide by Leonard Evelev, 1988.

1.13 Warping an *alforja* with red and white stripes. The weaver has long experience and strong toes to hold the dovetail stake in this manner. Celina Calle, Chicticay, Azuay province. Slide by Lynn A. Meisch, 1977.

1.14 Warping with two yarns of the same color at a time, using one cross stake. One ball of yarn is visible; the other is out of the photograph to the left. Luis Martínez, Pasa, Tungurahua province. Slide by Betty Davenport, 1988.

1.15 Warping on two cross stakes. The weaver supports the spindle between his toes. The younger generation watches and learns. Rafael de la Torre, San Luis de Agualongo, Otavalo area, Imbabura province. Photo by Lynn A. Meisch, 1984.

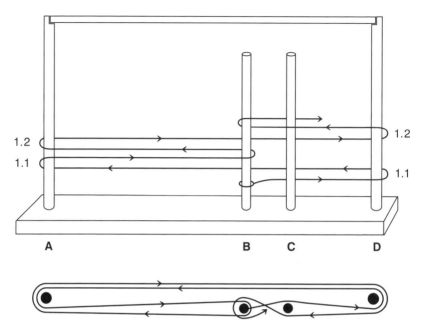

1.16 Diagram showing basic warping for plain weave. 1.1: Half round. 1.2: Second half round. Drawing by Arts and Letters Ltd., based on a drawing by Ann P. Rowe.

front to back around the dovetail stake on the first half round, it is carried in the reverse direction on the return, or vice versa.

If a warp yarn passes on one side of the cross stake in the first half round, it will pass on the opposite side on the return. A time-saving variation on this procedure is to warp with two yarns simultaneously, placing one in front and the other in back of the cross stake on each half round (Fig. 1.14). This procedure is common in warping two colors alternately, to produce a pattern of horizontal bars, but can also be used in warping one color alone, as shown in Figure 1.14.

If there are two cross stakes, the second one may be used to form the shed for the secondary shed rod (Fig. 1.15). Thus, in one round, the warp will pass behind the second cross stake in both directions, and in the next, it will pass behind both cross stakes in one direction and in front of both on the return. If only one cross stake is used in warping but the weaver wants to use two shed rods, the shed for the second shed rod is hand picked when the loom is set up (as in Azuay province).

The end of the warp yarn is usually simply tied to the dovetail stake. Another method is to tie an overhand knot in the end of the yarn and split the ply to put it over the stake (Redwood 1973: 12). If two yarns are used, an overhand knot is made with the parallel yarns, and the resulting loop is placed over the dovetail stake. Sometimes before warping begins, a strong cord is tied parallel to the dovetail stake to preserve the dovetailed join after the stake is removed.

Before removing the warp from the stakes, the weaver secures the cross by tying either one thread around the entire cross or a separate thread through each half. Or one or more shed rods may be inserted and tied on at this point (Redwood 1973: 14). On belt looms, the *cruzera* is usually inserted into the cross at this stage. The two sticks of the *cruzera* are already tied together at one end, and the other ends are inserted downward (or sometimes upward) through the cross and then tied together.

Often the weaver proceeds immediately from warping to setting up the loom, but sometimes the warp will be stored temporarily. In this case, the cross is secured with thread, and the warp is lifted off of all stakes except the dovetail stake by holding it near the end stakes. It is then twisted on itself and folded in half with one end loop put through the other to secure it. A yarn tie is put through the second end loop.

Setting Up the Loom

The Ecuadorian style of backstrap loom is relatively easy to set up. The first step is to insert the back loom bar into the circle of the warp and secure the loom bar to its support. The curved back loom bar of a belt loom is usually tied with a cord from each end that wraps around a vertical house post. A nail may be pounded into the back of the post to prevent the tie cord from slipping down. Such a loom may be temporarily set aside by rolling up the warp on itself, untying the cord from the post, and securing the roll by tying the cords around it.

Alternatively, looms have a heavy, straight loom bar tied with rope to two vertical posts. One end of the bar is slipped out of its ties, the warp is looped over it, and the bar is put back. It can be rolled up in the same manner as a belt loom, but the back loom bar is so heavy that, often, the rolled warp is stored with the back loom bar still tied to its posts (see Fig. 1.7, which shows one warp rolled up behind the one being woven).

The next step is to insert the front loom bars. Often the weaver will use only one loom bar while setting up the warp, but after the warp is spread out sufficiently, the roller bar is added.

The backstrap for belt looms is often a piece of cowhide with a hole in each end but can be made of almost anything sufficiently sturdy. A separate loop of rope or leather may be attached at each end, or a continuous ring of

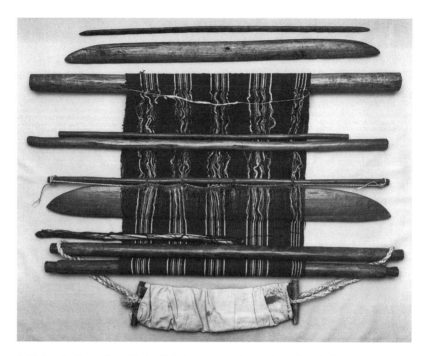

1.17 Poncho loom from Troje, Chimborazo province. Warp-faced plain weave wool, with wooden loom parts and leather backstrap wrapped with cotton cloth. The wide stripes are magenta. Warp: 69 (x2) × 60 centimeters (27 × 23½ inches). Length of back loom bar: 1.19 meters (47 inches). The Textile Museum 1970.22.1.

rope (the ends knotted together) may pass behind the backstrap and through the holes. The continuous ring of rope obviously prevents strain on the backstrap holes. A belt loom from Molobóg in Chimborazo province (Map 4) has a backstrap made from the sleeve of a heavy cable-knit sweater with a rope ring passing through the inside of the sleeve (The Textile Museum inventory no. 1988.22.13).

For larger looms, a thicker piece of leather is usual, but it is often difficult to see the foundation because of heavy padding with anything handy. A poncho loom from Troje, Chimborazo province, in the Textile Museum collection (Fig. 1.17) is typical. The thick leather backstrap is wrapped around a stick at each end. On each end, a rope is put through a hole behind the end stick and tied into a ring. For padding, a piece of heavy cotton cloth is put around the leather and sewn to itself to make a tube.

Some weavers sit on a mat or blanket on the ground with their legs straight out in front of them, while others use a low stool. We encountered two weavers in Chimborazo province who had made themselves a wheeled seat (Fig. 1.18).[3] Lynn Meisch reports that some Cañari weavers work standing up (Fig. 1.19).

Usually, the weaver braces his feet against something, to obtain greater tension with less back strain. On wide looms a foot brace is often built against the framework supporting the far loom bar (Fig. 1.5). The weaver places his feet directly against the brace or may set other items between his feet and the brace (Fig. 1.18). To get maximum tension on the warp, the weaver may lift his buttocks entirely off the ground and be supported only between the backstrap and his feet (see Fig. 2.9).

On belt looms the foot brace may be improvised. One weaver we recorded near Otavalo sets his axe handle against the wall and braces his feet against the top of the blade, padded with a folded cloth (see Figs. 4.21, 4.23). Another weaver (José Manuel Bautista, Agato, Otavalo area) uses a series of wooden blocks, adjusting their position to accommodate the amount of warp rolled onto the front loom bars. Some belt weavers do not bother to brace their feet at all.

Securing the Dovetail Join

If a cord has been tied to the dovetail stake before warping, it needs to be secured only so that it does not pull out. The simplest method, sometimes used for belts, is simply to tie the two ends of the cord together. Another method (used by Antonio Cando Camuendo, Otavalo area, and in Cacha, near Riobamba) is to tie the ends of the cord around the outermost warp threads. More often, the ends are tied to a small stick. For wider fabrics, the ends may be tied to a stick, with another cord hitched at intervals to secure the join to the stick. The stick may be on the outside of the warp (Fig. 1.20) or it may be inserted into the triangular opening to the left of the dovetail stake on the warping board (Redwood 1973: 14). The stick may be removed after a certain amount has been woven.

In Saraguro, on some wider looms photographed by Lynn Meisch, the ends of the stick fixed to the dovetail join are tied by cords to the front loom bar and no roller bar is used (Fig. 1.21). We did not note this practice in other areas.

If no cord has been tied to the dovetail stake, then the stake must be replaced in some other way. The usual method is by means of an eye (a hole) in one end of the dovetail stake that allows it to act as a needle to pull a cord through (Redwood 1973: 14, Otavalo area; Carlos Conterón, Ilumán, Otavalo area; also in Pungalá, Chimborazo province).

For belt looms, a small stick may be used instead of a cord. If the dovetail stake is bamboo, the smaller stick can simply be inserted into the hollow of the

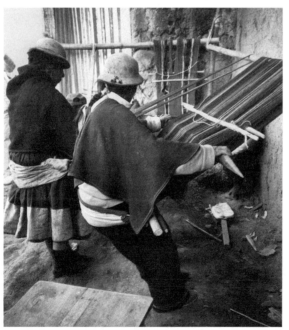

1.18 Weaver using a rolling seat. Note the ad hoc nature of the foot brace. A single large shed rod is used. San Juan, Chimborazo province. Slide by AlJean Thompson, 1989.

1.19 Weaving standing up in Cañar province. The loom has a single shed rod. Juan Tenesaca and his wife, Cañar, Cañar province. Photo by Lynn A. Meisch, 1993.

1.20 Poncho loom showing the dovetail cord tied to a stick. There are two shed rods. The tenter is a stick with the bark still on it. Manuel Curay, Nitón, Tungurahua province. Slide by Leonard Evelev, 1988.

1.21 Weaving an *anaku*, with the stick securing the dovetail cord tied to the front loom bar. One large shed rod is used. Daniel Chalán, Las Lagunas, Saraguro area, Loja province. Slide by Lynn A. Meisch, 1978.

bamboo and the bamboo then removed (as does Antonio Santa Cruz, Otavalo area). One Otavalo weaver we observed, José Manuel Bautista, uses a dovetail stake with the end only slightly hollowed out. With the warp under tension, he places the small stick into this hollow and pushes the dovetail stake out quickly. This maneuver is rather tricky and would take practice. Luis Virgilio Pupiales, in Paniquindra in eastern Imbabura province, holds the old stick in his left hand and the new one in his right and transfers each loop of the warp individually from one stick to the other with his fingers. Once the small stick is in place by any of these methods, a cord is tied to each end of the stick over the warp to ensure that loops do not slip off.

Making Heddles

Heddle-making methods are remarkably consistent throughout highland Ecuador, but a different method is used for belt looms and wide looms. The sword is turned on edge to hold the shed open in each case.

In belt looms, the heddle cord is looped in half hitches around the heddle rod. The weaver begins by tying the end of the heddle string to the left end of the heddle rod and then putting the rod through the shed (right to left) and out the other side. He makes the heddles from left to right, by drawing the heddle string up between two warp yarns with one finger of his right hand, twisting it to make a loop, and passing the loop over the heddle rod form-ing a half hitch (Figs. 1.22–1.23). Then he makes another half hitch over the heddle rod before proceeding to make the next heddle. When the free end is pulled tight, the loops change to the aspect at right in Figure 1.23. When all the heddles are made, he secures the string around the right end of the heddle rod. Sometimes the weaver ties the two ends of the heddle string together (as does José Manuel Bautista, Otavalo area). The half hitches secure the heddle loops at a fixed size, which facilitates opening the shed.

In wider looms, the heddle string winds around a heavy cord or thin stick, which is, in turn, tied to the heddle rod. The heddles are made by forming loops around a short gauge that is later withdrawn. The following description is based on the process used in Azuay province (Fig. 1.24) (see also Penley 1988: 74).

A cord that will carry the heddle loops is put through the hollow center of a bamboo gauge and secured to the right end of the gauge with a small plug. The other end of this cord is tied to the left end of the heddle rod. The heddle thread is put through the shed right to left and tied around the end of the gauge. Then the weaver makes the loops, starting at left, by hooking the first finger of his right hand around the heddle string between warp yarns and

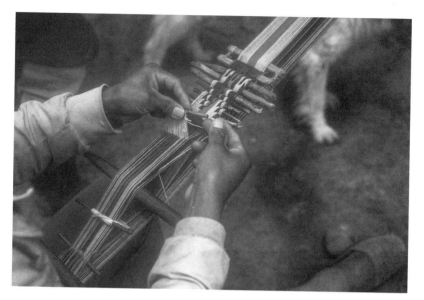

1.22 Making heddles on a belt loom. A finished heddle rod has been pushed down toward the dovetail join. The sticks above the heddles show the sheds for the pattern (see Chap. 7). Luis Virgilio Pupiales, Paniquindra, eastern Imbabura province. Slide by Laura M. Miller, 1989.

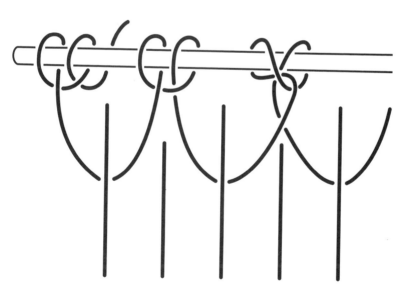

1.23 Diagram showing belt-loom heddles. The manner of looping is shown at left and the final configuration, when the loops are pulled tight, is shown on the right. Drawing by Arts and Letters Ltd., based on a drawing by Ann P. Rowe.

1.24 Making heddles on a wide loom using a bamboo gauge. Preparing to weave a warp-resist-dyed shawl. Manuel Maldonado Pérez, Gualaceo, Azuay province. Photo by Lynn A. Meisch, 1993.

wrapping it in a spiral around the gauge front to back. As the gauge becomes crowded with loops, they are slipped off the back and onto the cord. When all the loops are made, the gauge is removed and the cord is tied to the right end of the heddle rod. The cord is further secured to the heddle rod by another cord that forms half hitches over both the cord and the rod at intervals. A solid dowel with a hole in one end may be used instead of bamboo for the gauge (as is done in Quero).

The Troje loom in Figure 1.17 has the cord carrying the heddles secured to the heddle rod using four loops. Each loop consists of a separate leather strip with the ends tied together in a large overhand knot. The loop is put around the cord and rod, and the knot is inserted through the end of the loop like a button in a buttonhole.

In other looms, the heddles are looped over a thin metal rod (instead of a cord) bound to the main heddle rod. This system is used in a Cañari loom (The Textile Museum 1989.22.1), in Pualó and in Pungalá (Fig. 1.25).

A slightly more elaborate version of this system is used in the Otavalo area for weaving heavy wool fabrics (Fig. 1.26). A second heddle rod, thinner than the one on top of the warp, is placed parallel to the gauge. The heddle string is wound in a figure eight around the thin stick and the gauge. Both the holding cord and the thin stick are bound to the heddle rod as described. The extra winding helps keep the heddle loops even in size, to facilitate opening the shed.

Miscellaneous Matters

The exact order in which the various sticks are added to the loom is somewhat variable. For instance, the *cruzera* or shed rod(s) may be added before or after the warp is removed from the warping stakes; the dovetail join may be attended to either before or after the heddles are made. Descriptions of the habits of some individual weavers are included in subsequent chapters (see, for example, Abel Rodas in Chapter 2 and Herlinda Vera in Chapter 3).

In some areas a tenter is used to maintain the width of a wider fabric as it is being woven (Figs. 1.5, 1.7). The tenter is a stick with points or metal hooks at each end that pierce the fabric at each edge. It lies on top of the fabric near the working edge and is moved up periodically as the weaving progresses. We recorded tenters in every province where we recorded backstrap looms, but not all weavers use one.

The looms used in Azuay for weaving the cotton warp-resist dyed shawls have a rod near the far end of the warp around which each warp yarn winds for one circle, called a *coil rod* (see Chapter 3). This rod helps secure the slippery cotton warp and maintain an even width for the fabric. Coil rods are found on looms with circular warp and dovetailed ends in other parts of the world also, such as Mexico and Indonesia (Johnson 1979; Bolland 1979). The coil rod is not used for the cotton shawls woven in Rumipamba in Cotopaxi province, however (see Fig. 3.5).

For wide looms, the length of the shuttle is approximately the same as the width of the warp, though in belt looms it may be wider. The yarn is wound on in a long spiral lengthwise and is wound horizontally around the ends of the stick to secure it before changing direction (Fig. 1.27). This method of winding a shuttle is characteristic of the entire Andean area and also of Mesoamerica. Rather than using a stick shuttle, belt weavers often wind the weft yarn around the hand in loops and then crosswise around the loops.

Changing Sheds

For wide fabrics, we recorded the use of two shed rods in Imbabura (Otavalo area and Paniquindra), in Cotopaxi (Pualó and Rumipamba), in Tungurahua (Nitón and Quero), and in Azuay province. It probably occurs elsewhere, too. The sheds are usually secured with a separate loop of string. We recorded

1.25 Tying the heddle rod to the heddles, which are over a thin metal rod. The lower of the two swords will be left in place while the first weft passes are inserted, in order to make a fringe. Preparing to weave a child's poncho. Segundo Gushpa, Pungalá, Chimborazo province. Photo by Lynn A. Meisch, 1989.

1.26 Making heddles with a figure-eight over a rod. Weaving a scarf with a different color on each face (see Chap. 6). Antonio Santa Cruz, Peguche, Otavalo area, Imbabura province. Photo by Laura M. Miller, 1989.

1.27 Winding yarn on a shuttle. Antonio Santa Cruz, Peguche, Otavalo area, Imbabura province. Slide by Ann P. Rowe, 1989.

single shed rods in Cacha, San Juan, Pungalá, Mapahuiña (near Achupallas), and Chunchi in Chimborazo province, as well as in the Cañar and Saraguro areas (as used by Daniel Chalán). A weaver from Simiátug (Bolívar province) recorded in Pasa (Tungurahua province) was also using only one shed rod, secured by a string tied to both ends.[4]

If two shed rods are used, the usual technique for opening this shed is to bring the secondary shed rod forward against the heddle loops first, strum the warp, then push the secondary shed rod back and bring the primary shed rod forward, again strumming the warp (e.g., as in Quero, Tungurahua and in Azuay). The position of the two shed rods may be exchanged again to prepare for opening the heddle shed.

Another technique, recorded in Paniquindra, is to put the primary shed rod on top of the secondary one, strum with a pick both in front of and behind the heddle rod, and then bring the primary shed rod forward, move the secondary one back, and strum again (Fig. 1.6). The weaver also lays the pick sideways under groups of warp yarns and draws it forward to help open the shed.

In Cacha, where one shed rod is used for weaving warp-resist patterned ponchos, the weaver brings the shed rod forward against the heddle rod and moves them both back and forth slightly, after which he strums the warp in front of the heddle rod with a pick. In Saraguro, the weaver opens the shed by bringing the one shed rod forward against the heddle rod and strumming the warp with the tip of his sword.

For plain-weave belts, where the front stick of the *cruzera* serves as a shed rod, the shed is opened by inserting the sword flat next to the front *cruzera* stick, turning it edgewise, and moving it forward. It is then removed and re-inserted in front of the heddle rod. The left hand may be inserted into the shed behind the heddle rod in order to keep it open while replacing the sword.

On wide fabrics, the heddle rod shed is nearly always opened with the general technique shown in Figure 1.10. In Paniquindra the secondary shed rod is slightly behind the primary one, but the weaver still holds the primary (Fig. 1.10). More often, when there are two shed rods, the sword is rolled over the primary shed rod, with the secondary shed rod in front and not engaged. If there is not much unwoven warp left, the weaver may roll the sword over both shed rods together.

For belts, relaxing the warp tension and pulling on the heddle rod may be sufficient, sometimes supplemented by strumming the warp with the sword or a pick. The weaver may also scrape the heddle rod forward and back a few times. The heddle rod may be pulled to the left side, however, rather than lifted upward (as does José Manuel Bautista, Otavalo area). In this case, strumming may be done inside the shed or on the back of the warp instead of on top.

The sword may be inserted into the shed with either edge forward, but is usually first brought toward the weaver with the blunt end facing him or her and then turned and beaten with the sharp end forward. Some weavers hold the shed open by turning the sword with the sharp edge up, but others place the blunt edge up.

The sword is the most carefully made and valued part of the loom, and we spoke with several weavers who prized weaving swords inherited from their fathers. For poncho looms, heavy hardwoods such as that of the chonta palm of the Oriente are especially esteemed, but since chonta is not easy to get, *arrayán* (S., myrtle) is often used instead. Some weavers wax their sword periodically by rubbing it with a candle, to make it work smoothly and to help prevent the warp yarns from sticking to each other and fraying around the heddles. We also found one man ironing his sword to dry it out. The pick is most often made of wood, but bone ones (usually from a cow) are occasionally seen.

Finishing

Although weaving usually begins at the dovetail join, belts are not customarily woven all the way to the end of the warp. When the length of the remaining unwoven warp becomes too short to manipulate the various sticks easily, the weaver substitutes a smaller sword. This treatment often suffices, or the weaver may then remove the back part of the *cruzera*. These tricks make it possible to weave up to eight-ten centimeters (three-four inches) from the end. The last weft pass may contain multiple yarns.

The weaver then removes the loom parts. Generally, the heddles are removed while the warp is still under tension. Once the heddle rod has been taken out, the string forming the heddles can simply be unraveled by pulling on it. If the string is strong enough, it is wound on itself and saved for future weaving. The *cruzera* is also removed with the warp under tension. Then the belt is taken off the back loom bar and the front loom bar and the roller bar are removed. Last, the dovetail cord is pulled out, freeing the ends of the belt.

In some areas, a belt may be used without further finishing, but, more often, the long loops at the last end of the weaving are either corded or braided. If the belt is sold, this work is usually done by the person who buys the belt rather than the weaver. To cord the loops, small groups of them are rolled between the hands, first in one direction to ply them, and then in the opposite direction to re-ply them (Fig. 1.28). The end of the cord is secured by a knot. For braiding, simple three-strand braids are generally used. In addition, ties may be put through the end warp loops on both ends of a belt. Except in Chimborazo province, however, the ties on the ends of a belt are not generally tied together when the belt is worn but are just secured by tucking them under previous wraps of the belt.

Some ponchos are woven leaving a short five-centimeter (two-inch) fringe on both ends. The fringe at the beginning of the weaving is created by inserting an extra sword into the warp against which to beat the first weft passes (Fig. 1.25). This technique is also used in Pualó and by Abel Rodas of Chordeleg, Azuay province (see Chapter 2). A similar technique is used in weaving the cotton shawls with longer fringe on both ends (Chapter 3). The weaving then stops before the other end has been reached. The poncho warp loop ends are generally corded as described for belts.

Many ponchos and blankets are woven all the way to the end, creating a four-selvedged fabric. When shedding becomes difficult, a smaller sword is first substituted for the large one. The Troje poncho loom in Figure 1.17 has two swords progressively smaller than the principal one. Smaller shed rods may also be used. The heddle rod is lifted while pressing down small groups of warp yarns with the thumb of the right hand. Once these shedding devices can no longer be used and have been removed from the warp, the weaver must use another method to insert the last weft yarns.

One technique is to use a single needle of metal or wood, as long as the

1.28 Cording the fringe on a belt. Polivio Sarango, Tuncarta, Saraguro area, Loja province. Slide by Lynn A. Meisch, 1979.

1.29 Cloth after the last weft has been inserted but before the loom bars and dovetail cord have been removed. Chunchi, southern Chimborazo province. Photo by Patricia Meloy, 1989.

width of the piece, to darn in the last weft yarns while the loom bars are still in place (Redwood 1973: 33). This technique is also used by Abel Rodas in Chordeleg and by blanket weavers in Quero (see Chapter 2). The final effect can be seen in Figure 1.29.

Saraguro and Chicticay weavers recorded by Lynn Meisch use a two-needle technique.[5] The loom bars are removed but the dovetail join is left in place. The weaver then puts his or her legs through the tube of woven fabric, centering the join on the lap and parallel to the legs, and the woven area is secured by the bend in the knees to keep it taut (Fig. 1.30). Two weft yarns are put through at a time, each threaded on a large wooden or iron needle. The weaver works away from himself or herself with both needles, putting one under a warp yarn and the second under the next warp yarn, and so on. The weft yarns are only periodically pulled through. When these two weft yarns have been inserted, the fabric is turned around and the process is repeated as needed. When the fabric is complete, the dovetail cord is pulled out so that the textile opens into a flat rectangle.

Other finishing processes that are sometimes used for ponchos include brushing them with a teasel tool to form a fuzzy surface nap and sewing on a

1.30 Using two needles to add the last weft yarns to a large bag. Miguel Quizhpe, Saraguro, Loja province. Slide by Lynn A. Meisch, 1977.

collar. Both of these techniques are described in the following section on the Pualó poncho workshop. Using the teasel plant (*Dipsacus fullonum*) and the napping procedure are a European technology dating to at least Roman times and introduced to Ecuador after the Spanish conquest for finishing sheep's-wool fabrics. Backstrap-loom woven blankets are also often napped in Ecuador. The finely woven Cacha ponchos are the only style of Ecuadorian poncho with a separately made fringe sewn on after weaving. This technology is described in Chapter 3. *Alforjas* are usually finished by sewing a simple three-strand braid to the edges.

Loom Terminology

The terms used by the weavers for the various parts of the backstrap loom are quite variable from one area to another. Several are of obvious Inca origin, recorded also in the Cuzco area of Peru both early in the colonial period and in modern times (González Holguín 1608, 1952; A. Rowe 1975). Other terms are Spanish. Still others are of uncertain derivation. They, like *anaku* or *kushma*, may belong to a northern dialect of the Inca language (see A. Rowe 1997: 12, 25), or they may derive from one or another of the indigenous languages of Ecuador.[6] For such terms, as noted earlier, no source (Q. or S.) is indicated.

The most common term for the sword, *kallwa*, is of obvious Inca origin. The pronunciation is variable, however. Not only is the "ll" pronounced "zh" in central and northern Ecuador, but sometimes the stress is changed to *kalluwa* and sometimes the final "a" is dropped (in both the Salasaca and Chibuleo areas). In Carchi province, the sword is called *sobrechonta*, from the Spanish *sobre* ("over") and *chonta*, a heavy palm wood often used for this purpose (Jaramillo 1988a: 13; 1991: 137).

The Inca term for weft, *mini*, is also commonly found, for example, in the Otavalo and Saraguro areas and in Cotopaxi, Tungurahua, Chimborazo, Cañar, and Azuay provinces.

The Inca term for warp, *allwi*, is less often found in Ecuador, though we recorded versions of it in Cacha in Chimborazo province (*awlli*, pronounced "*awzhi*") and Cañar (*awllishka;* Meisch 1980). Instead, *shaya*, Quichua for "standing" or "waiting," is often used, for example, in Imbabura and Chimborazo provinces (Majipamba, Troje, Molobóg), and in the Chibuleo and Salasaca areas. In Saraguro, warp on the warping board is called *awllina*, and on the loom, *shaya puchka*, standing or waiting yarns. A term derived from the Spanish *urdimbre* is also sometimes used.

The Inca term for heddles, *illawa* (Q., pronounced "*izhawa*" in northern and central Ecuador), which may be combined with *kaspi* (Q., stick) for heddle rod, is used in the Salasaca and Saraguro areas, as well as in Chimborazo, Cañar, and Azuay provinces. A common term in Imbabura and Carchi provinces is *ingil* (or *ingil kaspi*). In Cotopaxi province, we found the term *pugsa*, a term also used by the weaver from Simiátug, Bolívar, now living in Pasa. In Rumipamba, Cotopaxi province, the Taipe family called the heddles themselves *pugsa* and the heddle stick *ingil kaspi*.

The term for *shed rod* is often Spanish. The wide use of *cruzera* has already been mentioned, and this term is sometimes also used for regular shed rods. In Imbabura, however, the shed rods on a wide loom are *pasín* and those in the Textile Museum's Troje poncho loom (Fig. 1.17) are labeled *pasaj* (*jatun pasaj* and *uchilla pasaj; jatun* Q., large; *uchilla* Q., small). In El Tambo, Cañar, the shed rod is called *bauladura* (S., *baúl*, trunk or chest); in Azuay, *masa* ([?] S., mortar; mass or volume); in the Saraguro area, *tupa* (Q., measurer). In Cañar the *cruzera* sticks are called *tinki*, sometimes pronounced *tinke* (Q., union, joining).

The term for the front loom bars in Imbabura and Cotopaxi is *kumil*, with a related term, *kumuel*, used in Carchi for both loom bars (Jaramillo 1991: 132). In Cacha, Chimborazo province, the front loom bar is *sij* (or *tsij*). Elsewhere in Chimborazo and in Cañar, it is *pillu kaspi, pillug*, or *pilludor* (with a Spanish suffix), from *pilluy* (Q., to wrap). The Salasacas call front loom bars *kaspi watarina* (Q., *watay*, to tie). The Chibuleo and Simiátug weavers use the Spanish-derived *pechera* or *pichera* (from *pecho*, chest), and nearby Nitón, the term used is *pecho*. *Mestizo* weavers in Pungalá and Quero use the Spanish *envolvedores* (from *envolver*, to wrap around). In the Saraguro area, the front loom bars are called *jillik*.

The curved back loom bar found on belt looms in Imbabura province may be called *aru* (S., *aro*, hoop) or *panga* (Q., leaf, blade). A straight back loom bar for a wider fabric is also *panga*. In the Salasaca area, the back loom bar is *charidora* (Q. with S. suffix, holder) and in Chibuleo it is *apari* (Q., to carry). In Cotopaxi and parts of Tungurahua provinces, the Spanish terms *cargador* or *travilla* are used. The weaver in Pasa used the term *macho*, also a Spanish word. In much of Chimborazo, Cañar, and Azuay provinces, the back loom bar is *jawan*. In Saraguro, it is *altej kaspi*.

The term for the dovetail join is especially interesting, since this is not a feature of Inca weaving. In northern Ecuador the term seems quite variable. In the Otavalo area it may be called *tumansi* (Q., *tuma*, a going around), *itsig*, or *chakchador* (appears to be Q. with S. suffix), while in Paniquindra we recorded *tigrador* (*tigray*, Q., turn back, with S. suffix). In Cotopaxi province, it was variously *tinero* (Pualó) or *yaposo* (Collana area), and in Salasaca, it was *tandachishka* (Q., collected). On the other hand, in central Chimborazo province, it seems to be consistently *juból* and in southern Chimborazo, Cañar, and Azuay provinces, it is *bocar*. This distribution suggests that *juból* might be Puruha and *bocar* might be Cañar, although the latter is perhaps more likely from the Spanish *boca* (mouth). In Saraguro, the term used is *pitidor* (Q. with S. suffix). In some areas a Spanish term is used, for example, *engarce* in Quero; *remate* in Pungalá; and *cargador* in Chordeleg. In Nitón and Quero it was *topa*, perhaps from Spanish *topar*, to meet up with.

The term for the tenter is often Spanish, for example *ancho*, meaning wide (Pualó, Otavalo) or *anchero* (Rumipamba and Quero). Another Spanish term is *media*, usually meaning "stocking," but here probably referring to a measure (San Juan, Chimborazo province). *Saca* or *sacan*, meaning "it pulls out" or "they pull out" (Cacha Obraje, and Mapahuiña, near Achupallas in southern Chimborazo province), and *temblador* (Saraguro) are also Spanish. In Bulcay, Azuay, however, Penley (1988: 80) recorded the term *shin*. In Otavalo, sometimes the term *tupulina* is used and in Paniquindra, *tupuli*, presumably from *tupu* (Q., pin).

In the Otavalo area the most common term for the backstrap is *washakara* (Q., back, leather), a term also occasionally found in other places (Sevilla in southern Chimborazo province). The Simiátug weaver in Pasa used the term *garabato* (S., hook). In the provinces of Cotopaxi (Pualó and Rumipamba), Tungurahua (Quero and Nitón), and the northern two-thirds of Chimborazo, the usual term is *atamba* (Q.). Exceptions are the Collana area west of Salcedo, where the term used is *kanafata*, and Salasaca, where the Quichua terms *chumbi watarina* (belt tier) or *siki sinchun* (lower back cinch) are found. In southern Chimborazo, Cañar, and Azuay provinces, the term used is *chapirichij* (with Q. suffixes).

The term for shuttle is *fúa* or *púa* (S., sharp point, grafted shoot) in much of northern Ecuador, including Imbabura, Cotopaxi (but not Pualó), Tungurahua (though not Chibuleo), and the northern two-thirds of the Chimborazo provinces. The term used in Pualó is *enjoyador* (S.) and in Chibuleo *neillka* (pronounced *neizhka*). In southern Chimborazo, Cañar, and Azuay provinces and the Saraguro area, the usual term is *jisanchi*.

The distribution of *bocar* (for the dovetail join), *chapirichij* (for the backstrap), and *jisanchi* (for shuttle) correspond to what we know of pre-Spanish Cañar territory, so possibly these words (or the latter two) are of Cañar linguistic origin. The term *takti* for the end stakes of the warping board and *juka* for the heddle gauge has a corresponding distribution also. However, other terms used in the Cañar area are of broader distribution (*jawan* for the back loom bar and *pilludor* for the front); other terms are Inca.

There might also be an Imbabura cluster: *panga, pasín, ingil*, with *kumil* extending into the Panzaleo language area. *Ingil* and *kumil* both also extend into Carchi province.

The terms used for the warping board were in every case Spanish (e.g., *banco* in Azuay and *urdidor* in Pualó), suggesting that this was a Spanish introduction. The aboriginal technique was presumably to pound stakes into the ground.

Poncho Weaving in Pualó, Cotopaxi Province

LAURA M. MILLER We recorded a poncho-weaving workshop in Pualó, in Cotopaxi province (Map 3), in 1988, run by Segundo Mena (see Fig. 1.5).[7] He said he was sixty-seven years old and had been weaving since he was twenty-three. His wife, an older female relative, and his son and daughter-in-law also worked in the household to produce ponchos and blankets. Mena also said that he paid five weavers to work for him.

Most of his production is commissioned. In this case, he receives the wool yarn from his customer, who also selects the color. Mena charges 3,000 sucres (about $6.25 at 1988 exchange rates) for the labor of warping and weaving the poncho. His cousin also sells some non-commissioned ponchos for him in the regional markets of Saquisilí, Pujilí, Salcedo, Latacunga, and Ambato. A poncho sold in the market brings 10,000 sucres (about $21.00), while one sold from home costs from 8,000 to 10,000 sucres. Tourists purchase some ponchos, but most are purchased by rural men. The commissioned ponchos have more variety of color than those made for the market.

Segundo Mena buys materials for the market ponchos in the Otavalo and Saquisilí markets. At the Saquisilí market there is an extensive area where raw and spun cotton and wool are traded and sold. Mena uses a two-ply yarn and purchases it as paired singles, which either he or his family plies with a walking wheel (made with a bicycle wheel). The drive cord of the wheel runs in a figure-eight; the yarns are S-plied.

Once plied, the yarn is colored with synthetic dyes imported from Japan and Colombia. The skeins are dyed in the yard, using large copper pots covered with pot black and supported on rocks over an open fire. The wool is boiled in the dye solution for ten to fifteen minutes. After dyeing, the yarn is washed, dried, and placed on a swift (*china* S.) for winding into balls, ready for warping. Segundo Mena has a strict production schedule. He usually dyes early in the week to prepare enough yarn for his weekly production of eight ponchos.

Mena's wife warps the poncho on a warping board with two cross stakes.

To warp one side, or *hoja* (S., leaf), takes an hour, winding two yarns at a time placed separately over the cross stakes. Mena himself or his adult son weaves the poncho.

The loom posts are inside the house with a board placed in front of the posts as a foot brace (Fig. 1.5). The heddles are made by winding the heddle cord over a narrow metal rod (*pugsar*) with the help of a small gauge rod. The metal rod is in turn bound to the heavier wooden heddle rod (*pugsador*, the whole apparatus). The loom has two shed rods (*cruzero mayor* and *cruzero minor*, S.) and a tenter stick with L-shaped wire hooks at either end. The weaver places a sword into the first shed next to the dovetail cord to make space for a fringe.

A good weaver can weave four poncho halves in a day, enough for two ponchos. This is production labor: weaving tasks are not mixed with any other work. A nonspecialist weaver, having other daily and seasonal tasks to do, would not work at such a pace. Also, the weaving is relatively coarse, with 8 to 10 warp and 2.5 to 3 weft yarns per centimeter (20–25 warp and 6–7 weft yarns per inch). One finished poncho measures 1.46 × 1.35 meters (57½ × 53 inches), including the fringe (The Textile Museum 1988.19.14).

The two halves of the poncho are sewn together by one of the women. The warp end loops are left uncut, and groups of warp loops are given more twist and allowed to twist back on themselves, making a neat finish. Finally, the poncho is brushed to form a nap (Fig. 1.31). It is hung over a horizontal wooden rod supported by end posts in the yard, with the center seam along the rod. One of the women scrapes the surface using a pair of implements called *palmares* (S.) made up of twelve teasels (*cardones*, S.). She holds one implement on each side of the poncho and scrapes them both downward simultaneously.

A matching collar (*cuello*, S.) is also woven, by Mena's daughter-in-law, but not attached to the poncho in the Mena workshop. One such collar piece measures 64 × 10 centimeters (25 × 4 inches) (The Textile Museum 1988.19.15). The poncho and its collar piece are sold together and the new owner has the collar attached by a marketplace tailor who does all kinds of sewing jobs, from patching worn clothing to finishing ponchos with a treadle sewing machine (Fig. 1.32). We met one such man, Luis Zapata, who works in the regional markets of Latacunga, Pujilí, Saquisilí, and Ambato.

The collar is made by cutting a triangular section from the corner of each end of the rectangle, leaving a trapezoid shape. One triangle is used for the gusset (*aleta* S., fin) at the nape of the neck and the other forms a button flap (also *aleta*) on the front of the poncho. Since the collar pieces are cut, it is necessary to finish the raw edges. The tailor has a bag of scraps from which the owner chooses a color for the edging (*ribeteado* S.) of the collar. He cuts strips of cloth from the scraps and sews the edging on both the collar and the button

1.31 Raising the nap on a poncho with teasels. Mena workshop, Pualó, Cotopaxi province. Slide by William H. Holmes, 1988.

1.32 Sewing the edge binding on a collar for a poncho, using a treadle sewing machine. Luis Zapata, Latacunga market, Cotopaxi province. Photo by Laura M. Miller, 1988.

flap. He then opens up the center seam of the poncho and sews the triangular back gusset into place. He next sews on the collar, followed by the button flap. Last, he makes the buttonholes. We rarely if ever saw these button flaps buttoned, but this is the style of Cotopaxi ponchos.

The Vertical Loom in Carchi Province

ANN P. ROWE   The use of a vertical loom (Fig. 1.33) and the fact that women are the weavers relate the weaving tradition of Carchi province more to that found in southern Colombia (Cortés [1989]; Pfyffer 2002: 257–262).

We recorded vertical-loom weaving by Aida Clemencia Narváez Morilla in the town of La Paz in 1989.[8] The loom consists of a square frame, including both uprights and upper and lower horizontal bars separate from the loom bars. The frame is made of squared boards, with the crosspieces set within the uprights. A peg is inserted near the top of each upright. The top loom bar is tied with rope to the uprights so that it hangs below the pegs but the ties are above the pegs, to prevent slipping. The bottom loom bar is tied to the lower horizontal bar of the frame with twisted leather bands. The frame leans against the wall for support, with rags tied to the top of the uprights to cushion them against the wall. The weaver seats herself on a low bench to work.

The warp is wound in the same way as for other highland Ecuadorian looms, that is, passing around both loom bars with the ends dovetailed. In the La Paz loom, the cord holding the dovetailed join is tied to each end of a rod. The shed rod and heddle rod are unsupported. The sword, worn to a wonderful smooth patina, is pointed on only one end and is used for strumming the warp as well as for beating. The weft yarn is composed of several threads of different colors.

Jaramillo (1988a: 8–9; 1991: 131–132) reports that warping is done on the actual loom bars already tied to the frame, not on separate warping stakes. The dovetailed join is warped over a steel wire with an eye on one end through which the final dovetail cord is threaded. Two temporary cross sticks are used for the sheds. These extra sticks are held by a helper until enough warp has been wound to secure them. The warp is counted in groups of twenty complete rounds. After warping, a stick (called *kwarmal*) about 2.5 centimeters in diameter (1 inch) is added near one of the loom bars in order to increase the tension on the warp (not apparent on the loom we saw in La Paz). Then the heddles are made. The heddle string appears to be wrapped spirally around the rod and warp, unlike for Ecuadorian backstrap looms.

The weaver we visited said that the wool she used was handspun by her neighbor and that she herself had done the dyeing. She makes both blan-

1.33 Weaving a blanket on a vertical loom. Aida Clemencia Narváez Morilla, La Paz, Carchi province. Slide by Lynn A. Meisch, 1989.

1.34 Wool blanket with warp-resist-dyed designs in warp-faced plain weave. La Paz, Carchi province. 2.08 × 1.71 meters (6 feet 10 inches × 5 feet 7¼ inches). The Textile Museum 1989.22.33, Latin American Research Fund.

kets and ponchos, each consisting of two loom panels. The ponchos are warp striped in brown and white and have some stripes of white and black that had been carded and spun together. A collar is added. The one the weaver's husband was wearing was four selvedged, while the one she had made to sell had fringed ends.

The blankets (Fig. 1.34) are four selvedged and are in bright pink and orange, with warp-resist-dyed designs not unlike blankets made elsewhere in

Ecuador (see Chapter 2). Two we saw here had large-scale chevron designs, and one had stepped-diamond designs. There was also a baby blanket made of a single loom panel of four selvedges, without warp-resist patterning, 1.28 × .76 meters (50 × 30 inches). Pfyffer (2002: 253–256) reports that some full-sized bedcovers are a single wide piece, which is easier to produce on a vertical than on a backstrap loom.

Warp-Resist-Patterned Wool Ponchos and Blankets

Introduction

ANN P. ROWE   Although the wool ponchos and blankets described in this chapter have relatively simple patterns, the weavers use an ingenious technique likely to be indigenous, despite the fact that they do not identify themselves as indigenous. These textiles also have a widely scattered distribution, although the technique and finished products are similar.

In yarn-resist dyeing, selected areas of the yarns are protected from the dye by applying a liquid resist material or by compressing the selected areas with either binding or clamping. In Ecuador, only warp-resist dyeing is done (no weft-resist) and the technique used is binding. That is, after warping, groups of warp yarns are wrapped tightly at intervals with another yarn or other material, which prevents dye from penetrating under the bound areas when the skein is dipped into the dye pot. After dyeing, the bindings are removed and the yarns are put on the loom and woven. It is easy for the yarns to slip slightly out of alignment on the loom, so designs produced by this method often have blurred edges. Because in Indonesia bound-resist dyeing of yarns before weaving has been carried to fantastic heights of elaboration, the Indonesian term *ikat* is often used to name this process, but we prefer the more descriptive "bound-yarn resist." The simplest techniques are found on wool blankets and ponchos, in which only a small portion of the warp yarns are bound, so they are described first.

Worldwide, it is relatively common for yarns to be bound as if to produce a rectangle design and then, after dyeing, to be pulled unevenly to form a chevron. In Ecuador this process is facilitated by the use of the dovetail cord. The technique involves first warping the pattern stripes in the usual Ecuadorian way (described in Chapter 1), except that each stripe has a separate dovetail cord. Then, after removing the dovetail stake, each dovetail cord is pulled into a chevron shape, which pulls each warp yarn in the stripe with it. The warp is then bound in rectangular blocks and dyed. After the warp is unbound, the dovetail cords are pulled straight again to make the chevron designs, and the stripes are incorporated into the rest of the warp for weaving. Since the dovetail cord is such an integral part of the indigenous loom in the northern Andes, this technique is presumably indigenous as well.

The blankets with this kind of chevron patterning are made by people who identify as *mestizos* or, in Azuay, *cholos*. Such people are presumably at least partly of indigenous descent, since they use the indigenous loom, but they mostly do not currently dress in a distinctive way, and they speak Spanish predominantly. The retention of the indigenous loom in these cases is probably due to the primarily commercial and nondomestic nature of the enterprise and to the blankets' not being a visible sign of ethnicity, as clothing is.

The locations where these blankets are made include Quero in Tungurahua province (Map 3), Pungalá in Chimborazo (Map 4), and San Juan Pamba (just south of Chicticay) in Azuay. Ponchos with chevron designs are also made using a similar technique, notably in Azuay. It is possible that the fine old-style Natabuela ponchos (of Imbabura province) with chevron designs were made in this way as well (Català Roca 1981: 213, fig. 647; Jaramillo 1988b: 165, 167–168; idem 1991: 41–44; Pfyffer 2002: cover, 154), but unfortunately the technique died out without having been recorded. Related blankets are also made on the vertical loom in Carchi province (Figs. 1.33–1.34) and the neighboring department of Nariño in southern Colombia (Cortés [1989]; Pfyffer 2002: 251–262). This scattered distribution may result from the kinds of migrations known to have occurred during the colonial period, or from people's copying a desirable and widely traded finished product. Or there may be some other historical factor no longer apparent.

This chapter begins with description of three areas where we recorded the chevron-patterned textiles. The method of achieving the chevron motif is the same in all areas, though other aspects of the process differ, such as the material used for the resist and whether binding is on the warping board or the loom. These sections are followed by a description of a poncho style with other kinds of bound-warp-resist designs.

Ponchos in Chordeleg, Azuay Province

LYNN A. MEISCH   Ponchos with bound-warp-resist patterning (*ponchos amarrados* S., tied ponchos) are traditionally worn by *cholo* men in the Cuenca region for fiestas and other special occasions, including Sunday Mass and market day. These ponchos are made to order as a specialty of certain weavers in the region. By 1980 don Abel Rodas of Chordeleg, a small town 38.6 kilometers (24 miles) east of Cuenca, was the last warp-resist-patterned poncho weaver in his community (Meisch 1981b)(Fig. 2.1), and he was still working in the 1990s, when he was in his eighties. He learned the process from his father. In addition to warp-resist-dyed ponchos don Abel weaves warp-resist and striped blankets and solid-color and striped ponchos.

A man desiring a warp-resist-dyed poncho gives don Abel a deposit to buy materials, including 6 *libras* (6.6 pounds, 3 kilograms) of two-ply white handspun yarn from the Paute market. He also buys a *carga* (15–20 *libras;* 16.5–22 pounds; 7.5–10 kilograms) of walnut branches (usually identified as *Juglans neotropica*), cut from the neighbor's living tree, and 15–20 kilograms (33–44 pounds) of firewood, also from a local source.

Dyeing the Yarn for the Stripes That Will Later Be Resist Dyed

On the first day of work at his home, don Abel dyes the yarn for the stripes that will later be resist dyed. Each poncho half has one such band, about twenty centimeters (eight inches) wide. Don Abel buys synthetic dyes at stores in Cuenca and believes German dyes are best while Peruvian and Japanese dyes are poor. Skeins (*madejas* S.) for each different colored stripe in the resist-dyed band, a rainbow of nine or ten colors ranging from yellow to dark blue, are dyed in the same pot one after another without changing the water. After the initial preparation of the dye bath, all don Abel does is add a different dye for each successive stripe. Sulfuric acid (*vítriol* S.) is used as a mordant to help the dye bond to the fiber. Thirty limes (*limones* S.) or alum (*alumbre* S.) can also be used as a mordant but are more expensive.

Don Abel fills a medium-sized ceramic pot about three-fourths full of water, balances it on stones, and builds a fire under it. He fills a second, smaller, ceramic pot with about a liter (quart) of water, then adds a few bottle caps of sulfuric acid and some dyeing salt (*sal* S., salt, an unknown white mineral, possibly Glauber's salt or tartaric acid, sold with the synthetic dyes). The sulfuric acid, water, and dyeing salt mixture is added to the water in the larger pot, then about a tablespoon of yellow synthetic dye is mixed in. Master dyers, like master cooks, measure by hand and eye—a pinch of this, a scoop of that— as a result of long experience and seldom use formal measuring devices. Don Abel is able to obtain eighty colors using synthetic dyes and twenty shades of brown using walnut bark. I did not have a measuring cup or measuring spoons with me when I documented don Abel at work nor did I want to interrupt him, so I cannot give precise measurements.

2.1 Don Abel Rodas wearing one of his warp-resist-patterned ponchos. Chordeleg, Azuay province. Slide by Lynn A. Meisch, 1978.

After the skein has absorbed all the yellow dye, don Abel removes it and hangs it on a bush to dry. He dyes successively darker colors, then lighter colors, in the following order: (1) yellow (*amarillo* S.); (2) orange (*naranja* S.); (3) dark orange (*naranja oscura* S.); (4) bright red (*rojo* S.); (5) dark red (*rojo oscuro* S.); (6) maroon (*café* S.); (7) black (*negro* S.); (8) dark blue (*azul* S.); and (9) light blue (*plomo* S.)(Plate 7).

On the second day don Abel uses the walnut bark to dye the yarn for the body (*cuerpo* S.) of the poncho. The yarn is bought in skeins and is dyed without being rewound. He gives the walnut bark a good pounding with a rock to separate it from the branches (Fig. 2.2) and then pounds it until it is pulverized. Don Abel's dye pot is a huge iron tub (*tanque* S.). He balances the tub on rocks, builds a fire under it, then adds two medium-sized baskets of mashed walnut bark (see photo in Meisch 1981b: 28 *top*). After the yarn is added to the dye bath, it must boil for three hours, after which it is removed.

Next, he mixes sulfuric acid and dyeing salt with water in a small ceramic pot and adds this mixture to the big iron pot. Ecuadorian dyers have no qualms about mixing natural and synthetic dyes. To get the deep brown color he wants, don Abel adds two small scoops of powdered orange synthetic dye (*aroma* S.) to the pot, then returns the yarn and boils it for about another hour. Finally, he removes the yarn from the dye pot and hangs it on the line or on bushes to dry.

Meanwhile, the dry skeins of dyed yarn for the stripes in the warp-resist stripe are made into balls (*ovillos* S.) for warping. Don Abel sits on a low wooden stool and puts the skein around his legs while he winds the yarn around his left hand (see photo in Meisch 1981b: 30 *top right*).

Warping, Binding, and Dyeing the Resist Stripes

On the third day, the entire morning is devoted to warping and binding the yarns to be resist dyed (*guardas* S.). Don Abel's warping board (*banco* S.) is about 7.5 centimeters (3 inches) thick, 20 centimeters (8 inches) wide, and 1.22 meters (4 feet) long. The board has holes where the end posts (*palos* S.), cross stake (*cruz* S.), and dovetail stake (*cargador* S.) are inserted. The board is adjustable for textiles of different sizes; the end posts for a poncho are set one vara apart (84 centimeters, or 33 inches). Because the warp is circular with the ends dovetailed, the poncho is actually two varas long.

The resist-dyed chevron design is called a *plumilla* (S., little feather). Don Abel warps the stripes for both poncho halves and binds each chevron stripe separately. First, a dovetail cord (*bocar*) is tied to the top (through a small hole) and bottom of the dovetail stake, and warping proceeds as described in Chapter 1. Each stripe is divided in half in the middle. The warp yarn is broken

2.2 Mashing walnut bark on a stone mortar for dyeing poncho yarns. Abel Rodas, Chordeleg, Azuay province. Slide by Lynn A. Meisch, 1978.

2.3 Warping the stripes to be resist dyed, tying off the crosses for each stripe. In the background, a girl is making a plaited ("Panama") hat. Abel Rodas, Chordeleg, Azuay province. Photo by Lynn A. Meisch, 1978.

and tied around the dovetail stake, and a piece of yarn of a contrasting color (*guía* S.) is tied through the warp cross (Fig. 2.3). Each resist-dyed stripe is split because, when don Abel does the final warping, the stripe will be separated by a few solid-color stripes, which he will insert in the final warping of the poncho.

To make the chevron design (which is sideways on the warping board), don Abel first carefully slips the dovetail cord (still joining the warp yarns) off the dovetail stake while keeping the warp on the warping board. He then grasps the dovetail cord in the middle of the band and pulls it into a sideways V-shape. He measures the length of each slope of the chevron with a ruler to be sure both sides are equal.

Next, don Abel takes small bunches of maguey fiber and wraps the resist (Fig. 2.4). He makes eleven simple rectangular bindings about five centimeters (two inches) wide and knots them with a square knot, using a ruler to measure

2.4 Binding the resist on the patterned stripes. In the background don Abel's wife is making a plaited hat. Abel Rodas, Chordeleg, Azuay province. Slide by Lynn A. Meisch, 1978.

their width as well as the distance between the knots. After the warp has been bound, don Abel ties the ends of the dovetail cord together (so it will not slip out), removes the stripe from the warping board, and repeats the process with the second stripe to be patterned. Then he builds a fire under his gallon-sized ceramic pot, adds water, sulfuric acid, dyeing salt, and black synthetic dye as described above, and immerses the bound yarn in the dye bath (see photo in Meisch 1981b: 30 *left*). He rinses off any excess black dye in the stream that runs by his house. The two stripes are then hung on the bushes to dry.

In the afternoon, while the patterned stripes are drying, don Abel makes balls of yarn from the skeins of dark brown yarn dyed on the previous day. When the patterned stripes are dry, he cuts the knots in the maguey fiber resist and unwraps them, revealing blocks of rainbow-colored bands between larger blocks of solid black.

Warping the Poncho Halves

On the fourth day, don Abel warps both poncho halves. There are sixteen hundred warp yarns (*hebras* S., yarns) to each poncho half. The counting is done in front of the cross stake. Since half the warp yarns pass in front of this stake and half behind, eight hundred warp yarns are counted. On the loom, each poncho half measures 75 centimeters (29½ inches) wide. When the poncho half is woven it measures 72 centimeters (28¼ inches) wide, since the warp contracts slightly in width during the weaving.

First, don Abel warps the brown yarn for the main body of the poncho. Then, he warps a few passes of contrasting colors (black, navy, light blue, beige in The Textile Museum 1988.22.19) to make a border (*guarda* S.) for the resist-dyed stripe. He uses an already woven poncho to judge the width of these sections. Next, he puts the resist-dyed stripe on his backstrap loom and straightens the warp out from a V to a straight line. He attaches the dovetail cord to the front loom bar and beats on it with his sword. He uses the warp cross to make sure all the resist-dyed warp yarns are untangled and in their proper order side by side. As he does this, the feather motifs appear. He takes the resist-dyed stripe off the loom and carries it back to his warping board, where he ties the patterned stripe's dovetail cord to the dovetail stake on the warping board. Very carefully, yarn by yarn, he slips half the resist-dyed warp yarns onto the warping board to join the warp for the main body of the poncho.

Don Abel next warps a few passes of contrasting colors to make a stripe in the middle of the resist-dyed stripe (black, navy, light blue, beige, wider brown, beige, light blue, navy, black in The Textile Museum 1988.22.19). Then he slips the warp yarns of the other half of the resist stripe, yarn by yarn, onto the dovetail stake and around the cross stake and end stakes. Next, he warps a few passes of contrasting colors (beige, light blue, navy, black) to finish the border of the resist-dyed design (*media guarda* S., middle border). Finally, he warps another thirty centimeters (one foot) of brown yarn to complete the body of the poncho half. He ties the cross with a yarn of a contrasting color (for example, orange) and removes the cross stake. He ties the ends of the dovetail cord together around the dovetail stake and takes the warp off the warping board and, with the dovetail stake still attached, twists it and puts one end through the loop of the other.

Don Abel repeats the process for the second half of the poncho. In one instance, some of the brown yarn was finer than the rest (because it was spun by different spinners in the Paute region), so don Abel finished warping with two balls of yarn, one thinner and one thicker, alternating them so that the texture of the last section of the warp appeared the same as the rest.

Setting Up the Loom and Weaving

On the fifth day, don Abel weaves one of the poncho halves. The loom posts are set against the side of his house under an overhanging roof (Fig. 2.5). His

2.5 Weaving a warp-resist-patterned poncho, opening the shed rod shed with the sword. Abel Rodas, Chordeleg, Azuay province. Photo by Lynn A. Meisch, 1978.

loom and weaving tools were handed down from his grandparents and have a beautiful patina from years of use. His sword is chonta wood.

Don Abel slips the warp over both loom bars, attaches his leather back-strap, and begins to spread out the warp. He puts tension on the loom and inserts a narrow sword between his body and the dovetail stake (with its dove-tail cord). He slides the dovetail stake out of the warp and ties the dovetail cord to the small sword. He inserts a wider sword above the dovetail cord; it is left in place to preserve space (about ten centimeters [four inches]) for the warp fringe and to give him something solid to beat against. He uses a second sword (*kálluwa*) for weaving. He always inserts the sword with the blunt side toward him (Fig. 2.5) and holds the shed open by turning the sword on its blunt edge, with its sharp edge holding the warps up. Next, he inserts a shed rod in the shed above the cross.

Then don Abel makes the heddles (*illawa* Q.), as described in Chapter 1. The heddle rod is notched at both ends so that the cord carrying the loops can be tied to it. If don Abel has made a mistake (for example, catching a warp yarn from the wrong shed), he breaks the heddle string, corrects his mistake, and reties the string with a square knot.

Next, don Abel (or his wife) winds two-ply brown yarn for the weft (*mini* Q.) onto the shuttle (*jisanchi*), a thin stick about forty-five centimeters (eighteen inches) long. Before he starts weaving he waxes the warp and his sword with the remains of an old candle (*esperma* S., tallow), to help keep the warp yarns from sticking together. He doubles the weft and passes it from right to left in the shed rod shed. He makes a slip knot with the weft around the rightmost warp yarn and another on the leftmost one after the shuttle is passed, then returns the doubled warp in the same shed. He opens the heddle shed and again passes the doubled weft. At the same time, he inserts a smaller secondary shed rod. He doubles the weft for the first ten passes then breaks it off at the left side of the warp and leaves the ends hanging (to be darned in later). This time, don Abel passes a single (two-ply) weft from right to left, making a slip knot with the loose end on the far right warp.

When about twenty-five centimeters (ten inches) are woven, don Abel removes the sword that he inserted against the dovetail cord to leave room for the fringe. He also removes the small sword holding the dovetail cord. He takes the dovetail cord and makes two half hitches around the four outside warp yarns on both the left and the right and then ties the dovetail cord together in the middle. He continues weaving with a single weft yarn for most of the body of the poncho half, using the sharp tip of a maguey leaf to line up the warp yarns in the resist-dyed stripe. As the weaving progresses, he uses a piece of yarn to measure the width and the length of the poncho.

When don Abel needs to join the ends of a broken warp yarn or the end of the old weft yarn to the beginning of the new, he uses a regular square knot rather than the weaver's knot. Sometimes the weft builds up unevenly. If so, he passes it back and forth on the same side (not all the way across) until it evens out.

When don Abel nears the end of the poncho half, he replaces the sword and the shed rod with smaller ones. He replaces the shuttle with a long, thin, wooden needle with an eye and a loop of string through the eye. He ties the weft to the string. For the last nine passes he doubles the weft. He leaves the end of the weft hanging, to be darned in later. He removes the loom parts and, last, pulls the dovetail cord out.

On the sixth day, don Abel repeats the process described above for the second half of the poncho. It would be appropriate to say that he rests on the seventh day, but the poncho is still not finished. And if the seventh day is a Sunday, don Abel frequently travels to the market in Paute to buy yarn for another order.

On the seventh day of work at his house, don Abel finishes the fringe. He twists two warp loops together in the opposite direction of the ply and then ties them. Using brown yarn the same color as the body of the poncho, he sews the two halves together from the bottom toward the neck, leaving an opening for the wearer's head. He inserts the needle from under the edge toward the body of the poncho back and forth across each half.

Next, don Abel takes out his warping board again, sets the end stakes about forty-five centimeters (eighteen inches) apart, and warps a small section about ten centimeters (four inches) wide for the collar and gusset, and sometimes a small tab in the front (*cartera* S.). He then weaves this. Don Abel leaves no fringe at the beginning but does leave room at the other end, not because he will make fringe but because the textile will be cut into two pieces and the ends hemmed.

When this piece comes off the loom, don Abel cuts it into two sections, one about thirty centimeters (twelve inches) long for the collar and the other about ten centimeters (four inches) long for a gusset at the back of the neck. He folds the ends of the collar back in a triangle and, using black cotton sewing thread, stitches them down with a herringbone stitch. He sews the gusset inside the back of the poncho, the raw edges with herringbone stitch and the selvedge edge with overcasting; from the right side the gusset forms a triangle. He sews the collar to the outside of the back of the poncho neck, then tacks down the edges of the collar and gusset on the inside, with overcasting. If don Abel includes a tab, he sews this on at the front of the neck, then continues the join up the back to meet the collar and up the front to meet the tab. The poncho is now finished and ready for use.

Blankets with chevron designs are also made in San Juan Pamba, just south of Chicticay, in Azuay province, as recorded by Laura Miller. The technique of pulling on the dovetail cord is the same as that described for Chordeleg. The resist binding is done on the warping board much as don Abel does it, but wool yarn similar to the warp, rather than maguey, is used for binding. The stripes are all bound together, as in Quero and Pungalá, rather than separately, as don Abel does. The variations evident in the stripes of the Carchi blanket (Fig. 1.34) reveal that these stripes were bound separately. The San Juan Pamba blanket recorded by Miller has white solid stripes and three chevron stripes in each half dyed red, with a narrow solid stripe through the middle of the outer chevrons.

Blankets in Quero, Tungurahua Province

LAURA M. MILLER   Heavy woolen bound-warp-resist patterned blankets called *cobijas* (S.) are woven on backstrap looms in *mestizo* communities of Quero and its barrio, San Vicente, not far south of Ambato (Fig. 2.6). Only some three or four families were making the blankets in 1988, but in the past, virtually everyone in these communities was involved. The advent of cheaper acrylic factory-made blankets in rural areas has depressed the market a great deal, and the weavers were attempting to sell blankets in the tourist market. Their children, however, are not learning the craft.

Andrés López V. of San Vicente, the weaver we recorded, then in his seventies, said that synthetic dye is used for the dark wine red color called *lacre* (S., sealing wax). He did not know of earlier dye sources for red. He also mentioned that walnut hulls and leaves were used for dye. In the past, they also used a plant called *kulkas* (see Chapter 9) as well as *aliso* (S., alder) for yellow for stripes in ponchos. Some blankets were made of undyed yarns, using white and dark yarn plied together to make gray, to contrast with white stripes.

Señor López's wife, Senaida Franco de López, travels to the Saturday market in Riobamba to buy wool; she buys both spun and raw wool. She used to go to Saquisilí, but in the late 1970s she could no longer find spun wool there, or, if present, it was too dirty. She can get wool in the Monday market of Ambato but prefers Riobamba, even though it is farther away. She buys synthetic dyes in the same markets as the wool.

The blanket is made in two halves, and each half (*hoja*, S., leaf) has three sections of resist-patterned warp. First, the sections to be bound and dyed are warped, each with its own dovetail cord.

Warping

Señora de López warps the blankets on a frame (*urdidora*), consisting of a base with two end stakes (*estacas* S.), a dovetail stake (*engarce*), and a cross stake (*cruzera*). A horizontal stick (*tope,* S.) is placed between the two end posts to keep them parallel.

Señora de López first wraps a dovetail cord (also called *engarce*) around a notch at the top of the dovetail stake and allows the longer end to trail down the stake. She ties the wool warp yarn onto the dovetail stake near the base and begins to warp to her right. After warping twenty pairs of yarns, she ties the warp yarn off around the dovetail stake. She pushes these warp yarns down on the dovetail stake and unties the dovetail cord from the notch at the top, allowing it to hang free. She then places another dovetail cord on the dovetail

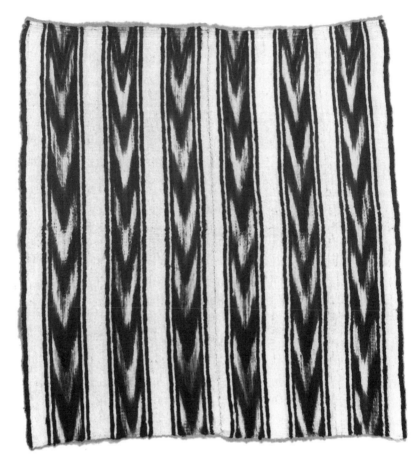

2.6 Warp-resist-patterned wool blanket in warp-faced plain weave woven by Andrés López V., San Vicente, Tungurahua province. 1.67 × 1.87 meters (65¾ × 73⅝ inches). The Textile Museum 1988.19.137, Latin American Research Fund.

stake and warps a second stripe in the same manner as the first, repeating the process again for a third stripe. Each group of twenty pairs of warp is called a *llama;* the dyed pattern is called *llama chaki* (Q.) or *pata de llama* (S.), both meaning "llama foot."

Señor López then prepares the warp for the resist. He moves the cross stake and the cross to his right, making room to manipulate the yarns at the dovetail. To preserve the cross, he places a cord (*engarce de los cruzeros*) through the cross of each section separately, after which he removes the cross stake.

He ties the ends of each dovetail cord together so that each is secured and makes a single loop. He then spreads the warp yarns out evenly along the dovetail cord, putting a few millimeters between each of the yarns along the cord. He next counts up ten pairs from the bottom and grasps the eleventh (center) yarn. He holds the bottom ten yarns in position with his left hand while he uses his right hand to pull the top ten yarns to his right. He offsets the topmost yarn by about eighteen centimeters (seven inches), and each yarn successively lower is offset by a somewhat lesser amount.

He repeats this process with the bottom yarns, so the dovetail cord forms a sideways V, with the opening to his right (Fig. 2.7). He adjusts the yarns with meticulous care, always checking to see that the space between the yarns on the dovetail cord is even. When he is satisfied, he bunches up the warp and wraps it with the ends of the dovetail cord, thus securing the position of the warp yarns. He prepares all three patterned sections in this fashion and is then ready to begin the resist-binding process.

Señor López takes out the top piece of the warping frame. All three sections are bound together and will be separated again only after they are dyed. He first wraps a strip of plastic called a *culebra* (S., snake) tightly around the warp for about ten centimeters (four inches), starting from the left (Fig. 2.8). This plastic had clearly been used several times before. He holds the plastic in place with maguey fiber cord. He starts wrapping the cord on his right and moves to his left. He pulls on the cord especially hard at his right side to secure the end so that the dye will not penetrate. He binds the desired length and then reverses direction, returning to the right side. On this second round, the bindings are not as closely spaced as before. When he reaches the spot where he began, he ties off the end.

He binds both sides of the warp together, making four bindings, so that there will be eight patterned sections. He then places a string (*cuenda* S.) through the loop in the warp where the end stake was, so that the warp will not tangle during dyeing. He lifts the warp, ready for the dye pot, from the warping frame. He can prepare four halves in a day, enough for two blankets. Once the piece is dyed and the bindings removed, he straightens out the dovetail cord, forming a V design.

When the patterned stripes are dry after dyeing, he adds them to the rest of the blanket warped by his wife. First, she warps plain white. The dovetail cord for this section serves as the dovetail cord for the whole blanket. She then places a resist-dyed stripe on the dovetail cord. The dovetail cord of each resist-dyed section has a loop at the end. She uses this loop like the eye of a needle, passing the new dovetail cord through it and pushing the warp yarns of the resist-dyed stripe onto the blanket dovetail cord. Warping continues in this manner. When finished, she twists the warp on itself and lays it aside.

2.7 Pulling the dovetail cord into a chevron. Andrés López V., San Vicente, Tungurahua province. Photo by Laura M. Miller, 1988.

2.8 Wrapping the plastic resist on the patterned stripes. Andrés López V., San Vicente, Tungurahua province. Photo by Laura M. Miller, 1988.

2.9 Weaving a warp-resist-patterned blanket half. The weaver is almost finished and is using a narrow sword. To get maximum tension, he lifts himself off the bench. Andrés López V., San Vicente, Tungurahua province. Photo by Laura M. Miller, 1988.

Weaving

The supports for the back loom bar are floor-to-ceiling posts (Fig. 2.9). With the warp on the loom bars, the heddles are made in the manner described for Azuay province in Chapter 1, using a gauge consisting of a solid short dowel with a flange at one end with a hole in it (*illawero* Q. with S. suffix, pronounced "*izhawero*"). Then the two shed rods (*cruzera mayor* and *cruzera menor* S.) are inserted. The sword is myrtle wood (*arrayán* S.).

The weaver also uses a wooden pick (*mishín*) to strum the warp and a wooden comb (*peine* S.). The use of a comb is unusual in Ecuador, since it is more often associated with weft-faced than with warp-faced weaving. It is particularly suited to techniques such as tapestry weaving, where the weft yarn is inserted through only a small portion of the warp at a time. Perhaps Señor López's ancestors wove tapestries.

Señor López opens the sheds as described in Chapter 1. Once the shed is open, he inserts the weaving sword into the shed with the wider side toward him and uses the comb to beat the previous weft into place. Then he turns the tapered edge of the weaving sword toward the ground, placing the sword on edge in order to pass the weft. He uses the sharp edge of the sword to beat the new weft into place. To obtain maximum tension, he may lift himself off his seat entirely (Fig. 2.9). As he reaches the end of the warp, he uses narrower swords (Fig. 2.9) and, finally, a long metal needle to pass the weft.

The blankets are finished by middlemen who also sell to the stores. The middlemen scrape the blankets with a pair of teasel brushes in order to raise a nap. Local customers like the nap, but tourists prefer the blankets without this finishing touch because they like to be able to see the handwoven texture.

Blankets in Pungalá, Eastern Chimborazo Province

ANN P. ROWE AND LAURA M. MILLER We visited Mariana Zavala and her son Rodrigo Pata, who weave ponchos and blankets on commission for neighbors who supply the yarn.[1] The blankets are called *cobija amarrada,* with large ones requiring 14 *libras* (15½ pounds, or 7 kilograms) of wool and smaller ones 9 *libras* (10 pounds, or 4.5 kilograms). We observed part of the process of making a smaller blanket, which would have seven stripes of a block design called *ladrillo* (S., brick) alternating with seven stripes of chevrons, called *pata de llama* (S., llama foot), separated by narrow solid stripes, in each half (*hoja*) of the blanket. The yarn to be resist dyed had already been dyed pink (*rosado* S.) and the overdye was maroon (*lacre* S.). All their dyes are synthetic, bought in Riobamba.

Señora Zavala warps all seven stripes for the block design at once, using two cross stakes, but ties the crosses and dovetail joins separately for each stripe (Fig. 2.10). The dovetail stake (*palo de remate* S.) is a metal rod with a string loop at the bottom, which señora Zavala uses to thread each dovetail cord through the warp sections. She works from bottom to top to thread the dovetail cords and from top to bottom to tie them off tightly. She then removes the warp from the warping board, twisting it on itself.

She puts the warp on the loom bars and uses the warping board as a foot brace (as her son is doing in Fig. 2.11). To measure the length of the bindings and the spaces between them, she uses a stick. The measure (*jeme* S.) is the distance between the thumb and first finger when the hand is outstretched. She places the middle of the stick at the dovetail join and begins to wrap above the stick. For the binding she uses a yarn that is identical to the warp and that

2.10 Tying off the stripes for the warp resist. Mariana Zavala, Pungalá, Chimborazo province. Photo by Laura M. Miller, 1989.

2.11 The warp on the loom bars ready to be bound. Rodrigo Pata, Pungalá, Chimborazo province. Photo by Laura M. Miller, 1989.

is later used for weft. She measures ten *brazos* (S.), the length from hand to hand with the arms outstretched, then the same length again, to double it. She folds the yarn in half twice, until she has eight strands, and the length becomes 2½ *brazos*.

The binding we observed was actually done by Rodrigo Pata, with his mother looking on and helping (Fig. 2.12). He passes the binding yarn around the warp, all the stripes together, and the end is passed through the loop at the other end and pulled very tightly. He wraps upward and counterclockwise. Señora Zavala told her son to wrap hard and not to twist the eight strands. When he has bound a *jeme*, he begins to wrap back toward himself. The return can be looser than the first binding. To tie off the binding, he divides the eight strands into two sets of four, wraps a little more, and ties the ends in a square knot.

2.12 Binding the resist. Rodrigo Pata, Pungalá, Chimborazo province. Photo by Laura M. Miller, 1989.

2.13 Making the chevron with the dovetail cord. Mariana Zavala, Pungalá, Chimborazo province. Photo by Laura M. Miller, 1989.

Señora Zavala put one section of the second half on the loom to show us how the chevron design was made (Fig. 2.13). She used the word *sesgueado* (S., slanted) to refer to the realignment of the dovetail cord.

She spreads out the warp yarns of the stripe on the far loom bar and ties the cross string loosely to itself so that the warp yarns can be moved. She counts from right to left to find the middle warp yarn of the section; there are seven pairs altogether. She separates the warp yarns along the dovetail cord and then carefully pulls the dovetail cord to make a V with the point away from her. She arranges the warp yarns along the inverted V, and ties the dovetail cord at the base of the V. As with the block design, all the stripes in one half are bound together and the measure is the same.

Poncho Rosado in Paniquindra, Eastern Imbabura Province

LAURA M. MILLER We could not observe warping and binding of the *poncho rosado* (pink poncho), but the weavers, Elias Pupiales and his son Luis Virgilio Pupiales, explained their techniques. Each half of the poncho (*hoja*) has three bound-warp-resist stripes, bordered by several green and red warp yarns, placed evenly in the pink field. The poncho we saw on the loom had a central stripe with lettering ("PROVINCIA IMBABURA") and side stripes with an undulating vine motif, called *uva guarda* (S., grape border) (Fig. 2.14). Other designs on these ponchos include *palma* (S., palm; a chevron pattern), *kingu* (Q., zigzag; M- or W- shaped motifs), and *anteojo* (S., eyeglasses; a curvilinear motif). The ponchos we saw on the looms in Paniquindra in 1989 were commissioned by men in La Florida and Paniquindra.

All the yarn is first dyed pink. The stripes to be resist dyed are warped first, and the resist bindings are applied while the yarns are on the warping board (*banco*). On the finished poncho, designs appear to be mirror images of each other, symmetrical about the center of the warp length, indicating that, when the resist bindings are put in place, both sides of the warp are wrapped in the same binding.

2.14 Warping a resist-dyed poncho. A similar warp is on the loom at right. Paniquindra, eastern Imbabura province. Slide by Laura M. Miller, 1989.

2.15 Adjusting the alignment of the resist-dyed warp yarns during weaving. Elías Pupiales, Paniquindra, eastern Imbabura province. Photo by Barbara Borders, 1989.

It was hard to tell if warp yarns from more than one stripe were bound together, for we were shown the resist-binding technique (*watana* Q.) on an already-dyed piece. For binding short areas (5–7.5 centimeters [2–3 inches] or less), the artisan wraps the warp with *chawar* (*Furcraea* fiber) strips, starting on his left and working to his right. When he starts to wrap, he leaves some extra fiber hanging at the right side. He wraps tightly, overlapping the fiber so that no dye will leak in. When he reaches the right edge of the area, he wraps extra-tightly and then works back to the left. When he reaches the starting point, he ties the fiber to the initial long end with a double knot and cuts the ends with scissors. When demonstrating this technique, Luis Virgilio Pupiales bound about five or six yarns, selecting them between the dovetail stake and closest cross stake.

For areas longer than 7.5 centimeters (3 inches), the artisan uses a cornhusk soaked in water and cut to the necessary length. The cornhusk wrap is held in place with *chawar.* The fiber is tightly wrapped and crisscrossed over the cornhusk, holding it in place.

After the resist is wrapped, the pink wool is overdyed with black. Black synthetic dye is purchased in Ibarra, and lemon juice is added to help fix the dye. After the resist stripes are dry, the entire poncho is warped, incorporating the resist-dyed stripes (Fig. 2.14).

Elias Pupiales weaves in an open area under the roof of his adobe house. The back beam (*panga*) is lashed to two stone posts sunk into the ground near the house wall. He uses a tenter stick (*tupuli* Q.) to maintain the width. The dovetail stick is bound to the warp with large half hitches using a cabuya yarn. He uses two shed rods (both called *pasín*) (see Figs. 1.6–1.11).

When weaving, Elias Pupiales is meticulous, and after every few weft passes he spends several minutes carefully adjusting the warp yarns so the resist design is as precise as possible. He uses a needle in his right hand to push against the weft and pulls the warp yarns into place with his left hand, to make the edges of the resist-dyed areas line up perfectly (Fig. 2.15).

CHAPTER 3

Warp-Resist-Patterned Cotton Shawls and Ponchos

Introduction

ANN P. ROWE Among the most striking and beautiful textiles in Ecuador are the bound-warp-resist and indigo-dyed cotton shawls with knotted fringe that are made in Rumipamba de las Rosas near Salcedo in Cotopaxi province (Map 3), and in Bulcay el Carmen and Bulshun (pronounced Bulzhun) near Gualaceo in Azuay province (Map 5). Formerly, similar shawls were made in Quichinche, San Juan (on the northern outskirts of the town of Otavalo), and Quiroga in Imbabura province (Map 2) (Jaramillo 1988b: 167–170; idem 1991: 42, 45–46; Pfyffer 2002: 211–212), but this production seems to have died out in the mid-twentieth century.

The Azuay shawls are made by *cholos* for sale to *cholo* women. The shawls in Imbabura were made for sale to women who were, like *cholos*, of intermediate socioeconomic class. These women were called *bolsiconas*, after the style of gathered skirt that they wore (*bolsicón* S.), similar to that still worn by *cholos* in Azuay (for a photograph, see Blomberg [ed.] 1952: 171). The Rumipamba shawls are also made for sale by people who now dress as *mestizos*. This pattern of manufacture is similar to that of the warp-resist blankets.

A simpler version of the Azuay shawl called *paño pacotillo* (S., poor-quality shawl) is used as a carrying cloth by some indigenous women of Chimborazo and Cañar provinces (Meisch in A. Rowe [ed.] 1998: 223, fig. 227) and the Rumipamba shawls are used as carrying cloths by indigenous women in Bolívar province and elsewhere. In Cotopaxi, however, it does appear that they were formerly used as shawls by indigenous women, while in Imbabura these shawls were apparently often buried with indigenous dead (Jaramillo 1988b: 169; idem 1991: 46).

Nonetheless, the predominant pattern of manufacture and use by people of intermediate social status correlates with the technological mixture that the shawls represent. They are woven on the indigenous style of backstrap loom, and the bound-warp-resist technique may also be indigenous, since some fragments of pre-Hispanic warp-resist-patterned cotton cloth with brown geometric designs have been found in Guayas province (Gardner 1979, 1982, 1985; Pfyffer 2002: 36–43). On the other hand, knotted warp fringe is not found in the pre-Hispanic American tradition, but, rather, is a common method of finishing the ends of treadle-loom woven cloth (see Chapter 8). In this technique, a set of elements is interworked by knotting adjacent elements with each other. The popular term is *macramé*, while that proposed by Irene Emery is *interknotting* (Emery 1980: 65).

How this style of shawl developed is unclear. In the absence of any documentation, possible influences from Asia or from Islamic Spain have been proposed (Martin 1993). The similarity of the Ecuadorian warp-resist-patterned shawls to others found in Mexico, Guatemala, and the north highlands of Peru around Cajamarca tends to support a Spanish colonial period origin. In Mexico this type of shawl can be traced as far back as the seventeenth century, and it may have been developed there (Davis 1991: 312–314). The usual manner of wearing it, with both ends draped over the left shoulder, is shown on creole and *mestizo* women in an eighteenth-century engraving of costume in Quito (Juan and Ulloa 1748 [vol. 1]: 378, lam. XIII; reprinted in A. Rowe [ed.] 1998: 46). But nineteenth-century Ecuadorian evidence for shawls with fringe on the ends is scarce.

These pieces require more complex grouping of warp yarns for binding than do those described in Chapter 2. We begin with the simpler Rumipamba shawls, but the technique of the Azuay shawls has been recorded in greater detail. The designs repeat across the width of the warp. Each individual design is made up of a series of components, and each component consists of a fixed number of warp yarns. Analogous components from the entire width of the warp are grouped for binding. In this way, the design needs to be bound only once. The term *selection system* applies to this grouping of analogous yarns from across the warp. The Ecuadorian systems are of notable ingenuity and economy of means.

The procedure used to select and group the patterned stripes in the indigo-dyed cotton ponchos of Cacha, in Chimborazo province, is similar in principle to that of Azuay. These ponchos are made by indigenous people for sale to other indigenous people. The fabric is woven on the backstrap loom, but the hole-and-slot heddle used to make the fringe band sewn to the outer edges is a European introduction (Sturtevant 1977). So, again, the technique is a hybrid. A hole-and-slot heddle is also used to make fringe for ponchos in the

Cuzco area of Peru, adding another similarity between the two areas to those of the warp-resist patterning and the poncho form. As noted in the Introduction, the available evidence suggests that the poncho, like the fringed shawl, spread through the Andes during the eighteenth century.

Macanas in Rumipamba de las Rosas, Cotopaxi Province

LAURA M. MILLER   We had known that warp-resist-patterned shawls were made in the Salcedo area of Cotopaxi province, and we finally located one of the four remaining weaving families in 1988 in a rural community called Rumipamba de las Rosas.[1] The family consisted of a couple, Nicolás Taipe and María Quilo de Taipe, their adult daughter María, and her husband, Segundo Taco. Señora de Taipe's parents were farmers, and she learned the processes of weaving and dyeing when she married and moved to Rumipamba. Señor Taipe learned these skills from his father.

The Rumipamba *macanas*, as these shawls are known, have white designs on a blue background, including *kingu* (Q., zigzag); *pata de cabra con mosquito* (S., goat hoof with mosquito), also called *pata de llama con moscas* (S., llama foot with flies); *cocos* (S., diamonds); *ladrillo* (S., brick); and *paiteña* (S., a kind of onion) (Figs. 3.1–3.3; A. Rowe [ed.] 1998: 121, fig. 111).

Marketing and Use

Macanas were sold at the weaver's home for 1,200 sucres ($2.52 at the 1988 exchange rate), and in the Salcedo market for 2,000 sucres ($4.20). It takes about three hours to warp and tie one *macana* and about five hours to weave it. The Taipe family bought their materials from the same middleman to whom they sold their product in the market, and their earnings were low. One of the shawl-weaving families was not working when we were there due to lack of money to buy materials.

In 1988 we saw only one elderly woman in the Saquisilí market wearing a *macana* (A. Rowe [ed.] 1998: 117, fig. 102). The shawls are, however, in common use as carrying cloths in Bolívar province, especially in the Guaranda area (Map 4) (A. Rowe [ed.] 1998: 165, fig. 154). Designs most often seen in the Guaranda market are *pata de cabra* and one similar to *ladrillo* but with very narrow resist white portions. *Macanas* are sold in the Guaranda market with unknotted fringes. Before wearing, the fringe is knotted in six or seven rows of simple overhand knots, without fancy designs.

Señora de Taipe remembered the past when the *macanas* were taken to Ambato, Riobamba, and Cuenca to be sold. In the 1980s the shawls were some-

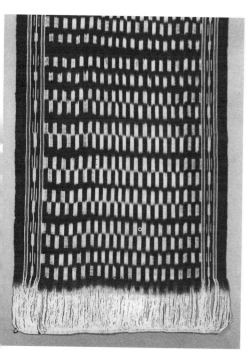

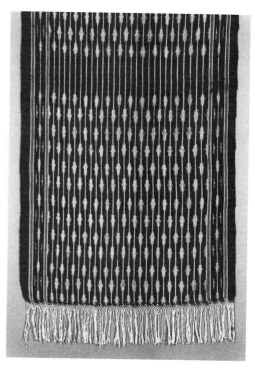

3.1 Warp-resist-patterned cotton shawl with *adrillo* pattern; warp-faced plain weave with unfinished fringe. Woven by Segundo Taco, Rumipamba, Cotopaxi province. Overall size: 1.89 × .74 meters (74½ × 29 inches). The Textile Museum 1988.19.5, Latin American Research Fund.

3.2 Warp-resist-patterned cotton shawl with *paiteña* pattern; warp-faced plain weave with fringe interknotted with overhand knots. Rumipamba, Cotopaxi province, purchased in the Otavalo market. The wide unpatterned area near the top is the middle of the shawl. Overall size: 1.83 (including fringe) × .74 meters (72 × 29 inches). The Textile Museum 1986.19.45, Latin American Research Fund.

times sold in the tourist craft sections of the Otavalo and Riobamba markets. They were also sold in artisan stores in Quito but were seldom seen in Cuenca. In the summer of 1989, an entrepreneur began to make carrying bags from this fabric, to be sold in some of the fine craft stores in Quito.

Warping and Dyeing

The shawls are warped on a board called a *banquillo* (S.). The entire piece is warped in white cotton and, while it is still on the warping board, groups of yarns to be bound together for the resist are separated. For a simple design, such as *ladrillo* (Fig. 3.1), which consists of alternating blocks of white on a blue ground, the warp is divided into only two groups of yarns. The *paiteña* design (Fig. 3.2) also requires only two groups of yarns. More complex designs, such as *coco* (Figs. 3.3 and 3.4) or *pata de cabra con mosquito* (Fig. 3.5) are formed with four groups of yarns, and the selection system is more complex.

In the selection process for the *ladrillo* design, all the warp yarns for the half of the rectangles that will line up horizontally are grouped together (here called A for convenience), as are all the warp yarns for the alternate rows of rectangles (here called B). Cords called *contando* (S., counting) are used to select the groups; the counting cord is tied on to the bottommost warp yarn on the warping board, and the warper counts out *pares* (S., pairs) at the dovetail cord. A *par* is two warp yarns, but yarns from both in front of and behind the dovetail stake are included, so it is actually four yarns. In the *ladrillo* design, each rectangle requires four *pares*, so when looking at the finished piece, each brick of the design is sixteen warp yarns wide. The counting cord is placed behind four *pares* for the first line of rectangles (A) and in front of four *pares* for the second line of alternate rectangles (B), and so on across the entire warp.

Two *macanas* can be warped, one above the other, on the warping board. Threads from both shawls are placed in the same two groups (A and B), and the two pieces are bound and dyed together, to save time and labor.

While separating the A and B groups, the warper also selects warp yarns to remain completely white; these form the warp-parallel borders along both side selvedges. Once separated, these warp yarns are twisted together and placed over the end stake of the warping board.

After the counting cord is placed, the warper physically separates the A warp yarns from the B. Using the selection created by the counting cord, she works across the entire warp (i.e., in a weft-parallel direction), gathering all the A yarns in front of her right thumb and the B yarns between her right thumb and forefinger. Once finished, she shifts the warp to her right on the warping board, which allows her to separate the groups along the entire warp. Each of these groups (or pattern units) is called a *soga* (S., rope).

For more complicated designs, like the *pata de cabra con mosquito* or *coco*, there are four *sogas*. These designs are composed of seven components symmetrical about a central line (Fig. 3.4). The yarns in the component labeled 1 on Figure 3.4 are grouped in one *soga;* those of 2 and 3 are grouped in the second and third *sogas*, respectively. The group marked 4 is the central axis and is alone in a *soga*. When bound, the design is a half diamond, having been folded along a central axis. When dyed and opened, the design appears as a full diamond (Fig. 3.3). We did not see a four-*soga* design being warped and

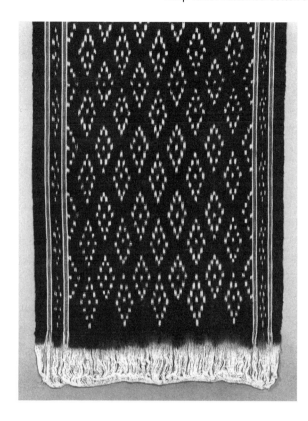

3.3 Warp-resist-patterned cotton shawl with *coco* pattern; warp-faced plain weave with unfinished fringe. Woven by Segundo Taco, Rumipamba, Cotopaxi province. Overall size: 1.84 × .75 meters (72½ × 29½ inches). The Textile Museum 1988.19.6, Latin American Research Fund.

bound. Either the technique used in Azuay province or that of Tacabamba, Department of Cajamarca, Peru (see Miller 1991), or another could be used.

After the *sogas* are formed, the resist bindings are put on. The warp is shifted on the warping board so that the dovetail cord (*cuenda* S.) is centered on the left end stake. The dovetail end will be the shawl fringe, and the center of the shawl lies at the right end stake. The artisan places the first binding one handspan from the dovetail cord. Since the Rumipamba shawls have white designs on a blue ground, the resist bindings cover a relatively small area, and only a few hours are needed to prepare one warp for dyeing. The strips of maguey fiber used to bind the warp were deep blue from reuse.

The artisan wraps the fiber tightly around a group of warp yarns and works toward the right and then back to the left, finishing with a square knot. The long ends are cut with a kitchen knife. The artisan measures *cuatro dedos* (S., four fingers) from the first binding and places the next binding on the same *soga*. Another resist binding is placed on the other *soga* between the two bindings on the first *soga*.

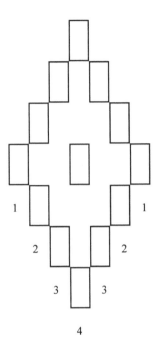

A

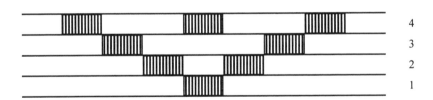

B

3.4 Diagram of binding the *coco* design in a Rumipamba shawl. A: The finished design with the *sogas* (pattern units) numbered. B: The design as it would appear in a bound warp on the warping board, ready for dyeing. Drawing by Ann P. Rowe, based on a drawing by Laura M. Miller.

Warp yarns on both sides of the warping board are bound together. The artisan starts at the dovetail and fringe end (usually the left) and wraps to the right. When she or he reaches the far right, the thick end-stake of the warping board prevents placement of the last bindings at the center of the warp. A small stick (*palito* S.) is placed along the right warping post, the *sogas* are slipped off the post onto this much smaller stick, and the final resist bindings are made. Before dyeing, the small stick is removed and replaced with a maguey fiber cord.

After resist binding, the artisan takes the warp off the warping board and securely winds the yarns for the white warp stripes around the dovetailed end of the warp so they and the dovetailed end can be held out of the dye.

The cotton warp yarn comes from the factory with sizing that prevents the dye from penetrating the fibers. Therefore, the bound warp is washed before dyeing using lather made by beating a *Furcraea* leaf. The weaver and his wife also work over the bound warp, using their thumbnails to open the unbound areas, so that the dye can penetrate more easily. (For the indigo dye preparation, see Chapter 9.)

The yarn is dipped in the dye pot six times. Between dippings, the warp is hung on a hook next to the door, and the couple continues opening up the unbound portions of the warp with their thumbs to facilitate dye penetration.

After dyeing, the warp is allowed to dry for five minutes, and then the maguey-fiber resist bindings are cut off, separating the two shawls that have been bound together. The warp yarns left white are then washed in water with *Furcraea* lather and the whole warp is allowed to dry in the sun.

Weaving

The shawls are woven on the backstrap loom (Fig. 3.5). In the home of the Taipe family, two looms are set up facing each other, and the back loom bar is only a foot from the ground. The weaving process is as described in Chapter 1, using two shed rods and a pointed stick (*mishín*) to strum.

The shawls are woven with dark blue cotton weft. The family purchases the yarn in long cut lengths that are probably factory ends. Children knot the ends together into a continuous weft yarn and roll it into a ball.

Paños in the Gualaceo Area, Azuay Province

ANN P. ROWE   The elaborate warp-resist-patterned shawl (*paño* S.) with long knotted fringe is the glory of the *cholo* woman's costume in Azuay province (Figs. 3.6–3.8) (see also Meisch in A. Rowe [ed.] 1998: 256–259). Since the 1980s, fewer local women have been wearing these shawls, and some artisans, with the encouragement of CIDAP in Cuenca, are producing yardage for clothing or simple shawls, scarves, and belts for the tourist market (Pfyffer 2002: 198–202).

The techniques used have been described previously by various authors (Meisch 1981a; Penley 1988; Miller 1989, 1991). The present summary is provided for the sake of completeness in this volume and to facilitate comparison with the other warp-resist dyeing techniques we recorded. Some new details and variations are included, from my own observations in 1986 (with Laura Miller as guide), from additional information from Meisch and Miller, and from my study of Textile Museum shawls.

Although worn throughout the Cuenca valley, the shawls are made chiefly in the non-nucleated villages of Bulcay and Bulshun near Gualaceo, about forty kilometers (twenty-five miles) east of Cuenca. The warping, binding, and dyeing are usually done by a woman, the weaving by a man, and the knotting of the fringe by a second woman. The first two processes are often done by wife and husband. The knotting is frequently done by women specialists in

3.5 Weaving a warp-resist-dyed cotton shawl with the *pata de cabra con mosquito* design. Segundo Taco, Rumipamba, Cotopaxi province. Photo by William H. Holmes, 1988.

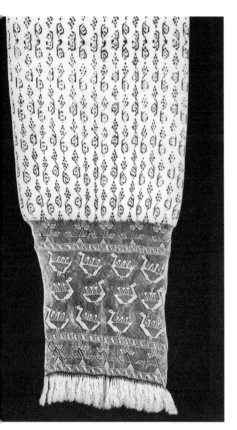

Warp-resist-patterned cotton shawl, warp-
[fac]ed plain weave with fringe interknotted with
[over]hand knots. Gualaceo area, Azuay province,
[pro]bably first half of the twentieth century. The
[cen]ter of the shawl, with the design reversal, can
[be s]een at the top of the photograph. Overall size:
[2.9]5 (including fringe) × .76 meters (116 × 30
[inch]es). The Textile Museum 1988.17.27, Latin
[Am]erican Research Fund.

3.7 Warp-resist-patterned cotton shawl (*paño
zhiru*), in warp-faced plain weave with fringe
interknotted in overhand knots. The ground areas
are mottled (*zhiru*). The knotted design includes
the coat of arms of Ecuador. Gualaceo area, Azuay
province, dated 1937. Overall size: 2.97 (including
fringe) × .79 meters (117 × 31 inches). The Textile
Museum 1988.17.26, Latin American Research
Fund.

Gualaceo, who often work while tending fruit stands in the market. Formerly,
children of both sexes assisted their families by knotting fringe (Miller and
Proyecto 1986: 14–15). Design innovation, however, in both resist designs and
fringe knotting, is credited to men (Miller and Proyecto 1986: 17–18, 24).

Traditionally, a male or female entrepreneur would provide materials; commission the warping, weaving, and knotting of the shawls; and then sell the

finished product (Miller and Proyecto 1986: 13, 17). In other cases, however, a couple would buy the materials themselves and warp, dye, and weave the shawl before selling it to a woman who would knot the fringe (Miller and Proyecto 1986: 15, 21).

The warp in the finest examples is white cotton (Figs. 3.6–3.7) that, in the late 1970s, was processed in Ambato (Meisch 1981a: 1). One eight-pound cone (30/2) has enough yarn for about four shawls.[2] A less-expensive style uses a striped layout and a colored warp. By the 1980s, however, cotton had become so expensive that the latter style became more common, using bright pink or red wool, bought dyed or home dyed with synthetic dye (Fig. 3.8). Although these shawls are called *cachemira* (S., cashmere), the wool is simply fine sheep's wool and not the fine undercoat hair of goats.

Warping and Binding

The warp for the complete shawl is wound on stakes on a warping board (*banco* S.). Between the end stakes (*takti*) are a dovetail stake (*cargador* S.) and a cross stake (*masa*) to the right. When the warp is entirely wound, the artisan adds thick cotton organizing cords (*cuendas* S.) in order to group the warp yarns for binding.

Each cord marks one component of one motif in each place where it is repeated. Often, these cords are different colors, presumably, to help the artisan keep track of the eventual design. The cords are used both to separate the counted components from other components in the same pattern unit and, later, to unite the analogous components in all the pattern units. The principle is similar to that described for the Rumipamba shawls, but the more complex designs require multiple counting cords. Up to twenty-four may be used in a single shawl.

The warp yarns are counted in pairs (*pares*), defined as a yarn passing on both sides of the dovetail stake. Thus, the Bulcay/Bulshun pair is half as many yarns as the Rumipamba pair. The counting is most easily done at the dovetail stake (Figs. 3.9, 3.10). Design components are typically between three and five pairs of warp yarns, and the number may vary between one part of a design and another.

Starting at the side of the board to the warper's left, the first cord is tied to a pair or more of warp yarns near or at the bottom, passed behind the warp yarns to be bound for that component, then returned to the front to pass over the warp yarns that are not needed for that part of the pattern. The second cord, to the right of the first, is passed behind both the warp yarns to be bound for the first component and those for the second component. The third cord is passed

3.8 Warp-resist-patterned wool shawl (*paño cachemira*), in warp-faced plain weave with fringe interknotted in overhand knots. The weaver has inadvertently reversed the two rightmost central patterned stripes. The lettering in the fringe reads "Un Recuerdo" (a remembrance, *top*) and "Señorita" (young woman, *bottom*). Gualaceo area, Azuay province, purchased new in the Cuenca market in 1986. Overall size: 2.70 (including fringe) × .77 meters (106¼ × 30¼ inches). The Textile Museum 1986.19.57, Latin American Research Fund.

3.9 Starting to put counting cords (*cuendas*) in the warp for two shawls to be resist dyed. Ana María Vera, Bulcay, Azuay province. Photo by Laura M. Miller, 1988.

3.10 Continuing to insert counting cords in the warp. Ana María Vera, Bulcay, Azuay province. Photo by Laura M. Miller, 1988.

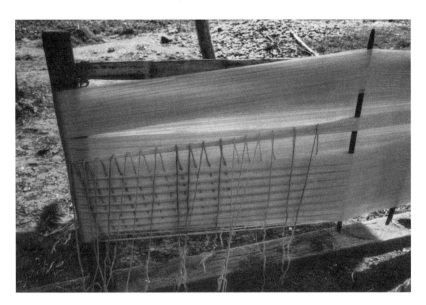

3.11 Warp with counting cords inserted. Arcelia Pérez, Bulcay, Azuay province. Slide by Lynn A. Meisch, 1977.

behind those for the first three components, and so on (see Fig. 3.11). Diagonals are thus formed by passing the cords, for example, behind four pairs, then eight, then twelve, and so on. Although the cord passes behind all previous components, not all are bound together. Selection of warp pairs for an asymmetrical design is called *selección en S*, according to Penley (1988: 55), but we did not encounter this terminology.

If the motifs repeat in bilateral symmetry around a central component (sometimes called *selección de rosa* [Penley 1988: 60]), the cord passes first in front of a group of warp pairs at the bottom that will be the central component, and then behind each of the other components in turn or in reverse. In the usual case of two alternating motifs or one motif in offset rows, the cords are first put in place for the first motif. Then, to the right of those, another set of cords is inserted for the second one. If the shawl is to include any plain stripes, the counting cords pass in front of them so that they are excluded from the bundles to be bound. Often, two shawls are warped and bound at the same time.

When all the cords have been started (Fig. 3.9), the warper returns to the left and counts the warp pairs for each component of the subsequent pattern units in the same manner as the first (Figs. 3.10–3.11).

Celina Ulloa of Bulshun, an elderly woman whom we recorded in 1986, uses a variant method, inserting the cords as she winds the warp (Fig. 3.12). As soon as the border is warped, she begins inserting counting cords. She first inserts a leftmost pink cord. Then she adds a blue and a yellow cord for the border X design and flips the ends to the back. She then uses alternating green and yellow cords for a bilaterally symmetrical design, with the center counted first and the ends hanging down on her side of the warp. For subsequent repeats, she flips the cords to the front or back between winding the warp. She works very fast from long experience.

When all the cords have been inserted through the entire warp, the artisan unties them from the bottom and ties the two ends of each cord together (Fig. 3.13). She then replaces the cross and dovetail stakes with yarn. She may pass a yarn through the shed on each side of the cross and tie the ends together or use separate yarns for each shed (Fig. 3.13). She then removes the cross stake. For the dovetail stake, the end of a cord is passed through a hole through the bottom of the stake and the stake is drawn through the warp loops like a needle.

It is then easy to move the warp around the end stakes until the dovetail join is at one end of the warping board, usually the artisan's left, but in Figures 3.14 and 3.15 it is on the right. To relax the tension on the warp sufficiently to remove the dovetail stake and rotate the warp, she may temporarily remove the top horizontal bar. If there are stripes in the shawl that will remain undyed, she gathers these warp yarns and separates them from the rest of the warp before rotating it (Fig. 3.14). They are then twisted and tied to the stake next to the dovetailed join (Fig. 3.15).

She then pulls together all the warp yarns that are to be bound together. Beginning at the right (the center of the warp), she gathers all the warp yarns enclosed in the first counting cord into a single bundle, called a *soga* in this area as in Rumipamba. She then laces some maguey fiber around this bundle to hold it together, adjacent to the left warping stake. She follows the same procedure to group the warp yarns in the remaining counting cord loops, continuing to lace each bundle together with the maguey fiber next to the left stake. When the lacing is in place, she may remove the counting cords. Alternatively, as shown in Figure 3.15, Ana María Vera is pulling on all the counting cord loops together, a procedure that requires a variety of pushing and tugging motions before the *soga* lacing can be done. A finished *soga* lacing is visible on the right in Figure 3.16. The lacing twines around the *sogas*.

Most often, the yarns on both sides of the warping posts are bound together (Figs. 3.16 and 3.17). A disjunction in the design where it reverses in the center of the shawl is usually visible (Figs. 3.6, 3.8). In a few fine older shawls, however, the two sides are bound separately (called *dando la vuelta* S.), which obviously is twice as much work.

3.12 Warp with counting cords inserted as the warping progresses. Celina Ulloa, Bulshun, Azuay province. Slide by Ann P. Rowe, 1986.

3.13 Tying the ends of the counting cords together. Ana María Vera, Bulcay, Azuay province. Photo by Laura M. Miller, 1988.

3.14 Starting to tie off the fringe. Ana María Vera, Bulcay, Azuay province. Photo by Laura M. Miller, 1988.

3.15 Pulling on the counting cords to make *sogas*. Ana María Vera, Bulcay, Azuay province. Photo by Laura M. Miller, 1988.

3.16 Starting to bind the warp, showing lacing of the *sogas* at right. Arcelia Pérez, Bulcay, Azuay province. Slide by Lynn A. Meisch, 1977.

3.17 Almost finished binding the warp, with the warp bound to the insides of the warping stakes. Celia Rodas, Bulcay, Azuay province. Slide by Ann P. Rowe, 1986.

Untwisted maguey fibers are used to bind the resists. If the shawl has a white ground, the maguey fiber must be clean and not previously used, since it is the ground areas between the motifs that are bound. For the pink wool shawls, usually, it is the designs that are bound.

The maguey fiber is dampened before binding. The fibers are wrapped as tightly as possible around the warp, first in one direction and then the other, and the ends tied in a square knot. A mottled effect (*zhiru*), is achieved by crisscrossing the resist instead of wrapping it parallel, so that the warp is not entirely covered (Fig. 3.7).

The horizontal crossbar is put back on the warping board to tighten the warp before binding. The binding begins at what would be the bottom of the shawl, leaving a distance from the left warping stake equivalent to the length of the fringe (fifteen inches, or thirty-eight centimeters), and proceeding toward the right (Fig. 3.16). When the binding reaches about ten centimeters (four inches) from the right stake, the lacing holding the bundles is removed and a cord is inserted parallel to the stake. The warp can be lifted off the stake and reattached by lashing this cord to the stake (Fig. 3.17). The yarns to be undyed may also be tied to the other warping stake with a cord. The binding process can then proceed to the end of the warp, which is the middle of the shawl.

The warp is dyed with indigo (see Chapter 9), a black synthetic dye, or both. The warp is immersed except for the fringe and any stripes that are to be entirely undyed.

Arcelia Pérez of Bulcay (recorded by Lynn Meisch 1981a), dips her warp in indigo up to its fringe and then kneads it vigorously to help the dye penetrate *under* the resist. Subsequently, the still-wrapped indigo-dyed warp is carefully dipped in black synthetic dye and immediately rinsed so that the black does not penetrate the resist. When the warp is dry, the resist is cut away, and the result is areas of solid black, areas of mottled indigo (*zhiru*), and areas of white (Fig. 3.18).

For synthetic dyeing, the bath is hot and contains salt, alum, and lemon juice as mordants, as well as the water and dye. The warp is wetted and beaten, as for indigo dyeing, and dipped four or five times. It is then rinsed to remove the excess dye and hung to dry.

Synthetic dye alone is used for low-quality cotton shawls and for the pink wool shawls. For cotton shawls of intermediate quality, the warp may be dipped in indigo once or twice and then dyed with synthetic dye as above.

The bindings are removed when the warp is still slightly wet; otherwise, it is too difficult. One end of the warp is held in the hand and the other is hooked over the worker's foot (Fig. 3.19). The knots are cut with a knife and

3.18 Unwrapped warp, showing solid black, *zhiru* mottled, and solid-white areas. Arcelia Pérez, Bulcay, Azuay province. Slide by Lynn A. Meisch, 1977.

3.19 Untying a warp. Celia Rodas and neighborhood children, Bulcay, Azuay province. Slide by Ann P. Rowe, 1986.

the fiber unwrapped. During our visit, the neighborhood children all gathered around to help Celia Rodas unwrap her warp (Fig. 3.19). Alternatively, the warp is hung over a nail on a house post to be unwrapped (Penley 1988: 71, photo 41). The two warps are then separated and hung again to dry.

A cotton shawl may be treated with a bluing agent at this stage. Meisch (1981a: 3) reports that a mixture of lime, water, and commercial bluing is used. Then the warp is rinsed and hung to dry again.

Weaving

The following description of setting up the loom is based on the procedure used by Herlinda Vera Ulloa, of Bulcay, recorded by Laura Miller and me in 1986, and photographed by Miller in 1988. As noted in Chapter 1, women weavers are unusual in her community.[3] The order señora Vera uses differs slightly from that described by Penley, reflecting individual variation among weavers, but the basic procedures are the same.

After she inserts the loom bars and puts on the backstrap, she ties the cord through the dovetail join through a hole in each end of a sword-shaped stick inserted into the warp on one side of the join. She places a small shed rod through the warp on the other side of this join (both sticks are visible in Fig. 3.20). She then spreads the warp, bundle (*soga*) by bundle, with her fingers. She holds the shed rod and gently strums the warp with a wooden pick (*pijchi*) above and below the dovetail join in order to even it out. Then the roller bar is added.

Señora Vera next inserts the coil rod (*tormentador* or *templador* S.), to help keep the dyed warp yarns from shifting out of position and blurring the design (Fig. 3.20). She releases the tension on the warp by leaning forward slightly, places the stick on top of the warp (above the cross), and wraps groups of warp yarns around it, two *sogas* (ten warp yarns each) at a time. Once inserted, it is easy to move the coil rod forward and back, and she does this every so often. Above the coil rod, she inserts a bamboo stick under alternate groups of *sogas* on the coil rod (*guía* S.), picking up the shed with her fingers (Fig. 3.21). Other weavers may not use this extra stick. Both sticks are pushed up toward the back loom bar.

Señora Vera inserts the main shed rod (*masa mayor*) into the shed marked by the yarn loop and removes the yarn. She again strums the warp and inserts the sword (*kayllwa* Q.) into the front shed and removes the small shed rod. She turns the sword on edge and strums the warp again. She unties the dovetail cord from the sword-shaped stick and turns the ends of the cord into the warp. She now removes the sword-shaped stick, adjusts the front loom bar

3.20 Inserting the coil rod into the warp. Herlinda Vera Ulloa, Bulcay, Azuay province. Photo by Laura M. Miller, 1988.

3.21 Weaving a warp-resist-dyed shawl. Herlinda Vera Ulloa, Bulcay, Azuay province. Photo by Laura M. Miller, 1988.

and the roller bar, and rolls them over so that the dovetail join is hidden and the area that will be at the top of the fringe is conveniently placed for weaving. She rubs wax on the warp and makes the heddles as described in Chapter 1.

To insert the secondary shed rod (*masa menor* S.), señora Vera inserts the sword-shaped stick with holes in each end into the heddle shed, removes the regular sword, and reinserts it behind the cross, turning it on edge. She brings the main shed rod forward against the heddles. She picks up alternate groups of two or three warp yarns from those that pass over the shed rod (in front of the heddle rod) and inserts the secondary shed rod behind the main shed rod. She does this by pushing the pick up, inserting her fingers into the shed, and then substituting the shed rod for her fingers. She then removes and waxes the sword.

She leaves the sword-shaped stick with the holes in each end in the heddle shed to provide a base against which to beat the first few shots of weft. When the warp is advanced again, this stick is removed. The first and last few weft shots usually consist of a doubled yarn. Changing sheds is done in the usual manner, described in Chapter 1.

Knotting the Fringe

When the weaving is completed, the weaver removes the loom sticks and dovetail cord, and the shawl fringe is ready for knotting, the most time-consuming part of making the shawl. Fine fringes can take up to three months to knot.

The shawl is folded crosswise and placed on a table or stand with its fringe hanging over the edge. The shawl is covered with cloth, and weights (e.g., rocks) are added to hold it down. In the case of Gualaceo market vendors, the weights may include the produce they are selling (Fig. 3.22).

Commonly, every other warp yarn is cut near the woven edge so that it is doubly long. The cutting may be done either above or below the first row of knots. Alternatively, the warp end loops are all cut at the ends where the dovetail cord was, and as the ends become short another yarn is knotted in. When all the knotting is finished, the ends from the joining knots are cut off.

Extra yarns are often added at the edge of the woven area after the first row of knots has been tied. A group of four new doubled yarns may be added after every four to six knots of warp (as in Textile Museum examples). Penley (1988: 82, 153) describes a technique in which a group of two new doubled yarns is added after every other knot in the first row.

The knot is a simple overhand knot (*toglla*), in which one group of warp ends (commonly, four yarns) is tied around an adjacent group (Fig. 3.23). In

3.22 Knotting the fringe on a warp-resist-patterned shawl. Concha Cambisaca, Gualaceo market, Azuay province. Photo by Lynn A. Meisch, 1978.

the next row of knots, the two groups of yarns that were tied together in the previous row are tied with the groups on either side, creating a diamond mesh (see also Harvey 1972). The designs are made simply by varying the spacing of the knots, with the knots forming the background of the designs farther apart than those within pattern areas. To outline the figures, two knots are tied with the same two groups of threads to make an even larger mesh. The knots in the pattern areas are spaced as closely as possible, so that the effect is of horizontal rows of knots, rather than a mesh.

A less time-consuming way of working the fringe is to knot a plain mesh and then embroider it (Meisch in A. Rowe [ed.] 1998: 256, fig. 242; Pfyffer 2002: 197). Sometimes, ribbon is interlaced in a fringe with a simple knotted design (A. Rowe [ed.] 1998: iv). On a few older shawls, the fringe is not made with the warp threads but is a separately made textile that has been sewn on. Presumably, the original warp fringe had become worn or stained and the owner had it replaced. The available examples are made with crochet or embroidered square mesh.

When the knotting is complete, extra yarns are added at the bottom to make a thicker fringe, ten to twenty centimeters (four to eight inches) long. A series of loops are wound and one end of the loops is cut. The yarns are put through the last row of mesh, folded in half, and wrapped for a distance

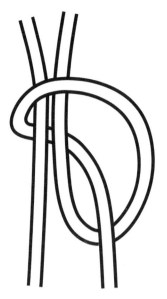

3.23 Overhand knot used to tie the fringe on warp-resist-patterned shawls. Drawing by Arts and Letters Ltd., based on a drawing by Ann P. Rowe.

adjacent to the fold to form tassels that hide the original warp ends. The last step on some shawls is to starch the fringe, with maize starch or a commercially sold starch, which makes the design stand out more clearly. Starching eventually causes the fibers to weaken and break, however.

Kokomuro Poncho in Cacha Obraje, Central Chimborazo Province

LAURA M. MILLER AND ANN P. ROWE   The *kokomuro* poncho (Fig. 3.24), called Cacha poncho outside of Cacha, is worn in several areas of Chimborazo province as festival and market-day dress for men. It is made in Cacha Obraje and Pucara Quinche, two of the sixteen Cacha communities that lie in the dry hills southwest of Riobamba (Map 4). The technique was demonstrated for us in Cacha Obraje in 1988 by Manuel Janita Pilco.[4]

The *kokomuro* poncho has eight prominent bound-warp-resist stripes, called *watashka* (Q., tied), four on each half of the poncho. The stripes are made in white cotton dyed with indigo in diamond and chevron designs. Previously, the rest of the poncho was also cotton, but since about the 1960s, red or black wool has been used. By the late 1980s, red (or blue) acrylic yarn had become usual. A separately made fringe is sewn to all four edges.

Unfortunately, we were not able to record warping, but it was clear that, unlike with the shawls, the yarns for the tied stripes are warped alone. Presumably, as in the ponchos and blankets discussed in Chapter 2, separate dovetail cords are used for each stripe. Also unlike the shawls, the warp for these stripes is placed on the loom bars and tensioned using the backstrap before binding (Fig. 3.25). By the time we observed, colored cords had been put through the warp similarly to the Azuay shawls, and the ends of these cords had been loosely tied together. Thus, the warp had been divided and the yarns to be bound together had been selected. It was clear that all the stripes were being bound together. In addition, since the diamond is horizontally symmetrical around a central line, only half of it must be bound. The yarns are grouped

3.24 Poncho with cotton warp-resist-patterned stripes and red wool solid stripes in warp-faced plain weave. Cacha, central Chimborazo province, probably made in the 1960s or the 1970s. 1.29 × 1.27 meters (50¾ × 50 inches), including fringe. The Textile Museum 1986.19.102, Latin American Research Fund.

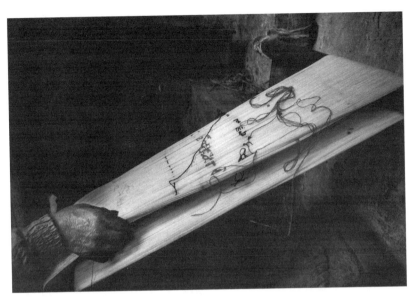

3.25 Warp for the patterned stripes of a poncho with counting cords inserted, ready for binding. Cacha Obraje, central Chimborazo province. Photo by Laura M. Miller, 1988.

3.26 Pulling on a counting cord to prepare for the second binding on a poncho warp. Manuel Janita Pilco, Cacha Obraje, central Chimborazo province. Photo by Laura M. Miller, 1988.

in such a way that, when the dyed warp is opened out, the whole design is present.

The artisan begins by tying all of the warp yarns together at the near end. Then he unties the uppermost colored cord marking the groups of warp yarns and separates the yarns enclosed in the tie from those underneath (Fig. 3.26). He wraps all the warp yarns enclosed in this tie. Then he takes the next colored tie and wraps all the yarns that were enclosed in it and repeats this procedure until the binding is complete.

Señor Janita uses groups of unspun *chawar* to bind the pattern. He twists the ends of the fibers together at the leading end by rubbing them between his palms. He crosses the two ends of the tie and wraps counterclockwise, pulling upward on the long end of the tie after each circumference. He spirals first upward on the warp, then downward, and then ties the two ends together.

The indigo dye (*tinta de baño* S.) is purchased in Ambato or Salcedo and is not available in Riobamba. Indeed, a Cacha *kokomuro* poncho weaver may go to Rumipamba, in Cotopaxi province, to use or "rent" the dye bath of *macana* weavers at a cost of 2,000 to 3,000 sucres ($3.75 to $5.50 at 1988 exchange rates). Though señor Janita in Cacha knew how to use indigo, he rarely readied his dye pots.

After the resist portions are dyed and dry, the rest of the poncho is warped, with the resist stripes added as the red portions are warped. Then the poncho is woven on the backstrap loom (Fig. 3.27). The loom has a single shed rod, and the weaver uses a wooden pick (*puntidor* S.; or *pikchi*) to strum.

A narrow band with loop fringe is sewn onto the selvedges of the poncho after it is taken off the loom. Señor Janita weaves this fringe band using a crudely made hole-and-slot heddle with six slats lashed to horizontal bars lashed to a Y-shaped frame made of a forked stick, the lower part of which is stuck into the ground (Figs. 3.28–3.30). Alternate warp yarns pass through a hole in the center of one of the slats or through the space between slats. He ties the end of the warp farthest from him to a forked stake at a convenient point. The remaining length winds down the length of the stake and into a ball at its foot (Fig. 3.28). We saw this loom in operation, but not the warping process.

Señor Janita kneels and controls the closest end of the warp with his hand. When he lowers the warp, the yarns in the holes of the heddle are above those in the slots, and he passes the weft through this shed (Fig. 3.28). When he raises the warp, the yarns in the slots of the heddle are raised above those in the holes, and he passes the weft through this shed (Fig. 3.29). He uses a small, smooth bamboo gauge, held in his left hand, to make the fringe (Fig. 3.30). It is actually the gauge rather than the end of the warp that he holds and pulls to create tension.

3.27 Weaving a poncho with warp-resist-dyed stripes. The weaver is inserting the sword into the heddle rod shed. Cacha Obraje, central Chimborazo province. Photo by Laura M. Miller, 1989.

3.28 Weaving a fringe band for a poncho: lowering the warp to create the shed below the holes in the hole-and-slot heddle. Cacha Obraje, central Chimborazo province. Photo by Laura M. Miller, 1988.

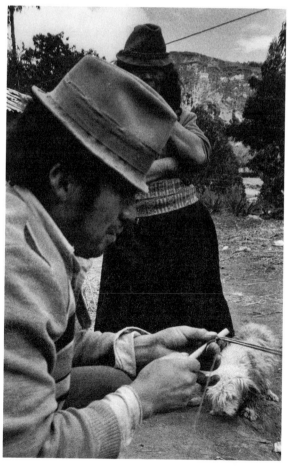

3.29 Weaving a fringe band for a poncho: lifting the warp to create the shed above the holes in the hole-and-slot heddle. Cacha Obraje, central Chimborazo province. Photo by Laura M. Miller, 1988.

3.30 Weaving a fringe band for a poncho: putting the weft yarn around the gauge rod to make the fringe. Cacha Obraje, central Chimborazo province. Photo by Laura M. Miller, 1988.

The ball of blue weft yarn rests on the ground at his right. He inserts his right hand into the shed and brings the cross forward, then inserts his left middle fingertip into the shed to hold it. With his right hand he takes the part of the yarn close to the fabric and inserts it through the shed right to left, around the gauge (over and under) and back through the shed left to right. The same motions are repeated for each shed.

CHAPTER 4

Belts with Supplementary-Warp Patterning

Introduction

ANN P. ROWE   It is startling how similar the belts woven with supplementary-warp patterning are throughout highland Ecuador, not only in their structure but also in color and design motifs. Indeed, this type of belt is one of the unifying elements of highland Ecuadorian weaving. Yet, we found the number of different techniques employed to produce them equally remarkable. It certainly appears that weavers in each area improvised their own methods to create a similar finished product.

These belts are woven in Carchi, Imbabura, Cotopaxi, Tungurahua, Chimborazo, and Loja provinces and before 1950 were also produced in Pichincha province (Stübel and Reiss 1888: pls. 14, 15, 17; Beals 1966: 65, 78). In southern Colombia, the indigenous people in the department of Nariño (example acquired by Joanne Rappaport in Cumbal in the late 1980s), as well as the Sibundoy (Cardale Schrimpff 1977: 45) and Páez (Nachtigall 1955: Abb. 189, 190), make similar belts. Chachis (Cayapa) fabrics from Ecuador's western lowland forest in Esmeraldas province are also patterned in this manner (Barrett 1925: pt. II, 261–262, pls. CXII–CXV; A. Rowe 1977: 39, fig. 37).

The structure is a warp-predominant plain weave with two ground-warp yarns alternating with one supplementary-warp yarn (Fig. 4.1). The supplementary-warp yarns often simply float over design areas on the front and behind background areas on the back. Larger solid designs may have the supplementary-warp yarns interlacing regularly over three weft yarns (forming a three-span float) and under one, with the floats commonly aligned in alternate pairs (Fig. 4.1). In larger background areas, there are often similar three-span floats on the back of the belt. In weaving, the supplementary-warp yarns are normally controlled separately from the ground-warp yarns. Varia-

4.1 Detail of a belt in white cotton plain weave with blue acrylic supplementary-warp patterning. *Left,* the front; *right,* the back. Otavalo area, Imbabura province. Width: 5 centimeters (2 inches). The Textile Museum 1986.19.24, Latin American Research Fund.

tions, such as using two colors of supplementary warp in some Salasaca belts or areas of supplementary weft in Natabuela belts, are unusual.

The plain-weave ground is almost always white cotton, and the supplementary-warp yarns are colored, formerly of wool, but since the 1970s mostly acrylic. There are side borders in plain weave without supplementary-warp yarns. These borders are predominantly white cotton but have some colored warp stripes that match or harmonize with the supplementary-warp yarns. In the central design area, horizontal bars of supplementary warp passing over one, three, five, or seven weft yarns separate the geometric and animal motifs.

Although there is nothing complex about it, the weave is actually rare among pre-Hispanic Peruvian textiles and has not been found, to date, among the few available pre-Hispanic Ecuadorian remains. The only postconquest examples known in the Andes outside of Ecuador and southern Colombia are a group of nineteenth-century ponchos from southern Peru and northern Bolivia made from strips that lack the end selvedges normally produced on indigenous styles of loom (A. Rowe 1977: 40, fig. 38). The belt style is definitely not Inca (cf. A. Rowe 1997). It may be native to Ecuador or it may be an innovation dating to the Spanish occupation. In either case, it is likely that its present wide distribution is at least partly the result of population movements or trade during the colonial period.

As noted, the weaving process has many variations. For weaving belts with hand-picked patterns, we recorded six ways to set up the loom for handling the supplementary-warp yarns. For weaving belts with loom-controlled designs, there are further variations. Although we have fewer data on warping, this process appears to be equally variable. For example, sometimes all crosses needed for the weaving are warped and sometimes not.

The methods of setting up the loom for hand-picked patterns can be divided into two groups: those where the ground-warp sheds are made using one heddle rod plus the front part of the *cruzera* (or shed rod), and those where the ground-warp sheds are made using two heddle rods. The methods of setting up the loom for loom-controlled patterns fall into both of these groups.

In the first group, the supplementary-warp yarns are controlled by an additional heddle rod, which is placed in front of the ground heddle rod (Molobóg, Chimborazo province), or in back of it (Salasaca and Saraguro), or in front of it but underneath the warp instead of on top (Nitón, Tungurahua province). The supplementary warp passes either over (Nitón) or under (Salasaca, Molobóg, Saraguro) the whole *cruzera*. The pickup is done near the fell, the woven edge.

In the second group, the supplementary-warp yarns pass under the back and over the front *cruzera* stick and also over an additional shed stick above the heddle rods. This additional shed stick may be loose, either in front of the *cruzera* (as in Cotopaxi) or on top of it (the method used by Otavalo weaver Antonio Cando), or it may be tied to the *cruzera* in front of the other two *cruzera* sticks (as do the Chibuleo, in Tungurahua province) or in between them (the method used by Otavalo weaver Carlos Conterón and in Natabuela). The pickup may be done just in front of this shed stick (as in Otavalo and by the Chibuleo), between the heddle rods (as in Cotopaxi), or at the fell (as in Natabuela).

Some of the variations appear to be of regional significance, while others are probably preferences of an individual weaver. We rarely found two weavers who worked in an identical way, though had we had a larger sample, one assumes more would have been found. The variation in the Otavalo area is particularly striking, and, indeed, each of the weavers we recorded was innovative in some way, so we refer to them by name, and not simply community, in the headings that follow. The degree of innovation seems to parallel the enterprising spirit of Otavalos generally. One can begin to see from this creative approach how Andean weaving reached such a high peak of technical development.

Supplementary Warp Controlled by a Second Heddle Rod (with Pickup)

Salasaca, Tungurahua Province

LAURA M. MILLER Salasaca belts are among the most finely woven of all supplementary-warp patterned belts in Ecuador. It takes a skilled weaver seven to ten days of steady work to finish a belt. Most belts are commissioned to weavers in the community or are woven for family members. Traditionally, belts were not woven for sale outside the community, but in the 1980s a few men were doing so as a result of Peace Corps encouragement (Fig. 4.2). Both men and women weave belts, but women tend to be the exception rather than the rule. In the 1980s fewer young men were weaving belts than formerly.

The belts have borders of plain warp stripes, zigzags (*kingu* Q.), and triangles (*punta* S.). The zigzags are said to represent the irrigation ditches that are the lifeblood of the dry Salasaca soil. The central section contains a fascinating array of designs made using pickup of the supplementary-warp yarns: birds, deer, geometric figures, horses, dancers at the Corpus Christi festival (A. Rowe [ed.] 1998: 133, fig. 120), monkeys, peacocks, and many more.

The yarns, both the cotton for the ground and the acrylic for the supplementary warp, are purchased in Ambato. The acrylic is overtwisted before use and rolled into balls.

The warper considers the juxtaposition of supplementary-warp colors very carefully by lining up the balls of acrylic yarn on the ground. Salasacas prefer muted tones: mustard yellow over canary yellow; dark wine purple over grape

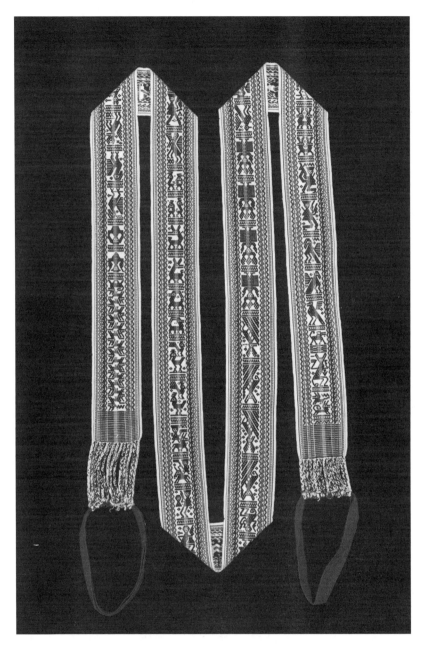

4.2 Belt in cotton plain weave, with acrylic supplementary-warp patterning. Woven by José Pilla Curichumbi, Salasaca, Tungurahua province. 2.67 × .07 meters (5 feet 5¾ inches × 2¾ inches), excluding ties. The Textile Museum 1988.19.2, Latin American Research Fund.

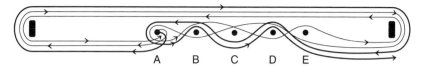

4.3 Diagram of warping for a Salasaca belt with supplementary-warp patterning. The finer lines represent the ground-weave yarns; the thicker line represents the supplementary-warp yarn. Drawing by Arts and Letters Ltd., based on a drawing by Laura M. Miller.

jelly purple; and maroon over fire-engine red. I was not aware of these preferences and used brighter colors for my belt. People commented that the colors were too bright: "These are not Salasaca colors." On one occasion, a woman I warped with was very pleased to have enough of two specific colors for her belt, namely, *morado negro*, a very dark purple, and *canela café*, a cinnamon bark color. She had purchased these acrylic yarns five to six years before and said that these colors were hard to find now.

To begin warping, the weaver pounds seven stakes into the ground (Fig. 4.3). Peach tree wood is used because it is especially hard. All the stakes are called *kaspi urdina* (Q., stick; S., for warping). They are saved and used for many warpings. The two outermost stakes are the strongest and largest, for they bear the tension of all of the warp yarns. In addition to the dovetail stake (A), there are three cross stakes for the ground warp crosses (B, D, E), and between the first and second of these is another stake (C) that separates the supplementary-warp yarns from the ground warp. The supplementary-warp yarns pass alternately behind and in front of each cross stake.

The length of the belt is determined by the distance between the two end stakes. Salasaca belts are generally one and a half arm's lengths long. One arm's length is from fingertip to fingertip, with the arms outstretched. A long pole is placed between the two end stakes to keep them from tilting toward the center. This pole determines the length of the belt. José Caizabanda, a full-time belt weaver, has several poles of varying lengths so as to produce belts of whatever length a client might desire. A belt I wove to practice the technique was only one arm's length long. My teacher had grave doubts about whether or not a North American woman could weave at all.

The warper ties a cord to the top of the dovetail stake to hold the join when the stake is removed. He then ties the white cotton ground warp to the dovetail stake and warps five pairs (each a complete round) of white cotton yarns, a pair of colored acrylic, a pair of white, and so on, until twelve pairs of ground warp have been warped for the plain-weave border. When putting on a new color, he simply ties this yarn to the dovetail stake. In Salasaca, warping usually begins toward the warper's left, away from the cross stakes, which are to the right of the dovetail stake.

Then the warper winds the supplementary-warp section, using one of the cross stakes to keep the supplementary-warp yarns separate (Fig. 4.3). He ties a colored yarn to the dovetail stake and warps a half round until he returns to the dovetail stake. He drops the colored yarn, picks up the white cotton ground warp yarn, and warps one complete pair (a round) with this yarn. He then picks up the colored yarn, pulls it taut, and warps in the opposite direction to the first half round, dropping this yarn when he returns to the dovetail stake. Next, he warps another complete pair with the white ground. The process continues in the same manner.

For the zigzag design, he uses five supplementary-warp yarns. After these five rounds, he warps one additional pair of ground warp, then selects the next color. He deftly breaks the yarn with a thumbnail and ties the new color onto the old, so that the knot lies at the dovetail stake. The central section contains thirty-two to forty supplementary-warp yarns. Usually, there is an area of contrasting colors of supplementary-warp yarns in the center of the central section, which bisects the designs.

He warps the other border in a similar manner to the first. An accomplished warper can prepare the warp for a belt in one hour. He then ties the crosses with string and the warp is lifted off the stakes. The last step is to ease out the dovetail stake, leaving the dovetail cord (*tandachiska* Q.) in place.

Another style of Salasaca belt, called *frutilla* (S., strawberry), consists of small diamond figures (Pl. 1). It is considered harder to warp and weave and therefore is more prestigious for both the weaver and the wearer. It is the only supplementary-warp patterned belt in Ecuador in which two colors of supplementary-warp yarns are used simultaneously. Each diamond shape, or *frutilla*, is made of two contrasting colors, one for the middle (*shungu*, Q., heart), and another for the outline. The warping is similar to that of the simpler belts, but with key differences.

For instance, if the center will be done in yellow and the outline in red, the warping is as follows. For the outline, three rounds of red supplementary warp (alternating with ground) are made, as described above. For the center section, a round of white ground warp is made, followed by a half round of red, followed directly by a half round of yellow, and then another round of ground warp. This sequence is repeated four times to complete the center section. Then three rounds of red supplementary warp are alternated with ground in the normal fashion. Thus, in the center of each diamond there are two supplementary-warp yarns between each two ground warp yarns, one for the center of the design and one for the outline.

4.4 Picking up the pattern in a supplementary-warp patterned belt. A simple shed rod is used instead of a *cruzera*. The two heddle rods are pushed together. José Pilla Curichumbi, Salasaca, Tungurahua province. Photo by Lynn A. Meisch, 1988.

On the loom, the center sections are controlled by one heddle rod, the outlines and other colors by a second heddle rod, and the cotton ground warp by a third heddle rod and the shed rod. I never saw the heddles installed on this kind of belt, but the yarns for the centers of the diamonds must have been separated by hand, for in the warping session I observed, there was no extra stake for these yarns. To weave the centers of the diamonds, it is necessary to pick up yarns from each of the two supplementary-warp heddle rods before opening the plain-weave shed.

The back loom bar (*charidora* Q. with S. suffix) is usually a straight bar tied to vertical posts supporting the end of the porch or a straight bar tied to a horizontal bar on the porch, but a few weavers use a curved stick tied to a house post. The weaver inserts the front loom bar (*kaspi watarina* Q.) and attaches the backstrap (*siki sinchun* Q.).

A bamboo stick, called *cruza* or *cruzana* (S.), is inserted behind the cross of the ground-warp threads. This stick is not the same as the *cruzera* in other Ecuadorian belt looms but a shed rod of comparatively large diameter, similar to those used for larger looms (Fig. 4.4). A yarn may be tied over the warp to both ends of the stick or to itself through the hollow core to prevent its falling out. One Salasaca weaver I recorded, however, does use a *cruzera* (marking the plain-weave sheds, with the supplementary warp underneath) in addition to a shed rod, in which case the *cruzera* functions only like cross sticks to hold the cross and to secure the warp (Fig. 4.5). Another weaver, Manuel Pilla, uses a second stick behind the shed rod, as large as the shed rod but not tied to it, to hold the other plain-weave shed as a cross stick (again with the supplementary warp underneath both) (Fig. 4.6). In any event, it is interesting that the *cruzera* is not as entrenched in Salasaca belt weaving as it is in other parts of highland Ecuador.

The weaver is then ready to make the heddles (*illawa* Q., pronounced "*izhawa*"), as described in Chapter 1. Eucalyptus branches are used for the heddle rods; they must be straight and strong. Some weavers use wire rods. Heddles are first installed on the ground warp (those not over the shed rod), and then on the supplementary warp (Fig. 4.7). Then the weaver makes sure that the dovetail cord, where weaving begins, is not too far from his hands. The roller bar (*kaspi watarina* Q.) is added and the backstrap refastened.

Two weaving swords are used, the *jatun kallu* (Q., pronounced *kazhu*), or *ruku kallu* (Q.), the big sword, or old sword; and the *wawa kallu* (Q.), or baby sword, a pickup stick. Both have handles. To create a shed for the weft, the weaver lifts the supplementary-warp heddle rod and slips his left hand under the shed. He uses the pickup stick in his right hand to pick the yarns needed to form the pattern. Once the selected yarns are on the pickup stick, he joins these to the shed rod shed or the heddle rod shed of the ground warp. The shed is beaten and then the weft is passed and beaten into place.

The weaver uses a great deal of force and usually beats the shed three or four times. Good belts are as stiff as leather. When people in Salasaca inspected the belt I made, they commented that I had not beaten hard enough. They recommended that, in the future, I eat more potatoes and *máchica*, toasted barley flour, to have the strength to weave better.

After weaving, the belt is finished by the woman who will wear it. Ribbon is passed through the dovetail loops where weaving began (Pl. 1). At the other end, the loops are much longer and are braided. The braids are called *chimba* (Q.). Either simple three-strand braids or round eight-strand braids may be used. The loops at the end of each braid are pulled over the end of the braid and ribbon is passed through these loops. The ends of the ribbon meet in their passage through the loops, forming a large loop that can be used to secure the belt.

4.5 Picking up the supplementary-warp pattern. This loom has a *cruzera* behind the shed rod. Salasaca, Tungurahua province. Slide by Laura M. Miller, 1984.

4.6 Weaving a *frutilla* belt. The loom has a lease rod as well as a shed rod, but they are not tied together, as in a normal *cruzera*. The weaver has picked the pattern and is about to lift the ground-weave heddle rod. Manuel Pilla, Salasaca, Tungurahua province. Slide by Laura M. Miller, 1984.

4.7 Detail of the crosses and shedding devices for weaving a Salasaca belt with supplementary-warp patterning. Slide by Laura M. Miller, 1984.

Supplementary Warp Controlled by a Second Heddle Rod (with Pickup)

Saraguro, Loja Province

ANN P. ROWE AND LYNN A. MEISCH   Lynn Meisch recorded three Saraguro weavers of supplementary-warp patterned belts in 1978–1979: María Asunción Quizhpe of Gunudel; Bolivio Guamán of Las Lagunas; and Polivio Sarango of Tuncarta (Map 6).[1] All use a similar technique and all use commercial cotton and acrylic yarns. It is cheaper to buy already-dyed yarns than to dye the small amount needed for one belt, and the weavers like the fine texture of the acrylic. The belt in Figure 4.8, however, was made as part of a natural-dye project in 1979 (see also Meisch 1982: 60, fig. 7; Meisch in A. Rowe [ed.] 1998: 266, fig. 253).

The back loom bar is straight and long enough to be tied to the same supports as are wider looms (Figs. 4.9 and 4.10). The dovetail join is held by a small stick or cord. Bolivio Guamán attaches a white thread to each of the two central supplementary-warp yarns to make it easier to pick up the designs.

The loom has a two-stick *cruzera*, which holds the ground yarns, with the front stick acting as a shed rod for alternate ground-warp yarns. Both *cru-*

zera sticks have a round profile and lack grooves. The remaining ground-warp yarns are controlled by a heddle rod. The supplementary-warp yarns are controlled by a second heddle rod placed behind the one for the ground warp. They pass under the *cruzera*. Polivio Sarango has a third stick under the *cruzera* under which the supplementary-warp yarns pass. A thread is tied from one end of the stick to another, under the supplementary-warp yarns to hold them in place (Fig. 4.9). The other weavers do without this extra stick.

The weaving sequence is as follows: lift the heddle rod with the supplementary-warp yarns, bring the shed forward with the sword, and then pick up the desired design at the fell (Fig. 4.10), leaving the pickup stick under the selected warp yarns. Then lift either the ground-weave heddle rod or the *cru-*

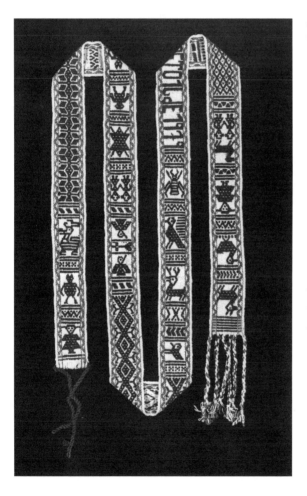

4.8 Belt in plain-weave white cotton with brown and olive green (natural dyes) wool supplementary-warp patterning. The use of natural dyes was a development project of the time. Woven by Ashuca Quizhpe, Gunudel, Saraguro area, Loja province, with lettering that reads "Agosto de 1979." 2.06 × .047 m. (6 feet 9 inches × 1⅞ inches), excluding tie. The Textile Museum 1988.17.11, Latin American Research Fund.

4.9 Inserting the weft in a supplementary-warp patterned belt. The *cruzera* contains an extra rod underneath in the center that holds the supplementary-warp yarns. The weaving is almost finished, and the dovetailed join is clearly visible. Polivio Sarango, Tuncarta, Saraguro area, Loja province. Slide by Lynn A. Meisch, 1979.

zera shed (alternately), push the pickup stick close to the heddle rod, insert the sword, beat (Fig. 4.11), then insert the weft. Repeat. The front heddle rod shed is opened by lifting the heddle rod with the left hand and pressing down on the front *cruzera* stick with the right hand.

Supplementary Warp Controlled by a Second Heddle Rod (with Pickup)

Molobóg, Eastern Chimborazo Province

ANN P. ROWE   Lynn Meisch and an Earthwatch team recorded both warping and weaving of a belt in Molobóg in the Licto area of Chimborazo province in 1988 (Fig. 4.12).[2] The weavers were Manuel Pilatacsi Minta and his wife, María Quizhpe.

The warping is done on stakes pounded into the ground behind the house (Fig. 4.13). Besides the end stakes and the dovetail stake (set to the left of

4.10 Picking up the supplementary-warp pattern in a belt. María Asunción Quizhpe, Gunudel, Saraguro area, Loja province. Photo by Lynn A. Meisch, 1978.

4.11 Beating the plain-weave shed in a supplementary-warp patterned belt. The pickup stick remains in the pattern and is pushed back toward the heddle rod for the opening of the ground-weave shed and weft insertion. María Asunción Quizhpe, Gunudel, Saraguro area, Loja province. Slide by Lynn A. Meisch, 1978.

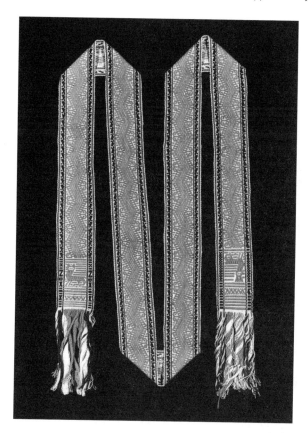

4.12 Belt in white cotton plain weave with orange (center) and blue (sides) acrylic supplementary-warp patterning. Woven by María Quizhpe, Molobóg, eastern Chimborazo province. 2.57 × .07 meters (8 feet 5 inches × 2¾ inches). The Textile Museum 1988.19.159, Latin American Research Fund.

the cross stakes), there is one cross stake set slightly in front of the others which has the supplementary-warp yarns in front of it, and a group of three other cross stakes to the right for the ground warp. A cord is tied to the top of the dovetail stake to hold the join when the stake is removed. Señor Pilatacsi warps a complete round of the white ground, then a half round of the supplementary warp, and so on. When changing colors, he holds down the end of the dormant yarn with his knee or foot.

When the warping is complete, the two-stick *cruzera* is inserted in the ground-warp cross between the two right-hand cross stakes, and a thread is looped around the supplementary-warp yarns (Fig. 4.13). The third cross stake marks the shed where the ground-warp heddle rod will be installed. The warping thus exactly matches the weaving setup, with a heddle rod for the supplementary-warp yarns in front, then a heddle rod for one of the ground-warp sheds, with the front part of the *cruzera* acting as a shed rod. The ends of the cord through the dovetail join are simply tied together in a bow, and not to a stick. The upper loom bar is curved.

4.13 Completed warp for a supplementary-warp patterned belt on the warping posts, with the *cruzera* sticks inserted between the rightmost cross stakes. The supplementary-warp yarns pass in front of the leftmost cross stake. Manuel Pilatacsi Minta, Molobóg, Chimborazo province. Photo by Lynn A. Meisch, 1988.

4.14 Picking up the pattern in a supplementary-warp patterned belt. Manuel Pilatacsi Minta, Molobóg, Chimborazo province. Photo by Lynn A. Meisch, 1988.

Señor Pilatacsi uses a narrow pickup stick to pick the design, from right to left, at the fell, holding all the supplementary-warp yarns up with the sword turned on edge (Fig. 4.14). Then the ground-warp shed is opened and the pickup stick pushed back toward the heddle rod, as in Saraguro. The weft is wound on itself into an oblong ball rather than on a shuttle. Señora Quizhpe weaves with the same setup.

Supplementary Warp Controlled by a Second Heddle Rod (with Pickup)

Nitón, Tungurahua Province

ANN P. ROWE   We were told that Manuel Curay, recorded by our Earthwatch teams, was the only weaver still working in Nitón in 1988. His weaving is most unusual in controlling the supplementary-warp yarns with an underneath heddle rod, making a sinking shed.[3] Don Manuel weaves ponchos as well as belts for his family and also for sale to other members of the community (Fig. 4.15; see also A. Rowe [ed.] 1998: 159, fig. 147). He buys acrylic yarn and retwists it.

He uses a curved upper loom bar (*travilla* S.) and a T-shaped foot brace, and his front loom bars (*pechos* S.) are secured to a cabuya backstrap (*atamba* Q.). A cord is put through the dovetail join and tied to each end of a stick (*topa* S.). He uses a two-stick *cruzera*, which holds the ground-warp sheds. The supplementary-warp yarns pass over both cross sticks (in contrast to the method used by the weavers described above) (Figs. 4.16–4.17). In front of the *cruzera* is a heddle rod (*illawa*, pronounced "*izhawa*") of the usual kind, controlling the ground-warp yarns that are under the front *cruzera*.

In front of this heddle rod is a second one (also called *illawa*), which controls the supplementary-warp yarns, but from the bottom, rather than the top (Fig. 4.16). That is, the stick to which the heddle loops are secured hangs below the entire warp, while only the ends of the loops around the supplementary-warp yarns are visible on top. This heddle rod is used after the pattern is picked up to lower the supplementary-warp yarns that are not selected for the pattern.

The weaving sequence, reconstructed from photographs, is as follows. The supplementary-warp yarns are lifted by inserting the sword (*kallwa* Q., pronounced "*kazhwa*") under them first behind the ground-warp heddle rod and then in front of it. Don Manuel holds the supplementary-warp yarns in his left hand as he picks up the pattern with a pickup stick (*escogedor* S.) in his right

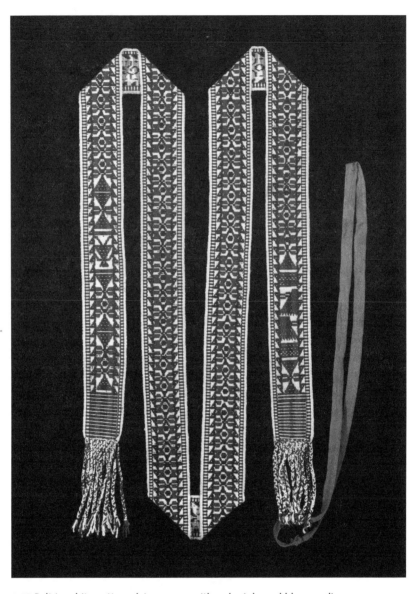

4.15 Belt in white cotton plain weave, with red, pink, and blue acrylic supplementary-warp patterning. Woven by Manuel Curay, Nitón, Tungurahua province. 2.83 × .065 meters (9 feet 3½ inches × 2½ inches). The Textile Museum 1988.19.76, Latin American Research Fund.

4.16 Picking up the pattern in a supplementary-warp patterned belt. The underneath heddle rod can be seen in front of the regular one. Manuel Curay, Nitón, Tungurahua province. Photo by Carol Mitz, 1988.

4.17 Inserting the weft in a supplementary-warp patterned belt. The T-shaped footbrace is also visible. Manuel Curay, Nitón, Tungurahua province. Photo by Carol Mitz, 1988.

hand (Fig. 4.16). The pickup stick is left in place at the fell while the ground shed is opened and the unused supplementary-warp yarns are lowered. The shed is held open by moving the pickup stick back toward the ground-warp heddle rod and turning the sword on edge (Fig. 4.17), and the weft, wrapped on its shuttle (*fúa*), is inserted.

For the ground-warp shed controlled by the heddle rod, the supplementary-warp heddle rod is lowered and then the ground-warp heddle rod is lifted. For the ground-warp shed controlled by the front *cruzera* stick, the ground-warp shed is first opened by inserting the sword in the shed behind the heddle rods, and again in front, and then by pulling down the heddle rod controlling the supplementary-warp yarns.

Supplementary Warp Controlled by Second Shed Stick (with Pickup)

Collage, Cotopaxi Province

A N N P. R O W E   Earthwatch teams recorded belt weaving in 1988 in the Collage-Quilajaló-Collana-Pilaló de San Andrés area, just west of Salcedo in Cotopaxi province.[4] The yarns, both cotton and acrylic, are purchased in the Salcedo market. The belts are made for sale and sold in the Salcedo market. Two styles of belts were recorded, one having pickup designs (Fig. 4.18), presented here, and the other having a design only of horizontal bars, discussed below.

The loom for pickup weaving (Fig. 4.19) has a two-stick *cruzera*, with a grooved back stick, to hold the ground-weave cross. The supplementary warp passes under the back stick, over the front one, and then over a loose shed stick set in front of the *cruzera*. In front of these sticks is a pair of heddle rods used for making the two ground-weave sheds. The pickup is done between the two heddle rods. The warp is made on a warping board with two cross stakes plus an additional stake to separate the supplementary-warp yarns.

One of the weavers, Rosa Toapanta Chicaiza, said that she warps ten pairs for a dancer design (*bailarín* S.), fifteen pairs for an elaborate zigzag design (*kingu* Q.), and six pairs for lettering (*letras* S.). She can warp ten belts between 9:00 and 12:00 AM and weave one belt of two *brazas* (S., an arm's length) with pickup designs between 7:00 AM and 5:00 PM. She weaves a belt without designs in one hour. The pickup designs are standardized and memorized. Besides those already listed, they include *venado* (S., deer), *pato* (S., duck), *coco* (S., diamond), *perro* (S., dog), *alacrán* (S., scorpion), and *sapo* (S., toad). The

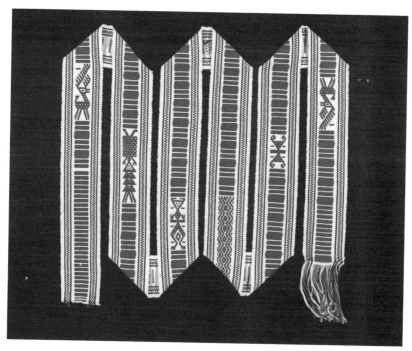

4.18 Belt in plain-weave white cotton with hot pink supplementary-warp patterning. Woven by Pedro Toapanta, area west of Salcedo, Cotopaxi province. 2.98 × .075 meters (9 feet 9¼ inches × 3 inches). The Textile Museum 1988.19.25, The Latin American Research Fund.

4.19 Picking up the pattern on a belt loom on which the supplementary-warp yarns are controlled by a second shed stick. Area west of Salcedo, Cotopaxi province. Slide by George Crockett, 1988.

zigzag border design is called *parangón* (S., comparison). In Collana, the deer is called *taruka* (Q.) and the dancer is called *danzante* (S.).

Supplementary Warp Controlled by Second Shed Stick (with Pickup)

Antonio Cando Camuendo, La Compañía, Otavalo Area, Imbabura Province

ANN P. ROWE Lynn Meisch and I recorded Antonio Cando Camuendo in the summer of 1986. He was a young unmarried man living with his widowed mother.[5] He had learned to weave from his father and was using his father's loom parts and tools, though, officially, these belonged to his mother. He weaves belts for sale and works very fast. As is typical of the Otavalo area, his back loom bar is curved.

He uses a two-stick *cruzera,* with both parts square in cross section and grooved, with the supplementary warp passing under the back and over the front (Fig. 4.20). In addition, an extra small sword is placed under the supplementary-warp yarns between the two parts of the *cruzera* and left there. He had put a shoelace through the dovetailed join and had tied the shoelace around the white edge warp yarns on both sides with a simple overhand knot.

He had memorized the designs so that he could weave a complete motif in about eight minutes. There were eight designs on the belt he was weaving, ranging from 2.5 to 4.0 centimeters (1 to 1½ inches) long with twenty to thirty-one weft passes.

He does the pickup just below the *cruzera,* since that is where the supplementary warp is raised (Fig. 4.20). His left hand either just holds the warp at the woven edge or holds either all the supplementary-warp yarns or the previous shed, just below the heddle rods. The heddle rods are pushed together for pickup of the warp yarns to be lifted together with the front heddle rod, and they are apart for the pickup of the warp yarns to be lifted together with the back heddle rod. He leaves the pickup stick behind the heddle rod that is about to be used and does not bring it forward (Fig. 4.21). The heddle rod is lifted and the sword inserted, beaten sharply once, set on edge, and the weft inserted. He then beats once more with the sword.

The most interesting aspect of his weaving is that, in addition to these supplementary-warp patterns, he was using supplementary-weft patterning in imitation of a belt from Natabuela, of the sort described below. He had been commissioned to weave this belt by someone in Natabuela and he had an

4.20 Picking up the supplementary-warp pattern. Antonio Cando Camuendo, La Compañía, Otavalo area, Imbabura province. Photo by Lynn A. Meisch, 1986.

4.21 Inserting the weft in the shed controlled by the front heddle rod. The pickup stick with the supplementary-warp pickup is between the two heddle rods. Antonio Cando Camuendo, La Compañía, Otavalo area, Imbabura province. Photo by Lynn A. Meisch, 1986.

old Natabuela belt as a guide, made from two different belts pieced together (Fig. 4.22). He was not copying this belt exactly, however, and had worked out his own technique for producing the structure. He seems to have used his own repertoire of supplementary-warp designs, some similar to and some different from the Natabuela ones, and he was using only two of the simpler of the several supplementary-weft patterns in the old belt. He was also copying the color scheme of the Natabuela belt (Plate 8). He was under the impression that no one in Natabuela now weaves this kind of belt. Obviously, very few do, or a weaver in La Compañía would not be asked.

Structurally, the supplementary weft is laid in the plain-weave shed (parallel to the ground weft) whenever it is not floating on the front to create the pattern. The supplementary weft passes back and forth across the entire width of the design band but does not extend into the plain side stripes. It is turned on the front of the fabric and is completely invisible on the back. Meanwhile, the supplementary-warp yarns are carried on the back in three-span floats horizontally aligned, with occasional five-span floats.

Señor Cando's method of picking up for the supplementary-weft pattern is unusual. He inserts the small sword used for picking up the supplementary-warp yarns under all of them above both heddle rods and leaves it there. He lifts one of the plain-weave heddle rods and inserts the large sword, turning it on edge. Then, using a steel needle on which the supplementary weft is threaded, he picks out from the lifted warps adjacent to the woven edge those that will pass over the supplementary weft (Fig. 4.23) and draws the supplementary weft through this shed. Then, from the opposite direction, he inserts the ground weft into the plain-weave shed held by the sword. To pick up the supplementary-weft shed going from left to right, he uses his left hand, since the weft is threaded on the needle. He uses nail clippers to trim the ends of the supplementary weft.

Every fourth passage of the ground weft, after the supplementary weft is inserted, he lifts the supplementary warp by bringing the small sword forward before putting the ground weft through the shed.

Supplementary Warp Controlled by Second Shed Stick (with Pickup)

Natabuela, Imbabura Province

ANN P. ROWE   In Natabuela and its neighboring hamlet Ovalos, belts are woven on a vertical loom, similar to the loom style seen in Carchi province.

4.22 Old Natabuela belt being copied by Antonio Cando Camuendo, La Compañía, Otavalo area, Imbabura province. Plain weave with supplementary-warp and supplementary-weft patterning. Photo by Lynn A. Meisch, 1986.

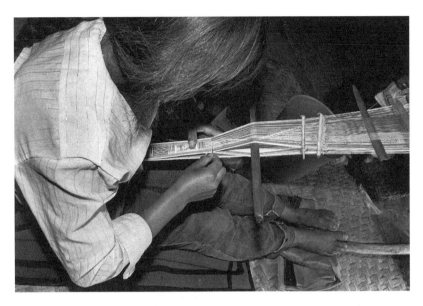

4.23 Inserting the supplementary-weft yarn with a needle. Antonio Cando Camuendo, La Compañía, Otavalo area, Imbabura province. Photo by Lynn A. Meisch, 1986.

The belts also differ from those made farther south in that they have areas of supplementary-weft patterning in addition to supplementary-warp patterning (Fig. 4.22; see also A. Rowe [ed.] 1998: ii, 83). Few still weave these belts, but in 1989 an Earthwatch team and I were fortunate to be able to record in Ovalos the technique used by José Miguel Limaico, who said he was seventy-eight years old.[6] He said he learned by watching a neighbor weave. His daughter said she also wove belts, but we did not see her working. Don José made the point that the vertical loom is easier on your back than the backstrap loom.

The loom is set up on a porch, leaning against the wall (Fig. 4.24). There are holes in the vertical posts for pegs that also pass through holes in the horizontal loom bars, which are placed in front of the vertical posts. There are two additional sets of holes below those used for the lower loom bar. Unlike the Carchi loom, there are no separate horizontal frame bars. Additional tension is obtained by inserting wooden blocks under the warp in front of the lower loom bar. The vertical loom posts are round and look like eucalyptus wood. The horizontal loom bars are squared off. The warp passes around the outside of the loom bars and is dovetailed in the same manner as in other Ecuadorian belts.

Don José uses a three-stick *cruzera*. All the sticks are round and smooth and the ends are tied together. The top one has half of the white ground-warp yarns over it, the same yarns as the top heddle rod. The middle *cruzera* stick has the supplementary-warp yarns over it, and the lower one has the supplementary-warp yarns and the other half of the white ground-warp yarns over it, the same ground-warp yarns as the lower heddle rod. The heddles appeared to have been made in the same way as in the belt looms of Otavalo and other areas. There is a small metal rod in the dovetail join. He uses a sword of the usual kind and a wooden pickup stick that is flat in cross section and pointed at both ends.

To weave the areas with supplementary-warp pattern, he inserts the sword under the supplementary-warp yarns at the *cruzera*, turns the sword on edge, and brings it forward. With his left fingers under the supplementary warp, he selects those wanted for the design with the pickup stick in his right hand, working near the fell (unlike in Otavalo) (Fig. 4.25), and leaves the pickup stick under the selected yarns. Then, he raises one of the heddle rods, pushing the pickup stick up against the lower heddle rod, inserts the sword in the shed, and brings it forward. He beats with the sword, inserts the weft, and beats again. This process is the same for each of the two heddle rods.

To open the heddle-rod shed, he places the narrow edge of the sword behind the heddle rod and pushes away from himself and up while pulling the heddle rod toward him with the left hand. He also sometimes pulls the warp yarns apart with his fingers from both sides, placing his thumbs on top of the warp and his fingers behind it.

To weave the horizontal stripes that frame the pickup designs, he first raises the upper heddle rod (all white) and then, for the next weft, the *cruzera* and the front heddle rod, which raises the supplementary warp as well as the other ground-warp yarns.

To weave the supplementary-weft patterns, he first opens the shed on the front *cruzera* by inserting the sword there and bringing it forward. He beats the sword down, inserts a ground weft, and beats again. Then he lifts the lower heddle rod, that is, he raises the same shed as before but without the supplementary-warp yarns. He selects the central warp yarns that will carry the supplementary-weft pattern and from these he picks up the warp yarns desired for the pattern (Fig. 4.26), inserts the supplementary weft and beats gently with the pick. Then he lifts the upper heddle rod, beats, inserts a ground weft, and beats again. He again selects the center warp yarns, from which he picks up the pattern and passes the supplementary weft. Then he repeats the sequence, raising the threads from the front *cruzera*. The use of the front of the *cruzera* secures the supplementary-warp yarns in over one, under one interlacing, without floats.

4.24 Vertical loom for belt weaving in Ovalos (Natabuela area), Imbabura province. José Miguel Limaico is inserting the sword under the first heddle rod. Slide by Ann P. Rowe, 1989.

4.25 Picking up the supplementary-warp pattern. José Miguel Limaico, Ovalos (Natabuela area), Imbabura province. Slide by Barbara Borders, 1989.

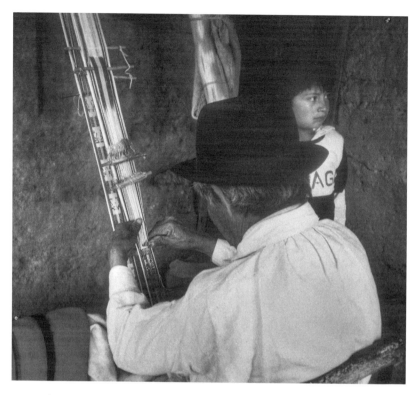

4.26 Picking up ground-warp yarns for the insertion of the supplementary weft. José Miguel Limaico, Ovalos (Natabuela area), Imbabura province. Slide by Ann P. Rowe, 1989.

Supplementary Warp Controlled by Second Shed Stick (with Pickup)

Carlos Conterón, Ilumán, Otavalo Area, Imbabura Province

ANN P. ROWE   Lynn Meisch and I recorded Carlos Conterón's belt-weaving technique in 1986, and he and his daughter Breenan demonstrated at The Textile Museum in 1999. Don Carlos (b. 1945) learned from his father to weave on the treadle loom but not on the backstrap loom. He still does treadle-loom weaving and has built his own loom. In addition, he teaches weaving to schoolchildren in several towns in the Otavalo area. He is also a farmer and community leader. He learned backstrap-loom weaving from a young man from Agato who demonstrated at the *colegio* (high school) in Quinchuquí in 1978. He weaves belts only for his family, a wife and five daughters (see A. Rowe [ed.] 1998: 74, fig. 60). Since this is not, for him, a commercial skill, he weaves much more slowly than the other weavers we recorded.

In 1986 he was using his carpentry bench as a warping board, although at the museum he just pounded stakes into the ground. For the patterned area, he warps a ground and a supplementary-warp yarn together and then a ground-warp yarn alone. He counts the supplementary-warp yarns in pairs at the warping stake, where they appear alone. He uses between fourteen and twenty-four pairs of supplementary-warp yarns for a belt.

He uses three cross stakes, corresponding to the three sticks of the *cruzera*. In 1986 he passed the supplementary-warp yarns (the darker ones in the photograph) in front of the first cross stake, behind the second, and in front of the third, with the plain-weave cross between the first two cross stakes and all ground yarns behind the third cross stake (Fig. 4.27). The cross between the first two cross stakes thus corresponded to that between the front and back sticks of the *cruzera*. However, since the center stick of the *cruzera* was to have only the supplementary-warp yarns over it, he had to separate these yarns from all those over the first cross stake and front *cruzera* stick by hand, and the right-hand cross stake was essentially not functional.

By 1999, however, he was warping with three cross stakes that exactly corresponded to the *cruzera* (Fig. 4.28). The supplementary-warp yarns (again the dark ones in the photograph) passed behind the first cross stake, in front of the second and behind the third, while the plain weave cross was made between the first and third stakes with all these yarns behind the second cross stake. In 1986 he told us that his teacher had used only two cross stakes and two *cruzera* sticks, and that he had done pickup for the *cruzera*. So don Carlos was working out for himself how to warp so as not to have to pick up any of the main sheds for the *cruzera*.

He adds the *cruzera* before he removes the warp from the warping board. The back part of the *cruzera* is slightly larger than the others as well as being grooved. Half of the ground-warp yarns pass over the front stick of the *cruzera* and the alternate ones over the back. He places one warp yarn in each groove of the back part of the *cruzera* for the belt borders and two in each groove for the central patterned area. The supplementary-warp yarns pass over the front two sticks. Although the ends of the *cruzera* are tied together, he also inserts a cord parallel to the first cross stake and ties the ends together before removing the warp from the warping board. He then adds the curved back loom bar and the front loom bar with the backstrap.

He next replaces the bamboo dovetail stake with a cotton cord, threaded through a hole near the end of the stake and pulled through as the dovetail

4.27 Warping a supplementary-warp patterned belt, detail. Carlos Conterón, Ilumán, Otavalo area, Imbabura province. Photo by Lynn A. Meisch, 1986.

4.28 Warping a supplementary-warp patterned belt, detail. Carlos Conterón, Ilumán, Otavalo area, Imbabura province. Slide by Ann P. Rowe, 1999.

stake is removed. One end of the cord is tied to a small wooden stick before it is put through the join, the other, afterward. The wooden stick is placed inside the shed next to the join.

He then adds the roller bar and adjusts the warp over the grooved part of the *cruzera*. Next, he puts on the two heddle rods, with the heddles made in the usual way. He still has to pick up the sheds for this purpose.

Before beginning pickup he also inserts a small square stick under alternate pairs of the supplementary-warp yarns (Fig. 4.29). This is placed above the center stick of the *cruzera* to facilitate the pickup of those designs with dotted grounds (three-span floats aligned in alternate pairs). It is secured by having a thread tied to both ends over the warp. In 1999 señora Conterón had incorporated this stick into her *cruzera* behind the stick with all the supplementary-

4.29 Picking up the supplementary-warp pattern. An extra shed stick with alternate pairs of warp facilitates pickup of large pattern areas. Carlos Conterón, Ilumán, Otavalo area, Imbabura province. Photo by Lynn A. Meisch, 1986.

4.30 Inserting weft in a supplementary-warp patterned belt. A graph paper pattern is used as a guide. The bone pick tied to the *cruzera* is clearly visible. This photograph was taken on a different day from Fig. 4.29, and this loom lacks the extra shed stick. Carlos Conterón, Ilumán, Otavalo area, Imbabura province. Photo by Lynn A. Meisch, 1986.

warp yarns. The pickup stick is made of a cow's leg bone and has a hole drilled into the blunt end by which it is tied to the cord on the ends of the *cruzera* by a string about fifty centimeters (twenty inches) long (Fig. 4.30).

Don Carlos does the pickup just in front of the *cruzera* (Fig. 4.29). With his left hand he holds the supplementary-warp yarns from the previous shed, dropping these as new ones are selected. He holds this new shed on his left forefinger while relocating the pickup stick to between the heddle rods, then in front of the heddle rods, and, finally, down to the woven edge, where it is left in place. Then he lifts the appropriate ground-weave heddle rod with the left hand, pushing down the warp with his right and inserting his forefinger into the shed to clear it. He pushes the pickup stick back against the heddles and inserts the sword into the plain-weave shed. He rocks the sword back and forth to move the cross down gently and then beats sharply three times. Then the sword is turned on edge and the weft inserted (Fig. 4.30). He beats once more with the sword, and then with the pickup stick beats the supplementary warp gently. He regards this last step as particularly important for good definition of the pattern. Then he inserts his left finger under the supplementary warp and removes the pickup stick and is ready to begin the next pickup.

He had been taught a number of designs by the man from Agato but also had gathered designs from other sources. He is literate and has a collection of design drawings he made on graph paper (Fig. 4.30) and also uses a collection of drawings of Otavalo belt designs that was made by an Ecuadorian anthropologist and published by the local Instituto Otavaleño de Antropología (Jaramillo 1981).

Supplementary Warp Controlled by Second Shed Stick (with Pickup)

Chibuleo, Tungurahua Province

ANN P. ROWE   In 1988 we were able to visit a belt weaver in the Chibuleo community of San Luis. Segundo Francisco Tiche said he weaves hair bands, too, but fortunately he had a belt on the loom when we were there. He weaves belts both for his family and for sale (Fig. 4.31). His loom is set up inside his house.

The back loom bar (*apari* Q.) is a straight piece of wood bound to two floor-to-ceiling vertical posts (*shaya kaspi* Q.) in the wall of the house. The space between these posts is only wide enough for belt weaving. A T-shaped wooden foot brace is built into the floor in front of the loom bar (under the

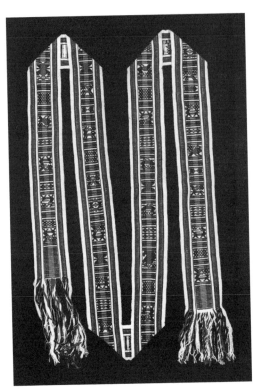

4.31 Chibuleo woman's belt. White cotton plain weave with purple and magenta acrylic supplementary-warp patterning. Woven by José Francisco Maliza Conceta, San Luis Chibuleo, Tungurahua province. 2.68 × .075 meters (8 feet 9½ inches × 3 inches). The Textile Museum 1988.19.111, Latin American Research Fund.

4.32 Inserting the weft in a supplementary-warp patterned belt. Segundo Francisco Tiche, San Luis Chibuleo, Tungurahua province. Slide by Betty Davenport, 1988.

blanket in Fig. 4.32). The front loom bar and roller bar (both *pichera* S. with Q. pronunciation) are of the usual kind.

He uses a three-stick *cruzera*. The back part is called *peine* (S.) or *ñakcha* (Q.), meaning comb. It is square in cross section and has a row of small nails sticking out of it. A cord is tied to the stick at both ends to help keep the warp yarns in their slots. The middle stick is called *cruzera* and is round in cross section. Each of the two back sticks holds half of the white warp yarns for plain weave. The front stick of the *cruzera*, slightly smaller than the others, is called *cruzera para dibujos* (S., shed stick for designs) and holds the supplementary-warp yarns, which also pass over the middle *cruzera* stick. There are two heddle rods, called *liso* (S.), each for one of the plain-weave sheds.

He does pickup behind the heddle rods and in front of the *cruzera* (Fig. 4.33), inserts the pickup stick, and leaves it in place for raising the heddle rods (Fig. 4.32). To lift the heddle rods, he releases tension on the warp, presses down on the warp with the sword behind the heddle rod he wants to lift, and pulls the heddle rod back and forth with his left hand.

Supplementary Warp Entirely Loom Controlled

Bar Design, Collage, Cotopaxi Province

ANN P. ROWE   These belts with a bar design, called *cajón* (S., box), are the simplest type of loom-controlled supplementary-warp pattern weaving. They actually mimic the effect of the belts woven in turn-banded 2/1 twill (see Chapter 5) but are simpler to weave, and we saw them being woven by children as young as seven. The looms were the same in the two households west of Salcedo in Cotopaxi province, where we recorded this technique in 1988, which were the same households mentioned above for belts with pickup patterns.

There is a two-stick *cruzera*, with a grooved stick forming the back part (Fig. 4.34). Alternate ground-warp yarns pass over the back part of the *cruzera* and under the front, while the remaining ground-warp yarns follow the reverse path. The supplementary-warp yarns pass under the back part and over the front part of the *cruzera* and then over a loose shed stick in front of the *cruzera*. This setup is much like that for pickup. In front of the shed stick is a heddle rod controlling the ground-warp yarns that are under the front part of the *cruzera*. The front part of the *cruzera* acts as a shed rod, unlike in the loom for pickup. The weaving sequence for a design of bars made of three-span floats is as follows: heddle rod shed alone; *cruzera* shed plus supplementary warp; heddle rod shed plus supplementary warp; *cruzera* shed plus supplementary warp; repeat.

Supplementary Warp Entirely Loom Controlled

Miguel Andrango, Agato, Otavalo Area, Imbabura Province

ANN P. ROWE   Miguel Andrango is a prosperous man who in the 1980s and the 1990s was spending a great deal of time in the United States. He is head of a weaving group in Agato that has experimented with backstrap-loom weaving techniques from other areas such as Guatemala, Peru, and Bolivia.

4.33 Picking up the supplementary-warp pattern in a belt. Segundo Francisco Tiche, San Luis Chibuleo, Tungurahua province. Slide by Betty Davenport, 1988.

4.34 Inserting weft in a belt with a loom-controlled supplementary-warp bar design. Area west of Salcedo, Cotopaxi province. Slide by George Crockett, 1988.

I first met him when he visited The Textile Museum for a weaving demonstration in 1978. The Otavalo style belt he was weaving on this occasion had a heddle-controlled chevron design (Fig. 4.35).

His two-stick *cruzera* separates the alternate threads of the ground weave (Fig. 4.36). The back part of the *cruzera* is in two pieces, the lower one with grooves so pronounced as to be slots. The warp yarns are secured in these grooves by a second stick that is tied directly on top of it. (Another belt loom he had lacked this top piece.) The front part of the *cruzera* over which the alternate ground-warp yarns pass is not grooved. All these sticks are square in cross section. The front part of the *cruzera* acts as a ground-weave shed rod, and a heddle rod is used for the alternate ground-warp shed.

In a reversal from the Cotopaxi loom just discussed, the supplementary-warp yarns pass through the slots of the back part of the *cruzera* and under the front part. In addition, a flat stick is inserted below the ground-warp yarns and above the supplementary-warp yarns underneath the *cruzera*. This stick is pressed down when the plain-weave heddle rod is lifted. The lifting of the supplementary-warp yarns is done using four additional heddle rods, located behind the ground-warp heddle rod. The sequence is first to lift a pattern heddle rod and to insert a pickup stick in front of the ground-weave heddle rod. Then the weaver opens the plain-weave shed, inserts the sword, and then the weft. His pickup stick was loose for this loom, but he had another loom in which it was tied to the cord connecting the ends of the *cruzera*.

Don Miguel did not indicate that he was innovative in this belt, though it is possible that he was. Collier and Buitrón (1949: 71) show an Otavalo man weaving a similar chevron-patterned belt, but he has the supplementary-warp yarns over the front part of the *cruzera* instead of the back. Accordingly, unlike don Miguel, his pickup stick is inserted just in back of the ground-warp heddle rod for weft insertion. Like don Miguel, he uses extra heddle rods for the supplementary-warp pattern, though the exact number is not clear in the photograph.

Don Miguel had looms set up for several other non-Otavalo techniques, including a Chinchero-style belt loom with complementary warps (Peru) and a Totonicapán-style belt with alternating float weave and supplementary weft (Guatemala). He had been to Chinchero and observed the technique there, but the method he later worked out for reproducing the structure and design differs from that found in Chinchero. He had not been to Guatemala so far as I know, but had simply worked out a way to reproduce these structures based on his observation of the finished product and his knowledge of Otavalo weaving techniques, in the same way that the La Compañía weaver imitated the Natabuela belt.

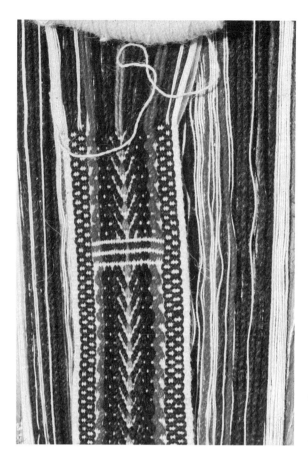

4.35 Unfinished belt with loom-controlled supplementary-warp chevron design. Woven by Miguel Andrango, Agato, Otavalo area, Imbabura province. Slide by Ann P. Rowe, 1978.

4.36 Weaving a belt with a loom-controlled supplementary-warp chevron design. Miguel Andrango, Agato, Otavalo area, Imbabura province. Slide by Ann P. Rowe, 1978.

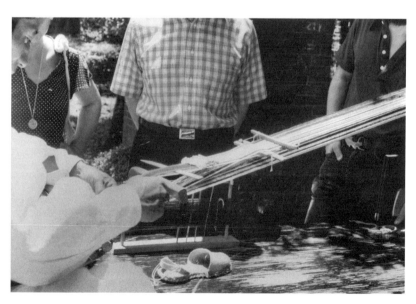

Supplementary Warp Entirely Loom Controlled

José Manuel Bautista, Agato, Otavalo Area, Imbabura Province

ANN P. ROWE José Manuel Bautista, recorded by Lynn Meisch and me in 1986, is from a relatively poor family in Agato and makes belts for sale to supplement his income. His belts were woven with finer yarns more closely spaced than most other Otavalo-area belts being made in 1986 and were also unusual in being made of polyester yarn (Fig. 4.37). He retwists the polyester on a walking wheel until it is very kinky. The designs on his belts are entirely heddle controlled, allowing him to weave very fast, so it takes him only two days to make one belt. He said he had learned only one of the smaller designs he uses from his father. The others he said he had worked out for himself. He said he had been weaving this type of belt for eight years. He also showed us another belt he had woven with a different principal design.

He uses a warping board designed specifically for belts. There are two cross stakes between which the ground-warp yarns and supplementary-warp yarns are separated, as well as the dovetail stake and end stakes (Fig. 4.38). The weaving cross is not made until later. For the plain-weave selvedges, however, a plain-weave cross is formed between these stakes.

For the pattern area in the center of the belt, he warps a complete round of the ground- and supplementary-warp yarns together and then a complete round of the ground warp alone. When winding the ground- and supplementary-warp yarns together, he separates them at the cross stakes. He warps a total of thirty-four supplementary-warp yarns. When the warping is complete, he ties a string around the cross of the two colors of warp and removes the warp from the board with the dovetail stake still in place.

He then inserts the loom bars and attaches the backstrap. He next inserts a two-stick *cruzera* to hold the cross between the ground- and supplementary-warp yarns, with the supplementary-warp yarns passing over the front part. He is thus the only weaver we recorded who did not maintain a ground-warp cross in the *cruzera*. The back part is grooved. When he is weaving, he arranges the warp yarns so that there are two ground-warp yarns in each groove (since two ground-warp yarns alternate with each supplementary-warp yarn). Each time he sets up the warp for weaving after it has been put away, he must readjust the warp yarns into the grooves.

He then forms the weaving cross of the ground weave by raising alternate white warp yarns with his fingers, working right to left. He inserts his sword into the first shed and brings the cross forward, then picks the second shed above the first, inserting his pickup stick. Then he makes the heddles for the

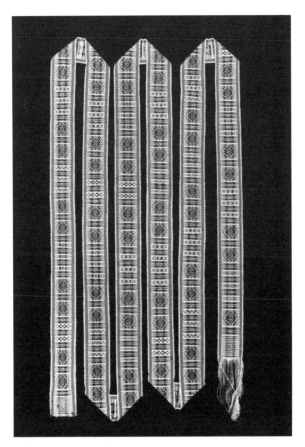

4.37 Belt in white plain weave with pink, blue, and copper colored supplementary-warp patterning, polyester yarns. Woven by José Manuel Bautista, Agato, Otavalo area, Imbabura province. 3.15 × .035 meters (10 feet 4 inches × 1⅜ inches). The Textile Museum 1986.19.13, Latin American Research Fund.

4.38 Warp for belt, detail. The cross stakes only separate the supplementary warp from the ground warp. José Manuel Bautista, Agato, Imbabura province. Photo by Lynn A. Meisch, 1986.

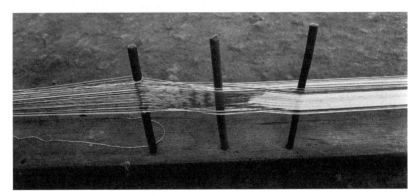

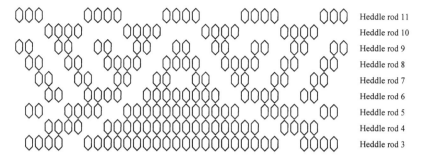

4.39 Diagram showing the use of the nine pattern heddle rods. José Manuel Bautista, Agato, Otavalo area, Imbabura province. Drawing by Ann P. Rowe.

plain-weave sheds. Next, he puts the nine pattern heddles on. He picks up the appropriate warp yarns just below the *cruzera* with a pickup stick, then makes the heddles before moving on to the next shed. He begins with heddle rod 9, and works forward to 3, and then does 10 and 11. The logic of this procedure is apparent in the diagram (Fig. 4.39). He frequently encloses two or four adjacent supplementary-warp yarns within the same heddle loop. These groupings are apparent in the diagram. In addition, in the center of heddle rods 3 and 4, there are two warp yarns in each heddle loop, while in the center of heddle rods 5 and 6, there are four warp yarns in each heddle. After making the heddles, the weaver replaces the dovetail stake used for warping with a small metal rod.

To begin, he weaves about 2 centimeters (¾ inch) of plain weave with heddle rod 2 and all the supplementary-warp yarns alternating with heddle rod 1. His weaving sequence for patterned areas is as follows. He lifts the desired pattern heddle rod and inserts the pickup stick into the shed, just behind the ground-weave heddle rod that is about to be lifted. Then he lifts the ground-weave heddle rod and inserts the sword. He beats down once, then inserts the weft (Fig. 4.40) and beats twice more with the sword.

When he wants to lift all the supplementary-warp yarns together for the horizontal bands, he grasps all of the pattern heddle rods together and inserts the pickup stick above the second ground-weave heddle rod. This stick is left in place for the horizontal bands, which are made using three-span floats, and is pushed back when the supplementary-warp yarns are below the ground weave between bands.

With seven of the nine pattern heddle rods, he weaves a large rayed diamond design, called *rombo* (S., diamond) (see Fig. 4.37). The sequence is 9, 8,

4.40 Inserting weft in a supplementary-warp patterned belt, which has the pattern formed by nine pattern heddle rods. José Manuel Bautista, Agato, Otavalo area, Imbabura province. Photo by Lynn A. Meisch, 1986.

7, 6, 9, 5, 7, 4, 9, 3, 7 (which is the center), then in reverse, 3, 9, and so on. He also weaves six small intermediate designs. The pattern heddle rod sequence for large checks is 10, 10, 11, 11, 10, 10. The sequence for a small X in the middle framed by a diamond and two chevrons is 7, 8, 9, 8, 7. The sequence for a horizontal zigzag (*kingu*) is 9, 10, 7, 11, 9. The sequence for X's separated by dots (*equis*, S., X's) is 7, 10, 9, 10, 7. The sequence for small checks (*lucero* S., morning star) is 7, 9, 7 or 7, 9, 7, 9, 7, depending on how many rows of checks are wanted. The sequence for small diamonds separated by colons (*coceado* S., kicked) is 9, 10, 8, 10, 9.

Supplementary Warp Entirely Loom Controlled

Cacha, Central Chimborazo Province

ANN P. ROWE The Centro Pastoral was founded in Cacha Machángara in 1979 to promote the teaching of belt-weaving techniques and to market the finished product in a village store and in a cooperative store in Riobamba. Many of the weavers who make and market belts through this organization are women (Jaramillo 1988a: 59).[7] Men needing cash income more often take wage labor outside the community.

A variety of small-scale diamond and chevron designs are woven with loom-controlled supplementary-warp yarns in Cacha. We saw weavers in four households making this kind of belt or hair band, but, unfortunately, most visits were too short to obtain complete information. There were general similarities but also some differences among these weavers. The back loom bar on one loom was straight but the others were curved. One heirloom loom bar was said to be a piece of deer antler and another also appeared to be of bone. Others were wood.

The main difference from the Otavalo manner of weaving loom-controlled designs is that the supplementary-warp pattern is not selected separately from the ground weave. No pickup stick is used, and the main sword is the only tool apart from the heddles and the *cruzera*. The ground-weave yarns and supplementary-warp yarns are lifted simultaneously. It follows that at least some of the heddle rods (or the *cruzera*) control both ground-weave and supplementary-warp yarns. For other sheds, a ground-weave heddle rod and a pattern heddle rod are lifted together.

Earthwatch teams recorded warping in the house of Ramón Paucar, who, though from Cacha, was living in Riobamba in 1988.[8] He uses only two cross stakes. In the photograph (Fig. 4.41), most but not all of the supplementary-warp yarns appear to be wound behind the first and in front of the second cross stake. There is also a ground-weave cross between the two cross stakes. We did not see him set up this warp for weaving. Carmen Conterón, a weaver I recorded setting up her loom in Cacha Machángara in 1988, picked up the sheds for each heddle rod, so her warping was probably similar to Ramón Paucar's.

Carmen Conterón was weaving a hair band with a pattern of chevrons or diamonds in the center stripe and lengthwise stripes on the sides using four pattern sheds (Fig. 4.42). She uses a two-stick *cruzera* (with square sticks) and four heddle rods (Fig. 4.43). In the central patterned area, most of the supplementary-warp yarns and half the ground warp are over the back part, and the other half of the ground-warp yarns plus the remaining supplementary-warp yarns are over the front part of the *cruzera*. The front part of the *cruzera* is used as a shed rod, and the ground-warp sheds are also lifted by means of the first and third heddle rods. The ground-warp shed controlled by the *cruzera* is the same as the front heddle rod, but the supplementary-warp yarns on these two devices differ (Fig. 4.44). The third heddle rod (with the opposite ground-warp shed) is lifted together with either the second or the fourth heddle rod, which control different groups of supplementary-warp yarns.

4.41 Warping a supplementary-warp patterned belt, using only two cross stakes. Ramón Paucar, Cacha, central Chimborazo province. Photo by Ed Healy, 1988.

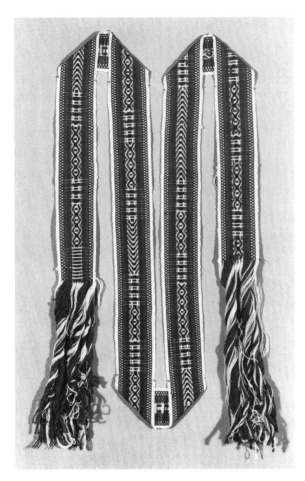

4.42 Hair band woven by Carmen Conterón, Cacha Machángara, central Chimborazo province. White cotton plain weave with loom-controlled supplementary-warp pattern in brown, green, red, blue, and magenta acrylic. 1.47 × .036 meters (4 feet 10 inches × 1⅜ inches). The Textile Museum 1988.19.134, Latin American Research Fund.

4.43 Making heddles for a loom with loom-controlled supplementary-warp patterning. Carmen Conterón, Cacha Machángara, central Chimborazo province. Slide by Ann P. Rowe, 1988.

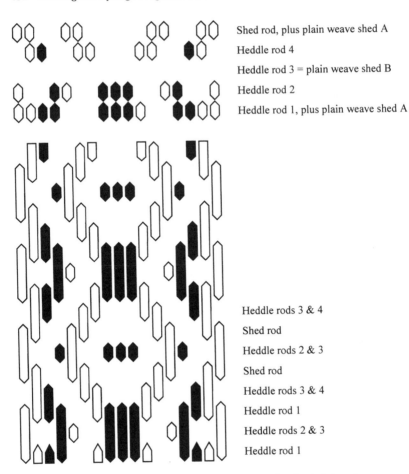

Shed rod, plus plain weave shed A

Heddle rod 4

Heddle rod 3 = plain weave shed B

Heddle rod 2

Heddle rod 1, plus plain weave shed A

Heddle rods 3 & 4

Shed rod

Heddle rods 2 & 3

Shed rod

Heddle rods 3 & 4

Heddle rod 1

Heddle rods 2 & 3

Heddle rod 1

4.44 Diagram showing the pattern and weaving setup for the hair band woven by Carmen Conterón, Cacha Machángara, central Chimborazo province. The plain-weave ground is not shown. Drawing by Ann P. Rowe.

The weaving sequence for the diamond design is as follows: 2 and 3, 1, 3 and 4, shed rod, 2 and 3, shed rod, 3 and 4, 1. The sequence for the horizontal bands (see Fig. 4.42) is 3, 1, 2–4, 1–2 and 4, 3, 1 (ending with an additional 3). Subsequent diamond designs begin with 1, followed by the sequence noted above. The sequence for the chevrons is 1, 2 and 3, shed rod, 3 and 4.

To create this setup, señora Conterón first inserts the *cruzera*. Then she picks up a shed that consists of the warp yarns of the plain side borders that are under the front *cruzera* stick and the ground-warp yarns of the center section that are over the front *cruzera* stick (omitting the supplementary-warp yarns), and inserts a temporary shed stick (Fig. 4.43). The heddle rods are all installed in front of this temporary shed stick.

Next, she picks up the ground-warp shed opposite this and installs what will be heddle rod 3. Next, she picks up the supplementary-warp yarns for and installs heddle rod 4, followed by heddle rod 2. She then opens the shed held by the temporary shed stick and inserts the first weft pass. She opens the next shed by lifting all three heddle rods (which includes all the supplementary-warp yarns), and the weft is again inserted. Several more weft passes are made in this manner, alternating the temporary shed stick and the heddles, ending with the temporary shed stick to form a heading. Then she picks up the ground-warp yarns opposite heddle rod 3 plus some supplementary-warp yarns and installs heddle rod 1. Above the heddles, she picks up another shed and then removes the temporary shed stick.[9] She is now ready to weave the pattern, starting with heddle rods 2 and 3.

Other Cacha weavers use a setup with some yarns passing over both sticks

4.45 Weaving a hair band like the one in Figure 4.42 but with a slightly different setup from that of Carmen Conterón. Some warp yarns pass over both sticks in the *cruzera*. Angélica Asqui Janita, Cacha Machángara, central Chimborazo province. Slide by Judith Kelly, 1988.

4.46 Weaving a supplementary-warp patterned belt with a loom controlled small diamond design. The weaver is opening the *cruzera* shed. Some of the supplementary-warp yarns seem to pass over both sticks in the *cruzera*. There are four additional heddle rods. Daughter of Ramón Paucar (see also Fig. 4.41), Cacha, central Chimborazo province. Photo by Jean Hayden, 1988.

4.47 Inserting a weft in a belt loom with loom control of the supplementary-warp patterning. There are four heddle rods and a larger shed rod over the *cruzera*. Cacha Obraje, central Chimborazo province. Photo by Laura M. Miller, 1989.

of the *cruzera*. A fifteen-year-old girl in Cacha Machángara, Angélica Asqui Janita, was weaving a design identical to that of Carmen Conterón, in which some white ground and some supplementary-warp yarns appear to pass over both sticks of the *cruzera* (Fig. 4.45). Her loom also has four heddle rods. She had been weaving since age twelve and can weave a belt a day.[10]

Ramón Paucar's daughter was weaving a belt with small diamond designs in both the center and side stripes, with some supplementary-warp yarns over both *cruzera* sticks, plus four heddle rods (Fig. 4.46). The number of heddles on each heddle rod on these looms appears similar in the photographs, but, unfortunately, there is no information about whether they were used individually or whether two were sometimes lifted together.

Laura Miller recorded a young woman weaving a supplementary-warp patterned belt in Cacha Obraje in 1989 (Fig. 4.47). She was weaving a design of chevrons (called *ñakcha*) in the center stripe and a series of diamonds with dots of color in the centers and corners (called *Quito*) in the side stripes. Her loom has a two-stick *cruzera* (made with round sticks) with a larger shed rod resting on top of it, plus four heddle rods. The threads over the shed rod also pass over the whole *cruzera*. Miller reports that ground-warp yarns are controlled by the heddle rod nearest the weaver and by the shed rod and that, at times, two heddle rods are lifted simultaneously. The setup may therefore have been similar to Carmen Conterón's, apart from the extra shed rod.

CHAPTER 5

Turn-Banded 2/1 Twill Belts

Introduction

ANN P. ROWE   One belt structure with definite pre-Hispanic roots and found in several areas of highland Ecuador in different variations has a horizontally banded appearance (Figs. 5.1–5.2). Typically, white (often cotton) lines alternate with one or two other colors that form warp floats, formerly of wool but by the 1980s usually acrylic. Unlike the supplementary-warp patterned belts, which have two white yarns for each colored one, these belts have two colored yarns for each white one. One of the colored yarns floats on one face of the fabric while the other floats on the opposite face. The weft is usually white. Similar banded effects can be and often are produced with supplementary warp, for example in the Otavalo area and in Cotopaxi province (Fig. 4.34; see also A. Rowe [ed.] 1998: 60, fig. 39, *left*), but with less possibility of color variation.

The simplest belts in this structure are woven in Saraguro in southern Ecuador (Fig. 5.1). The same color floats on both faces, but the colored yarn on each face is separate. Some are a combination of cotton and wool or acrylic, while others are all wool. A narrow version called *ñajcha chumbi* (Q., comb belt) is used as the inner belt for a woman, while a wider version was formerly woven as a man's belt (Fig. 5.1).

In the Otavalo area, on the other hand, the two floating yarns are each a different color and, since each is carried exclusively on one face of the fabric, one side of the belt is one color and the other is a contrasting color (Fig. 5.2). Red and pink as well as red and black are frequent combinations. The colored yarns may float over three or five weft yarns before passing under one, that is, in three- or five-span warp floats. The belt in Figure 5.2 has five-span floats; an example with three-span floats is illustrated in A. Rowe (ed.) 1998: 65,

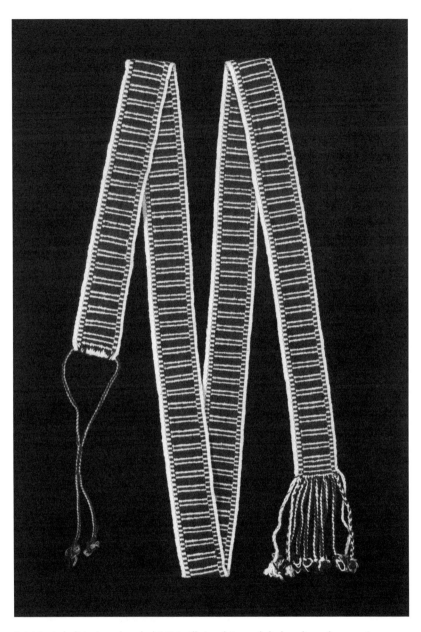

5.1 Man's belt in turn-banded 2/1 twill, in white and dark red wool yarns. Saraguro area, Loja province. Reproduction of an obsolete style woven between 1978–1985. 2.76 × .065 meters (9 feet ¾ inch × 2½ inches), excluding tie. The Textile Museum 1988.17.10, Latin American Research Fund.

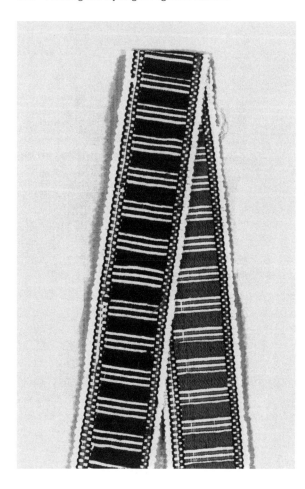

5.2 Detail of a belt in turn-banded 2/1 twill, in white cotton and red and black acrylic yarns. Woven by Ester Camuendo, La Compañía, Otavalo area, Imbabura province. Overall size: 2.94 × .045 meters (9 feet 7¾ inches × 1¾ inches). The Textile Museum 1989.22.17, Latin American Research Fund.

fig. 51, *center* (see also Figs. 5.1, 5.3 here). In the Otavalo area these belts are called *kanitillu chumbi* (Q., pronounced "*kanitizhu,*" cane belt). They are used not only as women's belts but also as hair bands and swaddling bands. I was able to record the technique in La Compañía in 1989 (see below).

A more complex variation of this structure occurs in belts of central Ecuador (Pl. 2). These belts have multicolored warp stripes, but there are still two colors of wool (or acrylic) floats in each area, one appearing on one face and one on the other. The two colors of floats in any given area, however, interchange faces at intervals to produce a checkered effect. The frequency with which the faces of the weave are exchanged may also vary, creating variations in the arrangement of the horizontal banding. Excluding the belt in Plate 2, four of The Textile Museum's six belts in this style are all wool, while two combine cotton with wool or acrylic. A different group of four has a pattern with a section of three narrow white ribs separated by two colored ones alternating with two wider colored bands (A. Rowe [ed.] 1998: 119, fig. 105, *left*). One of the belts does not employ exchange of colors (A. Rowe [ed.] 1998: 119, fig. 105, *right*).

We saw belts of this style being worn in Cotopaxi province in 1988 (Miller in A. Rowe [ed.] 1998: 122, fig. 112) but found no one weaving it there. Such belts were available for sale in the Latacunga and Saquisilí markets and were said to be imported from central Chimborazo province (Miller in A. Rowe [ed.] 1998: 118–119, fig. 105). In the central Chimborazo area this style is called *esterado* (S., *estera*, mat) (Bustos and Pilco 1987: 15). We also encountered a woman in the Guaranda market, Bolívar province, María Margarita Vayes, from Cuatro Esquinas, north of Guaranda, who made, wore, and sold this type of belt (A. Rowe [ed.] 1998: 166, fig. 156).[1]

Laura Miller and Lynn Meisch recorded this style of belt being woven in Nitiluisa in central Chimborazo province, which belongs to the San Juan costume area. The weaver, Santiago Sula Sisa, said that he had learned it from a man from Guaranda in the course of traveling with a musical group. He reported that learning this technique was facilitated by his previous familiarity with weaving the complementary-warp weave *kawiña chumbi* (see Chapter 7). His belts include sections of pickup that are not present in the other, similar, belts that we saw and seem to have been an innovation of his based on his experience with the *kawiña chumbi*.

Belts of this general structure were found in the graves of women sacrificed by the Incas at Pachacamac on the central coast of Peru (Uhle 1903: pl. 19, fig. 5; Wardle 1936: pl. VII). These belts are distinctive in pattern, however, and are more similar to bands still woven in southern Peru and Bolivia (A. Rowe 1977: 62–63) than to Ecuadorian examples. Thus, no direct Peruvian influence is likely for the Ecuadorian belts, but the technique is unquestionably pre-Hispanic.

Although this structure does not have a complicated appearance, it has no well-established shorthand name. The white warp yarns interlace over-1, under-1, but always over and under the same weft yarns, so that no complete plain weave is formed (Fig. 5.3). Of the two colors, one interlaces over-3, under-1, over-1, under-1, again, always over and under the same weft yarns (opposite the white), while the other interlaces over-1, under-1, over-1 (also opposite the white), under-3, so it is the opposite of the other color. Since each color passes over the same weft yarns each time, the three-span floats are horizontally aligned on both faces, producing horizontal bands of color separated by white bars.

5.3 Diagrammatic construction of turn-banded 2/1 twill: turned 2/1 horizontal herringbone reversed after every second weft and turned after every third, forming three-span floats in horizontal alignment. The use of monochrome yarns makes it a little harder to relate the construction to the Ecuadorian examples but it makes the twill interlacing easier to see. Note especially the weft interlacing order. From Emery 1980, fig. 215.

The structural basis for the weave is more apparent when observing the weft interlacing order (see Fig. 5.3). The weft yarns pass over 2 and under 1 or vice versa; the interlacing order can be abbreviated as 2/1. When such regular floats are in diagonal alignment, they form a twill weave. When the diagonal in a twill weave changes direction at regular intervals, it is called a *herringbone twill*. The change may be on either a horizontal or a vertical axis. In the banded weave, the direction of the diagonal changes after every second weft, on a horizontal axis. The weave is therefore a 2/1 horizontal herringbone twill (see also Emery 1980: 120–121).

When a twill weave has an uneven interlacing order such as 2/1, instead of an even one, such as 2/2, further patterning possibilities arise. These possibilities are based on the fact that, when a weft float occurs on one face of such a twill, a corresponding warp float occurs on the opposite face. The effect can be accentuated by making the warp (more visible on the warp-float face) and weft (more visible on the weft-float face) a different color. For example, the ubiquitous denim fabric is a 2/1 twill weave with a blue warp and a white weft, customarily worn with the blue (warp-float) face out. The enterprising weaver can make patterns by interchanging the faces of the weave, or turning it, so that areas of the weft-float face of the weave and of the warp-float face are juxtaposed on the same face of the cloth. In Figure 5.3, the weave is turned after every three weft yarns, so there are horizontal bands of the weft-float face alternating with bands of the warp-float face. In the belts, which are warp-faced and woven using white and colored yarns, the weft-float face is predominantly white, with a narrow colored bar through the middle, while the warp-float face is a solid row of colored warp floats.

The structural identity of the twill is obscured by the frequent reversal of the twill direction and the frequent turning of the weave as well as by the fact that the fabric is warp-faced. In *Costume and Identity in Highland Ecuador* (A. Rowe [ed.] 1998: 32–33), this structure is referred to simply as a twill-derived weave. I now propose a more precise and concise name, "turn-banded 2/1 twill," because the bands are formed by turning the 2/1 twill weave.[2] If there is any ambiguity, it could also be specified as warp-faced, since a weft-faced version is also possible.

In terms of understanding the techniques by which this structure is woven, however, a grasp of the warp interlacing order is sufficient. The belts have side edge stripes of warp-faced plain weave, so the technique actually involves weaving plain weave and twill simultaneously. As is typical of Andean weaving, an ingenious economy of means is employed.

La Compañía, Otavalo Area, Imbabura Province

ANN P. ROWE   The technique for weaving turn-banded 2/1 twill was demonstrated for us in 1989 by Ester Camuendo, who said her whole family weaves belts for sale.[3] They buy the yarns in Otavalo. There were three belt looms set up, one for a plain-weave hair band, one for supplementary-warp patterning, and one for the 2/1 twill belt. So as not to impose too much, I asked only to see the twill being woven. This belt was the same as that in Figure 5.2, with five-span floats of red on one face and of black on the other (see also Fig. 5.4). We did not see the warping, but the weaver told us that the white cotton yarns are warped separately and the red and black acrylic yarns together.

As the loom is oriented, the red floats on the upper surface and the black floats on the back. The setup is simple (Figs. 5.4–5.5). One heddle rod controls the white warp yarns as well as one of the edge plain-weave sheds. Above the heddle rod there is a white string tied around the red warp yarns alone, as well as a stick through this same shed. The stick is flat and pointed at one

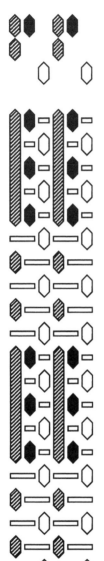

Cruzera

Shed stick

Heddle rod

5.4 Diagram of the turn-banded 2/1 twill weave used in Ester Camuendo's belt (Fig. 5.2). The vertical oblong elements are the three colors of warp, and the horizontal elements are the weft. Drawing by Ann P. Rowe.

end, so it probably functions as a pickup stick on other occasions, but here it is used as a shed stick. The white string is used only to mark the shed in case the stick is removed or falls out. A black string behind this is tied around the red warp yarns as well as around the edge warp yarns opposite those on the heddle rod, and so forms a shed loop.

5.5 Shed with only the white warp yarns up. Ester Camuendo, La Compañía, Otavalo area, Imbabura province. Slide by Ann P. Rowe, 1989.

The *cruzera* has two sticks with the ends tied together. The red and black pass over the front stick and the white over the back one. The back stick is grooved, and the weaver places two white warp yarns into each groove. The cross of the plain-weave edge is also held by the *cruzera*. The *cruzera* and the flat pointed stick were extracted from one of the other warps and added to this one before our demonstration began.

To create the areas where there are narrow bars on the front and black five-span floats on the back, the shedding sequence is as follows: heddle-rod shed (white threads up; Fig. 5.5); black shed loop (red threads up plus edge; Fig. 5.6); heddle-rod shed (white threads up); black shed loop (red threads up plus edge); heddle-rod shed (white threads up). This sequence is immediately followed by the one that creates red five-span floats on the front and the barred pattern on the back: shed on the front of the *cruzera* (red and black both up; Fig. 5.7); the shed stick and heddle rod (red and white are up; Fig. 5.8); the front of the *cruzera* (red and black up); the shed stick and heddle rod (red and white up); the front of the *cruzera* (red and black up).

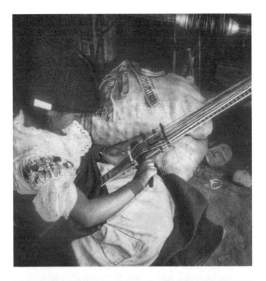

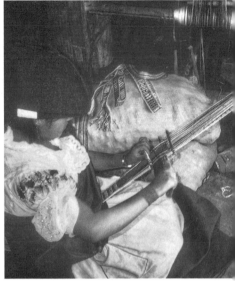

5.6 (above left) Opening the *cruzera* shed, with the red yarns up plus the border plain-weave shed. Ester Camuendo, La Compañía, Otavalo area, Imbabura province. Slide by Ann P. Rowe, 1989.

5.7 (above) Opening the shed with the red and black yarns up. Ester Camuendo, La Compañía, Otavalo area, Imbabura province. Slide by Ann P. Rowe, 1989.

5.8 Turning the sword on edge in the shed with the red and white yarns up. Ester Camuendo, La Compañía, Otavalo area, Imbabura province. Slide by Ann P. Rowe, 1989.

To open the shed with the black shed loop, the weaver merely lifts the upper part of the loop, afterward inserting the sword as usual. To lift the red and the black, she inserts the sword into the shed in front of the *cruzera* and turns it while moving the heddle rod back to make room for reinserting the sword in front of the heddle rod (Fig. 5.7). To lift the red and the white together, she brings the shed stick up against the heddle rod and raises the heddle rod (Fig. 5.8). She works rapidly, and the sheds are not difficult to open.

Nitiluisa, Central Chimborazo Province

ANN P. ROWE AND LAURA M. MILLER Santiago Sula Sisa, in sector Corona Real of *comunidad* Nitiluisa, demonstrated the warping and weaving of the more complex version of this structure in 1989 (Pl. 2). The demonstration attracted a large audience of interested neighbors. Miller described herself as "brain fried" after the session, but she and Lynn Meisch between them did manage to record all the relevant details.[4]

Señor Sula pounds the warping stakes into the ground in his patio, using a length of wood to determine the spacing of the end stakes. He uses three cross stakes to the right of the dovetail stake (*juból*) (Fig. 5.9). He ties a blue plastic string to the dovetail stake through a hole in the top, to hold the join when the stake is removed after warping.

He first warps the plain-weave edge of the belt. He ties the warp yarn to

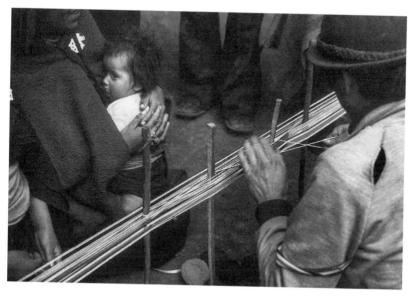

5.9 Warping a belt in turn-banded 2/1 twill. Santiago Sula Sisa, Nitiluisa, central Chimborazo province. Slide by Laura M. Miller, 1989.

the dovetail stake and begins warping to his right, passing the yarn in front of the first cross stake, behind the second, and in front of the third for the first half round; for the return, he reverses the pass of the warp yarn around the cross stakes, making one complete round (two warp yarns). He begins with four rounds of white cotton and then one of red acrylic. Warping with one yarn at a time in this fashion is called *chulla* (Q., pronounced "*chuzha*," one of a pair).

Continuing the plain-weave edge, he warps a stripe of pink alternating with blue yarns (a design called *grada* S.). The pink and blue yarns are warped together. The ends are laid parallel and an overhand knot is tied in the double strand, joining the two colors. The knot is placed at the dovetail stake, with pink in front and blue behind it. The pink is carried in front of and the blue behind the first cross stake. Their positions are reversed for the second and again for the third, and then are carried parallel around the end stakes. The pink is laid consistently below the blue. The weaver does two complete rounds (four warp yarns of each color), then a round of red and four more of white, then another two-color round in maroon and turquoise. This completes the plain-weave edge border.

For the central 2/1 twill area, the weaver warps the white simultaneously with one of each of the two colors of acrylic carried together (Fig. 5.9). He ties the two colors together and puts them around the dovetail stake in the manner described above. In passing the cross stakes, he first lays down the white, in front of the first cross stake, and then the two colored yarns behind. The white is laid behind the second cross stake, with the two colors in front, and the third cross stake is passed in the same way as the first. The return path in the round is the same, with the white again laid in first.

Señor Sula warps two complete rounds of each color combination, making a total of four warp yarns of each color in a single stripe. He counts the yarns in front of the third cross stake. To begin the second color combination, he breaks the yarns of the first colors and ties them to the ends of the second colors, all four yarns in one knot. The color combinations are magenta with green, blue with yellow, turquoise with maroon, purple with red, pink with navy, turquoise with maroon, yellow with purple, green with magenta (eight stripes of two rounds each). The weaver then warps the opposite plain-weave border with the colors in the reverse order from before.

To prepare the warp for transfer to the loom, he ties off each of the two crosses with separate cords. He next inserts a pair of *cruzera* sticks on either side of the cross between the second and third cross stakes. Thus, the white yarns pass over the back stick of the *cruzera* and the colored yarns over the front stick. Then the weaver unties the dovetail cord from the dovetail stake and ties the ends to a dark plastic tube. He pushes the dovetail cord through a hole in each end of the tube, using a shawl pin (*tupu* Q.). Then he ties the end of the cord around the ends of the tube. Now he can remove the cross stakes.

He then takes the warp to the loom and puts it around the back loom bar, which is a straight bar tied behind stakes fixed in the ground of the patio. He then installs the front loom bar and the roller bar. In this case, the back loom bar is supported by three stakes and accommodates two weavers. His wife spreads the warp out along the back loom bar. The weaver first makes the heddles on the shed held by the first cross stake with white cotton warp yarns of the central section and half of the plain-weave warp yarns from the two side borders (Fig. 5.10A).

To prepare for making the heddles, he inserts sticks into the two sheds marked by the cord between the first two cross stakes of the warping, after which the cord is removed. A black plastic tube (A) is inserted in the farther shed (the same as the front of the *cruzera*), and the sword into the nearer shed, on which the heddles will be made (Fig. 5.10A). The heddles are made like those more usual on wider looms, using a gauge (*payllador*, pronounced "pay-zhador") to form loops that are later tied to the heddle rod. When the loops are finished and the carrying cord is tied to the ends of the heddle rod, the weaver removes the sword and drops the heddle rod (h1) toward the front of the loom.

Next, he separates the colored yarns in the central section from those on the plain-weave edges and inserts a second black plastic tube (B) under those in the central section. He brings this tube forward so that it rests just behind the heddle rod and pushes the black tube in the *cruzera* shed (A) back toward the *cruzera* (Fig. 5.10B). He inserts his left hand under these yarns (in the area between tubes A and B) and, working from right to left, picks up each yarn of one color with his right hand, leaving the other color down. When finished, he inserts a third black plastic tube (C) into this shed and brings it forward (Fig. 5.10B).

Next, working in the area between tubes A and C, he picks up the yarns of the color that was down in the previous shed (Fig. 5.11). He inserts a white tube with a hole in each end into this shed (S1) (Fig. 5.10B). He ties a cord through each of these holes, which passes over the warp yarns and prevents the tube from falling out. He pushes this white tube and the black tube B (with all the central colored yarns) back toward the *cruzera* (Fig. 5.10C). Then he makes heddles for the first central colored shed that he picked, in the same manner as before, including lashing the loops to the heddle rod (h2 in Fig. 5.10C). This completes the creation of the necessary shedding devices.

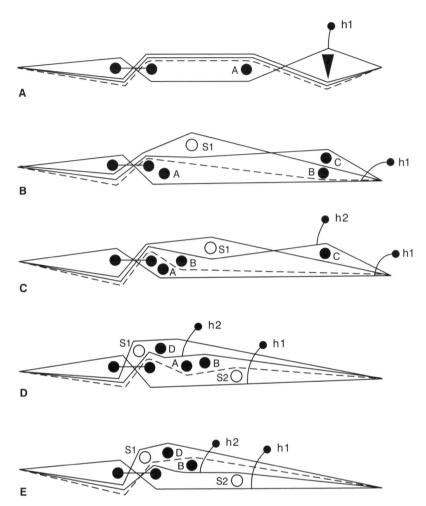

5.10 Diagrams showing the preparation of the warp for turn-banded 2/1 twill, as demonstrated by Santiago Sula Sisa in Nitiluisa. A: Position of the warp for inserting heddle rod 1 (h1). B: Position of the warp for separating the two float colors. C: Position of the warp for inserting heddle rod 2 (h2). D: Position of the warp for weaving the heading (shed rod shed open). E: Position of the warp for pattern weaving. The dotted lines show the position of the plain-weave edge yarns. Drawings by Arts and Letters Ltd., based on drawings by Ann P. Rowe.

5.11 Picking the second float color. Santiago Sula Sisa, Nitiluisa, central Chimborazo province. Photo by Lynn A. Meisch, 1989.

The weaver then moves the black tube B (with only the central colored yarns) forward slightly and replaces the black tube A, which holds the same shed as the front *cruzera*, with a length of bamboo (Fig. 5.10D). The bamboo functions as shed rod 2 (S2) while the *cruzera* remains passive in the warp. The weaver reinserts the black tube (A) into the same shed as and adjacent to the black tube B, under all the colored threads of the central section (Fig. 5.12). He inserts a fourth black tube (D) into the same shed as and directly in front of the white tube (S1) with a cord tied on it, that is, under the non-heddle-controlled center section (Fig. 5.10D).

Finally, the weaver lashes the heddle carrying cord to the first heddle rod (h1). He now removes black tube C, which held the second heddle-rod shed (h2 in Fig. 5.10D). He pushes all the other sticks up toward the *cruzera* to prepare for weaving.

He weaves a heading of plain weave, alternating between heddle rod 1 with the white cotton warp yarns (passing the weft left to right) and the bamboo shed rod 2 (weft right to left) (Figs. 5.10D and 5.13). After about sixteen weft passes, he removes the black tube B (from under all of the central colored warp yarns) and reinserts it so that it passes under the non-heddle-controlled central colored warp yarns (those over the white tube) and also under half of the edge yarns (opposite those on the heddle rod). B thus becomes shed rod 3. The black tube (A) that was in the same original shed as B is removed (Fig. 5.10E).

There are then one heddle rod (with white warp yarns [h1]) and two shed rods (bamboo [S2] and black tube B [S3]) that can be used to create sheds individually, and an additional three sheds are made using a combination of one of these with the second heddle rod or the other shed rod (the white tube [S1] in the same shed as black tube D). At any given time in this weave, two of the colors are up and one is down or vice versa. Figure 5.14 shows the white warp yarns on heddle rod 1 lifted.

To lift the white warp yarns plus the heddle-controlled color of the central section, the weaver simply lifts both heddle rods together. To lift the white warp yarns plus the non-heddle-controlled color of the central section, he first pulls the white tube (S1) forward until it abuts the heddle rods (temporarily removing black tube D), which raises the colored warp yarns, and then he inserts a pickup stick (*zhuti*), made of chonta palm wood, into this same shed in front of the heddle rods (Fig. 5.15). After moving the white tube back and reinserting black tube D in the same shed just behind the heddle rods, he lifts the first heddle rod and inserts the sword under both groups, to make the opening in which to pass the weft (Fig. 5.16). To lift only the colored threads on the second heddle rod plus the edge, he lifts the second heddle rod and then picks up the edge warp yarns from the bamboo shed rod (S2) using the sword (Fig. 5.17).

With these six possible sheds, he can weave two different regular patterns (Figs. 5.18A and B). For the one called *ladrillo* (S., brick; Fig. 5.18A), he uses the bamboo shed rod (S2, both center colors plus edge), then the two heddle rods (white plus one center color), then the bamboo shed rod (S2) again, then the white heddle rod alone (h1), then the color heddle rod (h2) plus edge warp yarns from the bamboo shed rod (S2), then the white heddle rod alone (h1). The sequence repeats as often as desired. In this sequence, the color on the second heddle rod floats on the upper working surface.

5.12 Inserting black tube A in preparation for weaving the heading. Santiago Sula Sisa, Nitiluisa, central Chimborazo province. Slide by Laura M. Miller, 1989.

5.13 Weaving the heading. Santiago Sula Sisa, Nitiluisa, central Chimborazo province. Slide by Laura M. Miller, 1989.

5.14 Beating the shed with the white warp up. Santiago Sula Sisa, Nitiluisa, central Chimborazo province. Slide by Laura M. Miller, 1989.

5.15 The pickup stick inserted under the colored warp yarns, selected from shed rod 1, which has been moved to just behind the heddle rods. Santiago Sula Sisa, Nitiluisa, central Chimborazo province. Photo by Lynn A. Meisch, 1989.

5.17 Picking up the edge warp yarns from shed rod 2 with the sword, together with those from heddle rod 2. Santiago Sula Sisa, Nitiluisa, central Chimborazo province. Photo by Lynn A. Meisch, 1989.

5.16 Beating the shed with the colored warp yarns selected in Figure 5.15 plus the white warp yarns on heddle rod 1 (shed rod 1 moved back toward the *cruzera*). Santiago Sula Sisa, Nitiluisa, central Chimborazo province. Photo by Laura M. Miller, 1989.

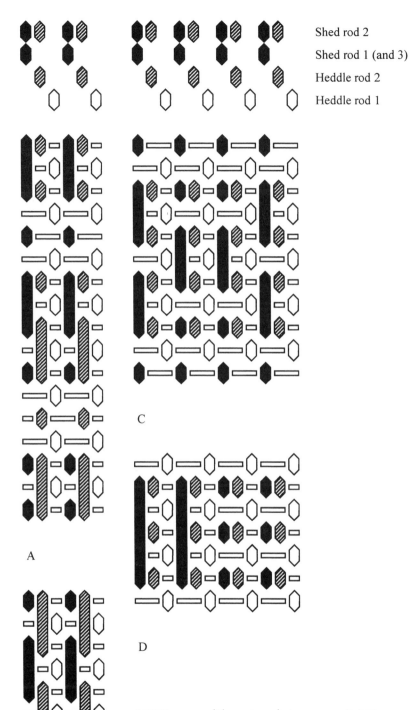

Shed rod 2

Shed rod 1 (and 3)

Heddle rod 2

Heddle rod 1

C

D

A

B

5.18 Diagrams of the various designs woven in turn-banded 2/1 twill weave by Santiago Sula Sisa, Nitiluisa, central Chimborazo province. A: *Ladrillo;* B: *Cuadro;* C: *Rombo chiquito;* D: *Letras.* Drawing by Ann P. Rowe.

To interchange the center colors and have the shed-rod color, instead of the heddle rod color, floating on the upper working surface, he lifts the bamboo shed rod (S2, both colors up), then the white heddle rod (h1) plus the yarns on the white tube (S1), then the bamboo shed rod (S2), then the white heddle rod (h1), then the black tube B shed rod (S3, with the shed rod color and edge warp yarns), then the white heddle rod again (h1), and repeats.

For the design called *cuadro* (S., square; Fig. 5.18B), in which all the three-span warp floats are on the upper working surface, the weaving sequence is the bamboo shed rod (S2), then the white tube (S1) plus the white heddle rod (h1), then the bamboo shed rod (S1), then both heddle rods, and repeat.

Normally, pickup is not done in this technique in Ecuador, but señor Sula wove two designs using pickup (Fig. 5.18C and D). One he called *rombo chiquito* (S., small diamonds; Fig. 5.18C), *nina kuru* (Q., firefly), or *ojo de pollo* (S., rooster eye). The pattern has a white border, made with the white heddle rod (h1). The sequence is the bamboo shed rod (S2), followed by the white tube (S1), from which he picks the pattern, inserts the pickup stick, and combines this with the white heddle rod (h1). The pickup stick is removed after the shed is beaten. These two moves are repeated, but a different pickup is made from the white tube (S1), then the bamboo shed rod (S2). Then the pickup from the white tube (S1) is repeated identically to the first one, then the bamboo shed rod (S2). At this point, the pattern can be concluded by raising the white heddle rod alone (h1), or the pattern can be extended by repeating the sequence.

His other pickup pattern, *letras* (S., letters; Fig. 5.18D), in which E shapes were formed, is made in a similar way; only the pickup itself is different. The pickup pattern does not appear on the reverse face of the fabric (see Pl. 2).

CHAPTER 6

2/1 Herringbone Complementary-Warp Weave Ponchos of the Otavalo Area, Imbabura Province

ANN P. ROWE

One style of poncho made in the Otavalo area is unusual in that it is a different color on each face, for example, light blue on one side and dark blue on the other, or blue and gray, or red and blue (Fig. 6.1). Sometimes, one face of the poncho is striped while the other is solid color (Pl. 3); rarely, one face is plaid (A. Rowe [ed.] 1998: pl. VIIIA). Since the ponchos are relatively large, they are often worn with one or both sides folded back on the shoulders, so that both colors are visible (Fig. 6.1). Although some examples are woven of fine yarn and are as supple as typical plain-weave ponchos, others are woven of relatively coarse yarn and are extremely thick.

It is likely that the style with plaid on one side is the origin of the similar machine-made ponchos worn by many middle-aged men in the Otavalo area since the 1950s (Meisch in A. Rowe [ed.] 1998: 69, 71, figs. 54, 57). Nevertheless, the available old photographs do not suggest that a handwoven version of this style was ever common. Since it is complex to weave, however, owning one was likely prestigious, as, indeed, is owning a plain one.

This style of poncho weaving is associated mainly with the town of Carabuela, although we also found two weavers from Agato who made them. The ponchos are customarily made for sale in Carabuela and, consequently, are worn over a wider area than the area in which they are woven, including eastern Imbabura province as well as the Otavalo area. In Cotopaxi province the style with stripes on one side is worn by men from Salamala and Macas, and in Tungurahua province the same style is worn by Salasaca men at the pre-Lenten festival of Carnival. One man we met in San Luis Chibuleo, Tungurahua province, wore a poncho that was red with some side edge striping on one side and a predominantly blue plaid on the other (A. Rowe [ed.] 1998: pl. VIIIA). These ponchos form only a small minority of those worn in a given area, including Otavalo. Fewer ponchos were being woven in Carabuela in

6.1 Miguel Andrango, of Agato, Otavalo area, Imbabura province, wearing a two-color complementary-warp weave poncho that he has woven. Slide by Ann P. Rowe, 1978.

the 1980s than formerly, since during the 1970s many younger men took up sweater knitting for the tourist trade instead (Meier 1985: 139).

The weave is a simple kind of complementary-warp structure that is structurally identical on the two faces (i.e., double faced).[1] A weave with complementary sets has two (or more) sets of elements in the same direction, usually of contrasting colors, that are co-equal in the fabric (Emery 1980: 150). In the variation found in Otavalo ponchos (Fig. 6.2), the warp yarns of one color interlace over two, under one (2/1), thus being visually predominant on the over-two face, while those of the other color interlace over-one, under-two, and thus are visually predominant on the opposite, or under-two, face. The alignment of the warp floats is diagonal, but the direction reverses, as in a herringbone twill, after every second element. The alignment of floats is thus similar to the weft-float face of the weave discussed in Chapter 5, only the herringbone is vertical instead of horizontal.[2] The structure can therefore be described as a complementary-warp weave with two-span floats in vertical herringbone alignment, or, more concisely, as a 2/1 herringbone complementary-warp weave.

Since the fabric is warp-faced, the warp color that floats over-two covers up the over-one color on that side. In addition, the over-three weft float tends to overlie its over-one neighbor. Thus, when densely packed, the weave has the appearance of warp-faced plain weave on both sides. A fine poncho in two shades of blue in The Textile Museum collection has warp yarns of the two colors alternating singly (ABAB warp order; Figs. 6.1, 6.2B), while a heavy striped example has the warp yarns of the two colors alternating two by two (AABB warp order; Pl. 3, Fig. 6.2C). The weaving process is essentially the same for both, however.

Although the structure is one of the simplest complementary-warp weaves possible, it is unknown in surviving pre-Hispanic textiles and has also not been reported ethnographically from elsewhere in South America. There is no reason why it could not be indigenous to the Otavalo area.

It is possible to make color patterns with this structure by interchanging the two colors from one face to the other. We encountered one weaver in Agato, Alejandro Quinatoa Santillán (b. 1906), who made ponchos exploiting this possibility by forming checked patterns in many different color combinations (Quinatoa 1982). He did not sell or wear them but made them only for his own artistic gratification. He wove most of them on a treadle loom, although this structure is usually woven on a backstrap loom. His work has not influenced others in the Otavalo area but is another example of Otavalo creativity and individuality.

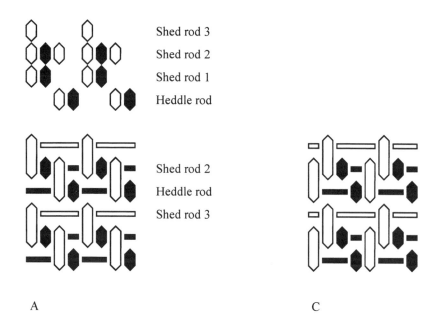

Shed rod 3

Shed rod 2

Shed rod 1

Heddle rod

Shed rod 2

Heddle rod

Shed rod 3

A

C

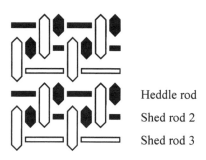

Heddle rod

Shed rod 2

Shed rod 3

B

6.2 Diagrams of the 2/1 herringbone complementary-warp weave. A: The version woven by Antonio Santa Cruz and José María Cotacachi, Carabuela, Imbabura province. B: The version woven by Miguel Andrango, Agato, and Carlos de la Torre, Carabuela, Imbabura province. C: The version found in Textile Museum 1988.19.37 (Pl. 3). Drawings by Ann P. Rowe.

The standard technique, without interchanging faces, is similar among all the weavers we recorded. José María Cotacachi, who is from Carabuela but who married into a Peguche family, and Antonio Santa Cruz, a compadre of his from Carabuela, demonstrated the entire process for us in 1989. José María Cotacachi said that the style his father wove was red on one side and blue or gray on the other. We also observed the weaving of Carlos de la Torre in Carabuela, who was making a poncho in two shades of blue. In 1978 I recorded some details of the technique used by Miguel Andrango, of Agato (Fig. 6.1), who customarily wears this style of poncho but does not weave them for sale (A. Rowe 1985: fig. 20 and note 59).

Warping

Warping was demonstrated by Antonio Santa Cruz, with a little initial advice from José María Cotacachi. The warp was for a scarf to be red on one side and blue on the other, with the red side facing up during weaving, so these colors will be used in the following description. There were also a few dark blue stripes on the red side, visible in the photo, but these will be ignored in the text.

The two end stakes for warping are pounded into the ground in the backyard of the house. They are held apart at the top by a bamboo pole placed between them, resting on notches. Señor Santa Cruz cut four fresh bamboo stakes to use for the dovetail stake (to his left) and the cross (to his right) and pounded these into the ground a bit (Fig. 6.3). He placed the middle stake slightly behind the others. The cross stakes correspond to the shed rods on the loom.

Señor Santa Cruz winds a red and a blue yarn simultaneously, separating them at the cross. He takes no care as to which color is on top. Leading both yarns from the front of the dovetail stake, he carries the red behind the first cross stake, in front of the second, behind the third, and so on, while he carries the blue behind all the cross stakes (Fig. 6.3). On the return pass, he carries the red in front of all the cross stakes and the blue behind the right stake and in front of the left two, then winds both behind the dovetail stake.

The warping continues in the same fashion. This procedure places alternate yarns of each color in front of the left cross stake, all the red and alternate blue in front of the center cross stake, and alternate red yarns in front of the right cross stake. In addition, there is a cross between the dovetail stake and the left cross stake. The weaver keeps track of the number of turns by counting the red threads over the right cross stake.

When warping is complete, he ties a string around the warp yarns held by each of the three cross stakes (Fig. 6.3). Then he removes the cross stakes and transfers the warp to the loom bars. He inserts shed rods into the sheds held by the ties from the cross stakes, after which he removes the ties. The first shed rod has over it half of the red yarns and half the blue ones. The second shed rod has over it all except the other half of the blue warp yarns (three-quarters of the entire warp), while the third shed rod has over it the same half of the red warp yarns as are over the first shed rod (one-quarter of the entire warp) (Fig. 6.4). The numbering is arbitrary, however, because the shed rods can all be moved past each other.

The weaver replaces the dovetail stake with a smaller stick by inserting the smaller stick into the hollow end of the dovetail stake and pushing. He next inserts the sword into the shed just in front of the dovetail stake, preparatory to making the heddles in the manner described in Chapter 1 for wider textiles (Fig. 1.26). Each heddle loop encloses two warp yarns, one of each color (half the warp). The warp yarns lifted are opposite those on the left cross stake (the first shed rod; see Fig. 6.2).

6.3 Completed warp for a scarf in the 2/1 herringbone complementary-warp weave. Antonio Santa Cruz, of Carabuela, Otavalo area, Imbabura province. Slide by Ann P. Rowe, 1989.

6.4 Shed rods in place, preparing to make heddles for the scarf in 2/1 herringbone complementary-warp weave. Antonio Santa Cruz, of Carabuela, Otavalo area, Imbabura province. Photo by Laura M. Miller, 1989.

Weaving Sequence

Two colors of weft are used, which are interlocked at the side selvedges. Señor Santa Cruz begins weaving by tying a red weft yarn around the rightmost warp and inserting it into the shed formed by the third shed rod, which lifts alternate red warp yarns (¼). Then he ties the blue weft to the rightmost warp and inserts it into the shed formed by the heddle rod (alternate threads of each color, ½). After interlocking the two yarns on the left, he inserts the blue weft yarn (left to right) into the shed formed by the second shed rod, lifting all the red and alternate blue warp yarns (¾). He then repeats this three-shed sequence (Fig. 6.2A), but with the direction of weft insertion and interlocking taking place in a longer sequence.[3]

To open the shed using the third shed rod with alternate red warp yarns over it, Señor Santa Cruz brings the shed rod forward against the heddle rod (cf. Fig. 6.5), leans back, and strums the warp in front of the heddle rod with his fingers. To open the shed controlled by the heddle rod, he first moves the previously used shed rod (with alternate red yarns) up to the top of the loom. Shed rod 2, with three-quarters of the warp over it, is now in front of the others (cf. Fig. 6.6). Then, with his thumb between the front two shed rods,

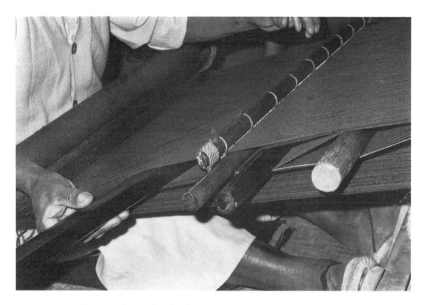

6.5 Inserting the sword into the shed with one-quarter of the warp up. Note that the shed rod with three-quarters of the warp over it has been pushed back. Carlos de la Torre, Carabuela, Otavalo area, Imbabura province. Photo by Jennifer Lantz, 1989.

6.6 Inserting the sword into the heddle rod shed with half of the warp up. Carlos de la Torre, Carabuela, Otavalo area, Imbabura province. Photo by Jennifer Lantz, 1989.

6.7 Beating the shed with three-quarters of the warp up. Carlos de la Torre, Otavalo area, Imbabura province. Photo by Jennifer Lantz, 1989.

he lays the sword over the back two shed rods and presses down, releasing tension, and lifting the heddle rod. To open the third shed, he brings forward the second shed rod with all the red and alternate blue warp yarns (3/4) over it (cf. Fig. 6.7), leaning back to get maximum tension and strumming the warps in front of the heddle rod with his fingers.

The weaving procedure used by José María Cotacachi on another occasion was similar except that, to open the shed with three-quarters of the warp up (equivalent to all the red and the alternate blue yarns, above), he uses both the second shed rod with these yarns and the first shed rod, which contains alternate yarns of each color (opposite the heddle rod). He rolls first one and then the other of these in front of each other near the heddle rod. The third shed rod remains toward the back of the loom. He noted that it required a lot of strength to open the sheds completely with this technique. He also pointed out that it was necessary to feel underneath the warp when opening the shed to make sure there were no gaps.

The weaving sequence of Carlos de la Torre (Figs. 6.5–6.7) and Miguel Andrango differs slightly from the preceding in that the use of the third shed rod (with alternate yarns of one color: 1/4, Fig. 6.5) is followed first by the second shed rod with three-quarters of the warp lifted (Fig. 6.7) and then by the heddle rod (1/2, Fig. 6.6). This sequence produces a reflection of the same structure (see Fig. 6.2).

Carlos de la Torre, who was weaving a panel for a full-sized poncho, uses a wooden pick to strum the warp and, to gain sufficient tension to open the sheds, he lifts his seat off the ground completely and supports himself between the backstrap and the foot brace (cf. Fig. 2.9). To open the shed with three-quarters of the warp lifted, he pushes the third shed rod with alternate yarns of one color to the back of the loom and places the two remaining shed rods on top of each other, strumming the warp with the pick. Then he brings the second shed rod with three-quarters of the warp forward and strums again (Fig. 6.7). He opens the other sheds in the manner already described.

CHAPTER 7

3/1 Alternating Complementary-Warp Weave Belts

Introduction

ANN P. ROWE   There are three distinct complementary-warp patterned belt styles in Ecuador, all made on the backstrap loom but each with different technical characteristics that, in turn, reflect a different historical context.[1] A consideration of their technical characteristics thus contributes significantly to our understanding of their origin. Two of the belt styles can be shown to have been introduced as a result of the Inca conquest, one by the Incas them-selves and one by a group of *mitimas,* or colonists, while the third is probably a local indigenous development.

As with the structure of the ponchos discussed in Chapter 6, there are two complementary sets of warp yarns of different colors that float on opposite faces. Instead of having two-span floats, however, both colors of warp in the belts interlace primarily in three-span floats: over three, under one or under three, over one (Figs. 7.1 and 7.2). And instead of being in herringbone align-ment, the three-span floats on each face are in alternating alignment. Thus, the structure can be described as "a complementary-warp weave with three-span floats in alternating alignment."[2] A more concise terminology would be 3/1 alternating complementary-warp weave.[3] Again, since the fabric is warp-faced, it appears solidly one color on one face and the other color on the oppo-site face. Unlike the structure used for ponchos, however, the two colors used in belts regularly interchange faces to form designs.

To weave this structure, a shed in which all the warp yarns of the surface color are raised to form the ends of the three-span warp floats (in weaver's jargon, a design row) alternates with a shed in which alternate warp yarns of each color are raised to form the over-one and under-one warp interlacings (in weaver's jargon, a tie-down or binding row). The variety of techniques used to

7.1 A complementary-warp weave with both faces formed by three-span floats in alternate alignment. The warp yarns are compacted sufficiently to nearly hide those that form on the opposite face, which are normally a different color. From Emery 1980, fig. 244.

7.2 Diagrammatic construction of the weave in Fig. 7.1. From Emery 1980, fig. 245.

form these sheds in the Andes affects the finished product in various ways, the most diagnostic of which is how the horizontal color changes are done. From such clues one can often infer something about the basic principles of the technique by which a finished textile might have been made, although there are so many variables that details can be provided only by field documentation.

One of the technologically simplest methods is found in parts of both southern Peru and Bolivia and is presented briefly here in order to help place the Ecuadorian techniques in perspective. The method has been documented in the Tarabuco area of Bolivia (Fig. 7.3) by Marjorie Cason and Adele Cahlander (1976: 154–159; see also Meisch 1986: Figs. 3, 16, 17). As shown in Figure 7.4, it employs an ABAB warp order, where A and B represent the two colors, with one shedding device (a heddle rod or set of heddle loops tied together) for lifting one color and one shedding device (a shed rod or shed loop) for lifting the other color, for a total of two sheds mechanically produced.

In Tarabuco the weaver uses a pickup stick to select the warp yarns she wants for the pattern.[4] For the color already lifted, the selection of warp yarns is easy; for the opposite color, the warp yarns have to be lifted from below and the yarns of the upper color dropped, one by one. Because of patterning and because the binding rows of the two colors are in successive weft shots, such hand selection (or pickup) is necessary for each weft pass, although if the color is to be the same all the way across, the design rows do not need to be picked. Because each color is controlled by a separate device, the three-span floats of the two colors are not horizontally aligned (see Fig. 7.4).

This method produces a neat horizontal color change with the ends of three-span floats lined up alternately with 1/1 interlacings (which I call 3/1 horizontal color change), since one simply lifts all the warp yarns of one color and then all of the other as provided by the shedding devices. Many surviving pre-Hispanic fabrics with complementary warps display this type of color change. Examples from the Inca occupation period from southern Peru exist both from the coast and from the highlands, including some pieces with Inca designs (Fig. 7.5).[5]

Hair bands woven in both Cacha and Majipamba in Chimborazo province have complementary-warp weave zigzag and diamond designs that are similar to these Inca examples (Fig. 7.6). In Cacha, the pattern in these hair bands is called "Cuzco" (Bustos and Pilco 1987: 2, 6; Jaramillo 1988a: 86–87), strengthening the possibility that they descend from Inca examples. As in the Inca and Tarabuco examples, the warp order in the hair bands is ABAB and the horizontal color changes are 3/1. Unfortunately, we were not able to record the weaving technique, although it seems likely that such small repeated designs are created by adding extra heddle rods, as is the case in creating similar

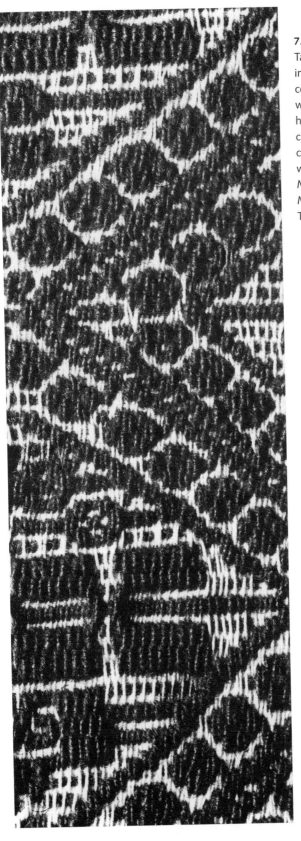

7.3 Detail of a Tarabuco-style textile in 3/1 alternating complementary-warp weave, with 3/1 horizontal color change, of white cotton and dyed wool. The Textile Museum 1985.27.98, Meadowcroft Bolivian Textile Collection.

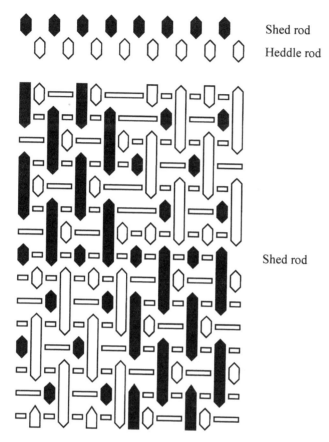

Shed rod

Heddle rod

Shed rod

7.4 Diagram of the 3/1 alternating complementary-warp weave used in the Tarabuco area of Bolivia, with 3/1 horizontal color change. Drawing by Ann P. Rowe.

supplementary-warp patterns in Cacha (see Chapter 4), rather than by using pickup.

Other 3/1 alternating complementary-warp weave Ecuadorian belts have different types of horizontal color change, reflecting different techniques. A second style is found in belts of two areas that are completely isolated from each other (Pl. 4). One area is in eastern Imbabura province in northern Ecuador, where Laura Miller and I recorded the technique in the village of Paniquindra, where the belt style is called *chumbi banderilla*. The other area is in Chimborazo province in central Ecuador, where the belt style is called *kawiña chumbi*. Miller recorded the technique in Troje and Cacha. In both areas, these belts are woven traditionally in wool, though by the late 1980s they were

7.5 Inca bag with stripes in 3/1 alternating complementary-warp weave and in warp-faced plain weave, of camelid hair. 23 × 18 centimeters (9 × 7 inches). American Museum of Natural History, New York 41.0/1532.

usually woven in acrylic. The colors used in the belts of the two areas are also strikingly similar (Pl. 4). In both areas, this style of belt coexists with the supplementary-warp style.

Unlike in the Tarabuco and Inca technique, the warp order is AABB. In addition, the basic structure is produced with four shedding devices, with each warp yarn governed by two of these devices, a principle that Franquemont (1991) calls dual-lease weaving (see Fig. 7.7). In the first two shedding devices there is one warp yarn of each color through each heddle loop. Each of the second two shedding devices controls yarns of one color, but, again, there are two warp yarns in each heddle loop. Alternate weft passes (the binding rows) are completely heddle controlled by using the first two heddle rods alternately. This technical feature causes the three-span floats of the two colors to line

7.6 Details of a "Cuzco" hair band from Cacha Machángara (*left*) and a hair band from Majipamba (*right*), both central Chimborazo province, with designs in 3/1 alternating complementary-warp weave very similar to Inca examples. White cotton and red and green acrylic (*left*) or wool (*right*). Widths: 3.3 and 4 centimeters (1⅜ and 1⅝ inches). The Textile Museum 1988.19.103 and 1988.22.11a, Latin American Research Fund.

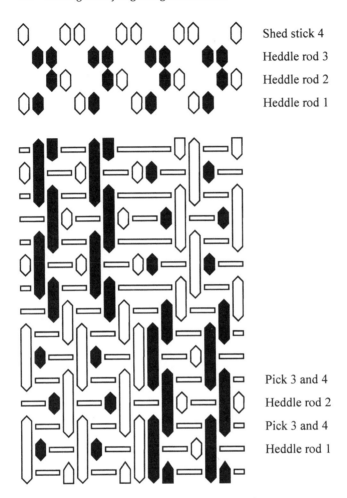

Shed stick 4

Heddle rod 3

Heddle rod 2

Heddle rod 1

Pick 3 and 4

Heddle rod 2

Pick 3 and 4

Heddle rod 1

7.7 Diagram of the 3/1 alternating complementary-warp weave used in the *kawiña chumbi* in Chimborazo province, with 2/2 horizontal color change. Drawing by Ann P. Rowe.

up with each other. The pattern is selected in the other weft passes from the other two sheds.

In this technique, the horizontal color change has two-span floats of each color which overlap on one weft pass (which I call 2/2 horizontal color change), since there is a binding weft pass between those in which the succeeding colors are raised. The dual-lease system also makes it convenient to weave a tubular edge, which is done in the *kawiña* belt, though not in the *banderilla* belt, which uses only two edge warp yarns. In both areas, the edge is customarily red.

The principal difference in the weaving of the two areas is the manner in which the designs are created. In Paniquindra, only three designs are made, using a total of seven additional heddle rods. An unfinished warp in The Textile Museum collection (1984.46.3), acquired separately from our fieldwork, has an arrangement of heddles identical to that used by the weaver we recorded in Paniquindra, suggesting that these designs are standardized there. In Chimborazo, on the other hand, a large variety of designs is created using pickup. Miller also recorded a slight difference in the warping procedure, described in the text that follows.

The dual-lease technique is also found today in the central and southern Peruvian highlands, as Franquemont has noted (1991: 287–288), and sometimes coexists with a complementary-warp technique related to that of Tarabuco. One small point of contrast between the Ecuadorian and the Peruvian examples is that in Peru a forked stick is usually used to hold the cross at the back of the loom, while in Ecuador the characteristically Ecuadorian *cruzera* is used instead. A variation of the dual-lease technique without the forked stick is also found in Bolivia near Lake Titicaca (Cason and Cahlander 1976: 72–76, with ABAB warp order). Textiles with 2/2 horizontal color change are found in some other parts of Bolivia, but fieldwork is needed to determine precisely what technique is used.[6]

In addition, Desrosiers (1986) has deciphered weaving instructions for this type of belt in a colonial document of the beginning of the seventeenth century, probably recorded along the northern shore of Lake Titicaca, and has found an identical archaeological belt preserved in the American Museum of Natural History in New York. Belts with a closely similar design and technique have now also been found in the Huamachuco area of Peru (Fabish and Meisch 2006: 55–56).

Some of the belts of the women sacrificed by the Incas at Pachacamac on the central coast of Peru and recovered by Uhle display the same structural features as the American Museum belt, providing documentation for their occurrence during the time of the Inca empire. One of these belts has designs also found in the Chimborazo belts (Fig. 7.8), although, since only two motifs are used, the patterns could easily have been heddle controlled.[7] All these belts, like the American Museum belt cited by Desrosiers, are woven with undyed camelid hair yarns.

Other archaeological textiles exist that show the characteristic 2/2 horizontal color change (A. Rowe 1977: 70, fig. 79, and p. 79, note 10), suggesting that a related method of heddle control was used. Of these, the fragmentary small poncho in the collection of the Los Angeles County Museum of Art shown in Plate 5 is remarkably similar to the Ecuadorian belts in color and to the Paniquindra belts, especially in design, and may represent a pre-Hispanic

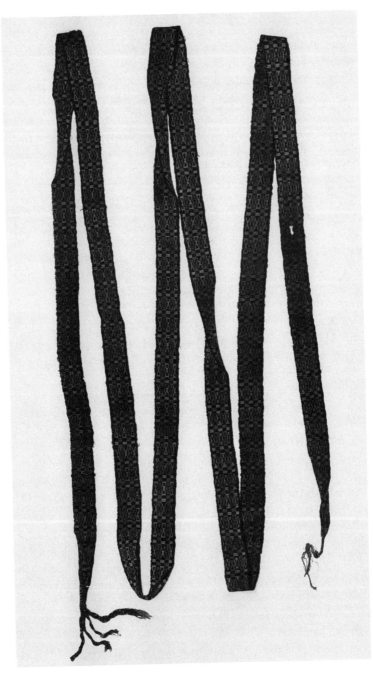

7.8 Belt in a provincial highland style found in the graves of the women the Incas sacrificed at Pachacamac. 3/1 alternating complementary-warp weave with 2/2 horizontal color change, of camelid hair. 4.655 × .033 meters (15 feet 3¼ inches × 1¼ inches). University of Pennsylvania Museum, Philadelphia 31517 (Uhle number 2438) (neg. # S4-142170).

antecedent.[8] The fragment was most likely preserved in Peru, although it has no provenience information.

The similarity between the colors and techniques that have been documented ethnographically in Ecuador is such that it is likely that the dual-lease technique was introduced into both regions by colonists (*mitimas*) from some common area of Peru or Bolivia during the Inca empire. Although the cultural traditions of such colonists were often obliterated by the intervening pressures of Inca, Spanish, and modern acculturation, this is a rare instance in which a feature that has survived to the present can be pointed to as plausible evidence of this Inca policy. Unfortunately, although colonial documents do tell us that *mitimas* were brought to both Imbabura and Chimborazo, the records do not tell us precisely where these people were from.

The name of the belt in Chimborazo province provides a possible clue, however. Kawiña (spelled Caviña, Cavina, Cauina, etc., in Spanish documents) is the name of an ethnic group and province of the Inca empire not far south of Cuzco.[9] Cieza de León describes it as near Quiquijana (1553, 1ᵃ pte., lib. 1, cap. 97, fol. 122v; 1984: 268). Although these people were not ethnic Incas, they were given Inca privileges, including allowing the men to wear large earplugs, cut their hair very short, and wear a black headband (*llawt'u*) (see also Guaman Poma de Ayala [1615] 1936: 85). It is thus possible that the Kawiña introduced this style of belt into Chimborazo (and Imbabura) province. Perhaps they made belts for trade to other peoples in the area, which might account for their names being attached to the style.

The third Ecuadorian technique for producing 3/1 alternating complementary-warp weave occurs in Cañar in southern Ecuador (Figs. 7.9 and 7.10). As with the technique just discussed, Cañari belts are woven with an AABB warp order, but the shedding is completely different (see Fig. 7.9). Alternate warp yarns of one color (white in the diagram) are put on the first heddle rod, the remaining ones of the same color on the second heddle rod. Alternate warp yarns of the second color (dark in the diagram) are put on the third heddle rod. The remaining yarns of the second color are controlled with the *cruzera*. The belts have plain-weave side borders.

The warping and weaving procedure recorded by Laura Miller is described in detail below. Here I will explain only the principle involved. For each weft pass, the weaver selects warp yarns for either the pattern or the ground color from one of the shedding devices. He selects the alternate color for the next weft pass. Because the two colors are picked sequentially, the three-span floats of each color are offset, unlike in the dual-lease technique. For each weft pass, the warp yarns picked for the previous weft remain lifted (held on a second pickup stick) and help guide the selection of the opposite color for the next

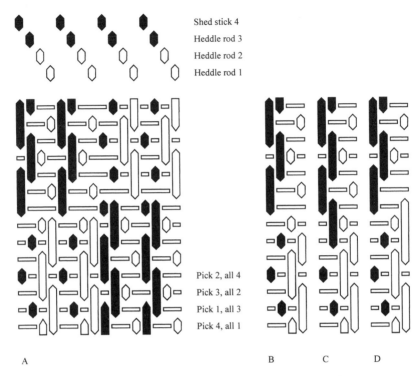

7.9 Diagram of the 3/1 alternating complementary-warp weave used in Cañar. A-D show variations of the horizontal color changes. Drawing by Ann P. Rowe.

weft. In addition, all the warp yarns of the color picked for the previous weft but from the alternate shedding device are lifted as well (Fig. 7.9A). The complete sequence is four weft passes, since there are four shedding devices.

This ingenious technique makes it possible to pick the design in groups of warp yarns the width of each design unit rather than having to handle each warp yarn individually, as in the pickup techniques described above (see Fig. 7.11, and Figs. 7.24 and 7.25, below). This makes it easier to use extremely fine yarn such as cotton sewing thread for the warp, as the Cañari often do.

Although the horizontal bars that separate the designs have 3/1 horizontal color changes and are double-faced, the horizontal color changes made with pickup are unlike those that result from the other techniques under consideration.[10] The transition is sharper on one face than on the other (see Fig. 7.10), so it is not double-faced. Since the technique involves lifting only half the yarns of the new color for the first weft pass, the remaining yarns of that color occur in floats that overlap the color change on one face (Fig. 7.9A–D). Analysis and description of these color changes is complicated by the fact that there are some four different variations, one in which the basic sequence of four shedding devices is strictly maintained (Fig. 7.9A), and three involving minor modifications of this sequence (Fig. 7.9B–D; see the Cañari belt section for descriptions). In each case, however, on the less-clear face, only half of the new color begins at the line of color change.

For the vertical color changes, the diagram for the Cañari belt (Fig. 7.9A) has been drawn to match those for Tarabuco and the *kawiña* belt (Figs. 7.4 and 7.7), with the clearer face below (showing warp floats) and the reverse and less-clear face above (showing tie-downs). In Tarabuco textiles and *kawiña* belts, the distribution of these two faces of the vertical color change seems to be somewhat random. In Cañari belts, on the other hand, an attempt is usually made to have all of the clearer vertical color changes on the same face as the clearer horizontal ones. That is, the warp floats of the two colors are generally

7.10 Detail of the front (*left*) and back (*right*) of a Cañari 3/1 alternating complementary-warp weave belt in red and white wool, showing the difference in the color change on the two faces. Width: 5 centimeters (2 inches). The Textile Museum 1986.19.64, Latin American Research Fund. See A. Rowe (ed.) 1998 (238, fig. 234) for a full view.

7.11 Weaving a Cañari 3/1 alternating complementary-warp weave belt. Nicolás Loja, El Tambo, Cañar province. Photo by Lynn A. Meisch, 1978.

immediately adjacent on the front but separated on the back. The diagram in Figure 7.9A would thus be more accurate if it did not show the reverse of this color change. The purpose of showing it like this in the figure is to make the comparisons as clear as possible.

Ingenious and logical as it is, the Cañari technique has not been documented elsewhere in the Andes, and I have not seen pre-Hispanic or modern textiles from other areas that have the type of horizontal color changes found in Cañari belts. A Cañari friend suggested to Lynn Meisch that plain-weave striped belts were older than the complementary-warp weave style in Cañar, although the time frame was vague. Possibly, then, this technique is not of great antiquity in the area. In fact, the system by which the heddles are organized is not unlike what one might use on a treadle loom, and it is possible that knowledge of treadle-loom weaving might have served as inspiration. Whether or not this is the case, however, the technique remains an excellent example of continuing Andean creativity on the loom.

Banderilla Belt in Paniquindra, Eastern Imbabura Province

LAURA M. MILLER   The 3/1 alternating complementary-warp weave belt called *chumbi banderilla* (Pl. 4) is made in the communities of La Florida,

Chirihuasi, and Paniquindra and worn by women in these communities as well as in Las Abras and Magdalena in eastern Imbabura province. This belt is highly prized. We spoke with one woman whose husband weaves and sells *banderilla* belts. She wore a supplementary-warp patterned belt of the Otavalo style but said that she would rather that her husband make a *banderilla* belt for her.

We recorded Luis Virgilio Pupiales warping and weaving this belt in Paniquindra in 1989. The three designs are *ojo* (S., eye), consisting of three small circles; *cruz* (S., cross), a row of diamonds joined horizontally; and *peinilla* (S., comb) or *ñajcha* (Q.), consisting of opposing blocks with a diagonal color division, placed in between the others (see Pl. 4). Seven heddle rods with preselected sheds govern these designs, so no hand picking is necessary. The designs are separated by a design of horizontal bars called *caña* (S., cane). The acrylic yarn used is purchased in Ibarra and then overtwisted using a walking wheel stored under the eaves of the roof.

The belt is warped on stakes pounded into the hard ground in front of the house. The weaver measures a yarn between his two fully outstretched arms and then folds it in half to determine the distance between the end stakes. He places the dovetail stake (*tigrador* Q. with S. suffix) to the left of the two cross stakes (*cruzeras*). After warping one round (two circuits of the stakes, one for each half of the cross) of red, the selvedge contrast color, he ties the purple and yellow yarns onto the red warp at the dovetail stake. Purple and yellow are warped together, separated only at the cross stakes.

Two strands of purple alternate with two strands of yellow at the cross, but the artisan warps with a single purple and a single yellow yarn together. To achieve the color pairing, therefore, a special motion is necessary: when he warps to the cross stakes from his right, he lifts the previous yellow yarn from the rightmost cross stake and holds it out of the way as he warps the purple yarn (Fig. 7.12). Thus, the previous purple and the newly warped purple are together, without an intervening yellow warp. He then replaces the previous yellow that he had held and warps the new yellow, yielding two yellow yarns together. Different warping techniques are used to achieve the same result of color pairing in the 3/1 alternating complementary-warp weave belts of both Chimborazo and Cañar, as described below.

After warping eight *pares* (S., pairs), or complete rounds, the artisan changes to red and green yarns, with red taking the place of yellow and green taking the place of purple. Eight pairs of red and green are followed by another eight pairs of yellow and purple, and then by a final round with red, as at the start. The warp ends with a final loop around the dovetail stake. The artisan adds a two-stick *cruzera* (locally called *cruzeras*) from underneath to hold the cross, after which he slips the warping stakes out.

7.12 Warping a 3/1 alternating complementary-warp weave belt. The two colors are carried together but manipulated into AABB order. Luis Virgilio Pupiales, Paniquindra, eastern Imbabura province. Slide by Barbara Borders, 1989.

The warp is suspended from a curved wooden back loom bar (*aro*, S., ring), hung from one of the wooden porch posts, with a nail in the back of the post to prevent the rope from slipping. The weaver inserts the front loom bar (*ku-mil*), and puts on the backstrap (*washakara* Q.), ready for heddle placement. He first picks all the sheds and places small sticks in them, afterward making the heddles.

The first step in picking the sheds is to make a new cross in which purple is paired with yellow and red with green. Working below the *cruzera*, the artisan makes this new cross on his thumb and forefinger (Fig. 7.13), then inserts small sticks. Each of these two sheds is called a *traba* (S., tie or bond). One red yarn on each selvedge passes over the first, and one over the second stick.

The next two sheds consist of the initial pairs made on the warping stakes. The shed of purple and green warp is called *morado y verde* (S., purple and green). Since this shed is the same as that over the front of the *cruzera*, he merely brings this shed down and inserts another small stick. The next shed consists of yellow and red pairs and is therefore called *amarillo y rojo* (S., yellow and red). For this shed, working from left to right, he picks up two yellow (or red) warp yarns between each two purple (or green) ones and again inserts a stick.

He then picks the pattern sheds, beginning with one called *peinilla primer grado* (S., first step of the comb). He holds the yarns over the front of the *cruzera* in his left hand and picks pairs of threads from right to left with his right hand. When purple is to show on one face, he simply passes it to his right hand. When yellow is to show, he exchanges the purple for the corresponding yellow from below. He inserts a stick into the completed shed and then begins the next one (see Fig. 1.22).

Peinilla de primer grado is followed by *peinilla de segundo grado* (S., second step of the comb) and up through *peinilla de quinto grado* (S., fifth step of the comb). The two remaining sheds are for the *ojo* and *cruz* designs. The yarns for each pattern shed are shown in the diagram (Fig. 7.14).

After pushing all the shed sticks up toward the *cruzera*, he adds the roller bar. He also replaces the large dovetail stake from warping with a smaller stick (*palito* S., little stick), transferring one pair of loops at a time from his right to his left. The weaver then replaces the shed sticks with heddle rods, as described in Chapter 1 (see Figs. 1.22 and 7.15).

To weave, the first two heddle rods (the *trabas*) are used in alternation with each other, and in alternation with the pattern heddle rods. For example, *traba* 1 is followed by pattern heddle rod 3, then *traba* 2, then pattern heddle

7.13 Picking up the new cross on the fingers, pairing the two colors, for a 3/1 alternating complementary-warp weave belt. Luis Virgilio Pupiales, Paniquindra, eastern Imbabura province. Photo by Barbara Borders, 1989.

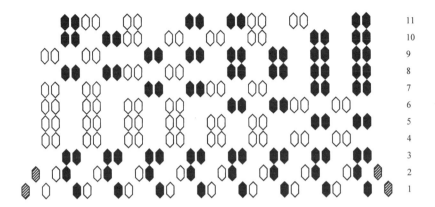

7.14 Diagram of the sheds in the 3/1 alternating complementary-warp weave belt of Paniquindra, eastern Imbabura province. Sheds 1–4 form the basic weave and 5–11 are the pattern sheds. Drawing by Ann P. Rowe, based on Textile Museum 1984.46.3, Latin American Research Fund, and photographs taken in Paniquindra.

7.15 Weaving a 3/1 alternating complementary-warp weave belt with designs formed by using multiple heddle rods. The landscape of the high valley is in the background. Luis Virgilio Pupiales, Paniquindra, eastern Imbabura province. Photo by Laura M. Miller, 1989.

rod 4, then *traba* 1, and so on. To open the sheds made by the *trabas*, the weaver lifts both heddle rods, pulling them apart, so that both sheds are opened. Then he twists them to the left and inserts the sword into one of them from the right.

Omitting reference to heddle rods 1 and 2, which alternate between the pattern heddle rods as noted, and numbering the pattern heddle rods 3–11, the weaving sequence for creating the patterns is as follows. The *ojo* design is woven with pattern heddle rods 3, 4, 3, 10, 11, 10, 3, 4, 3. *Peinilla* is woven with 4, 4, 4, 5, 6, 7, 8, 9, 3, 3, 3. *Cruz* is woven with 4, 3, 4, 11, 3, 11, 4, 3, 4. This design is followed by the sequence for *peinilla* in reverse.

Kawiña Belt in Central Chimborazo Province

LAURA M. MILLER   The *kawiña chumbi* or *kawiña* belt is woven and worn throughout most of Chimborazo province (Pl. 4; see also A. Rowe [ed.] 1998: 182, fig. 161). People say that wearing it gives a woman strength for hard labor in the fields. We documented *kawiña* belt warping and weaving in 1988 in Troje, a community south of Riobamba, just east of the Pan-American Highway.

The weaver we recorded, Francisco Mullo Cepeda, was disabled and no longer able to work in the fields. His wife, Ángela Yumisaca Yautibog, and children did all of the agricultural labor, and he earned money by weaving six *kawiña* belts a week, which his wife took to a vendor at the weekly Cajabamba market. The weaver had learned *kawiña* and other styles of belts and ponchos from his father, who had learned it from his father. As he told us: "It is the work of our ancestors." The acrylic yarn is purchased in Cajabamba, and all members of the family re-ply and overtwist the paired yarn (*kawpunchij* Q., paired or plied yarns) using a hand spindle made from a pampas grass stem (Meisch et al. 2005).

The weaver could no longer move freely, so his wife did the warping for him, usually at 6:00 AM every day. Since it was raining the day we observed, the belt was warped inside. Some of the warping stakes are wooden and others metal. They are pounded into the hard dirt floor of the house, using a larger piece of wood as a mallet. To establish the length of the belt, the warper measures *dos brazos y un codo* (S., two arms and an elbow) with a length of yarn. An arm's length is from hand to hand, with the arms outstretched, and the "elbow" is from the fingertips to the elbow. The yarn is then folded in half to determine placement of the second end stake. There are two cross stakes. Before beginning to warp, the warper ties a cord (*juból*) onto the dovetail stake

7.16 Warping a 3/1 alternating complementary-warp weave belt (*kawiña chumbi*). Ángela Yumisaca Yautibog, Troje, Chimborazo province. Slide by Carol Siegel, 1989.

(*estaca juból*), secured at top and bottom. The warp has outer stripes in yellow and blue and a center stripe in red and green. The selvedges are red and called the *jumba* in Troje.

The warper begins with red yarn, tying it onto the dovetail stake and carrying it to her right (away from the cross stakes). After four rounds of red, she changes to blue and yellow yarns (Fig. 7.16). She knots the ends together and places the knot at the dovetail stake. When passing the cross stakes, she places the blue yarn first, followed by the yellow. When coming from the left side to the right, through the cross stakes and to the dovetail, she warps the blue yarn to the dovetail stake and then back out through the cross stakes before she warps the yellow (Fig. 7.16). Thus, the blue yarns are in pairs at the cross stakes and dovetail stake, as are the yellows, achieving the same result as in Paniquindra but by a different method.

The warper counts the threads between the two cross stakes and continues warping until there are ten pairs. A pair of blues with a pair of yellows constitutes one pair. She ties the blue and yellow together and places this knot over the dovetail stake to finish this stripe. She then ties the red and green threads together and continues warping in the same way. Red follows the blue path and green follows the yellow path.

Ten pairs of red and green are warped, followed by ten pairs of blue and yellow, and then the red selvedge. The warper places a cord through both of the crosses and knots it. She also unties the cord parallel to the dovetail stake. She then lifts the warp from the stakes and twists it on itself for storage until her husband is ready to weave it.

The belt is woven using three heddle rods and a two-stick *cruzera* to hold the fourth shed and its reverse. In contrast to the procedure in Paniquindra, the weaver in Troje picks each design by hand, using a much greater variety of motifs.

After placing the warp on the loom bars, the weaver inserts the *cruzera* into the sheds created during warping. As in Paniquindra, he then makes a new cross of sheds in which yellow and blue are paired, in front of the *cruzera*. He makes the cross on his forefinger and thumb, from left to right, the same as in Paniquindra. A stick is placed in each shed, and then heddles are made (heddle rods 1 and 2). Each heddle loop contains two threads, whether of the same or contrasting colors. A third heddle rod is also made with yellow pairs and green pairs, as on the warping stakes. The fourth shed lifts the red pairs and blue pairs passing over the front part of the *cruzera*, which functions as a shed rod (Figs. 7.7, 7.17).

To weave, señor Mullo raises the heddle rod straight up with his left hand. He checks and clears the open shed with his right hand before inserting the sword (*kalluwa*, pronounced "*kazhuwa*") (Fig. 7.17). He beats the fabric, turns the sword on edge, and passes the weft. He beats again and then repeats.

To create the designs, he does pickup between the third heddle rod and the *cruzera* (Fig. 7.18). He lifts the third heddle rod, which controls the yellow and green pairs, and slips his right hand into this shed. He picks with his left hand, from left to right. Where yellow should show on the top face, he simply passes the yellow from his right hand to his left. If blue is to show, he allows the corresponding yellow to drop from his hand and picks up a blue from the front of the *cruzera* above. The picked shed stays on his left hand while his right hand places the sword into this shed. He uses the sword to bring the picked shed down to the woven area, through the other heddles. He then beats and passes the weft.

He picks every other pass. In general, the sequence is heddle rod 1, picked shed, heddle rod 2, picked shed, heddle rod 1, picked shed, and so on. He refers to heddle rods 1 and 2 as the *tapa* (S., cover). Between each figurative design, there are several straight lines, called *panzas* (S., bellies). These are created with the following heddling order: 3, 2, 4, 1, repeated for additional stripes.

Señor Mullo's repertoire includes such motifs as *pajaritos de la costa* (S., coastal birds), *equis* (S., Xs), *kuy tulluito* (Q., pronounced "*tuzhuito*," guinea

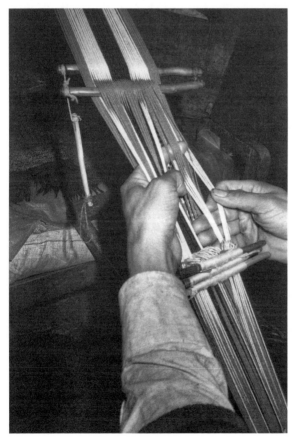

7.17 Lifting the third heddle rod for a 3/1 alternating complementary-warp weave belt (*kawiña chumbi*). Francisco Mullo Cepeda, Troje, central Chimborazo province. Photo by Laura M. Miller, 1988.

7.18 Picking up the pattern for a 3/1 alternating complementary-warp weave belt (*kawiña chumbi*). Francisco Mullo Cepeda, Troje, central Chimborazo province. Photo by Laura M. Miller, 1988.

pig skeleton), *pico para sacar piedras* (S., pike for removing stones), and *lampa* (Q., an implement used to dig holes in the fields). One belt had the words "Comunidad El Troje," "Canton Colta," and "Republica del Ecuador," as well as his name, his wife's name, and their birth dates.

In Cacha Obraje, the complementary-warp weave belt called *kawiña chumbi* throughout the province is called *kawiña chumbi cuatro pareado* (*kawiña* belt with four paired together) to distinguish it from the supplementary-warp patterned belts which are termed *kawiña chumbi dos pareado* (*kawiña* belt with two paired together). The arrangement of heddle rods for the *kawiña chumbi cuatro pareado* and the use of pickup is the same as in Troje.

Cañari Belts, Cañar Province

LAURA M. MILLER AND ANN P. ROWE   In the Cañari area, 3/1 alternating complementary-warp weave belts are worn to the exclusion of other kinds of belts and are called simply *chumbi* (Figs. 7.19 and 7.20). Laura Miller learned the technique from the late Antonio Loja Loja in Suscal parish, in the western part of Cañar province.[11] His technique is typical, although other weavers use minor variations. The belt is worn by men, over the *kushma* at the waist, holding it tightly to the body (Meisch in A. Rowe [ed.] 1998: 236, fig. 231). The belt is wrapped with the fringed free end hanging down in back.

The designs of Cañari belts are a fascinating syncretism of Christian symbols and motifs from the natural world. Common motifs include deer, rabbits, goats, and birds, while the Christian symbols include chalices, angels, crosses, the letters JHS, and many more. Often, these two groups of designs alternate along the course of the belt. A typical sequence would be deer, cross, bird, chalice, and so on. Symbolically, these belts represent the syncretism of Catholic and pre-Catholic spiritual traditions. Words are also used. Antonio Loja was literate and he noted with pride that he could charge more for his work because he could weave people's names and that of their community into the belts. A few weavers also include representations of modern vehicles such as trains and ships.

During the 1980s, prisoners in the Cañar jail wove belts and small hangings for the tourist market, and a distinctive jail style has evolved (Fig. 7.20). Christian symbols are not as evident as in belts for use, and animals predominate. The animals are more stylized, with elegant curves, than those figures seen in the countryside. In addition, the animals on jail belts often have prominent penises (although they do not appear on the belt in Fig. 7.20), whereas this is not a frequent element in belts for local use.

7.19 3/1 alternating complementary-warp weave belt, in black and white cotton sewing thread. Cañar province, dated 1982. 3.01 × .04 meters (9 feet 10½ inches × 1½ inches), excluding tie. The Textile Museum 1986.19.63, Latin American Research Fund.

Cañari belts are very finely woven, usually of cotton sewing thread. In an average belt, the warp count is approximately 50 yarns per centimeter (125 per inch). One brand of thread, Pinto, is somewhat coarse and not as shiny as the other brand, Sedal, which is more expensive and considered to be finer quality. Weavers making belts for the tourist market often use Pinto, whereas Cañari men who weave or commission belts for their own use often prefer Sedal.

In communities farther away from the town of Cañar, such as Suscal or Juncal, overtwisted acrylic yarn is often used instead of sewing thread (Fig. 7.10). After purchase in the local markets, it is overtwisted by women in the home. Because this yarn is thicker, designs on such belts tend to be simpler and more geometric. The technique, however, is the same.

Traditional color combinations are white and black or white and red. Other combinations such as red and black, black and yellow, or blue and white are now also used. Some Cañari men wear belts with four colors, for example, red and black on one face with green and yellow on the opposite face. These color divisions are stripes set up in the warping process, and the weaving process is the same, independent of color scheme. Often, the color division is ignored in the formation of the patterns.

To warp, the weaver drives five stakes, called *takti* (Q.), into a flat plot of ground near the house, although some weavers have a fixed warping board (*banco*). The dovetail stake is called the *chaki kaspi* (Q., foot stick). After warping, the dovetail stake is transferred to the loom and left in place until the weaving is completed. Two cross stakes are used, placed to the left of the dovetail stake in the example shown in Figure 7.21.

For this description, we will refer to a belt warped in red and white. After warping several rounds for the plain weave at the side edge of the belt, the weaver begins to warp the patterned area by tying a double strand of red warp and a double strand of white warp onto the dovetail stake. He then winds these yarns to the right, away from the cross stakes, and around the two end posts. As he approaches the cross stakes, he places both red threads in front of cross

7.20 3/1 alternating complementary-warp weave belt, in red and black cotton sewing thread. Woven in the Cañar jail. 2.55 × .05 meters (8 feet 4½ inches × 2 inches). The Textile Museum 1986.19.88, Latin American Research Fund.

stake 1 and behind cross stake 2. Then he passes the two white threads behind cross stake 1 and in front of cross stake 2, forming a cross (Fig. 7.21). At the dovetail stake, the two colors interlock with (link around) each other and then repeat the same path (Fig. 7.22). They must interlock because, otherwise, they would not be secured at the dovetail stake. The remaining pattern circuits are completed in the same way.

After the warp is finished and before it is taken off the warping stakes, a pair of cross sticks is inserted. These sticks are called *tinki* (Q.) in Cañar, rather than *cruzera*. Essentially, they replace the cross stakes and preserve the principal cross between red and white.

The warp is then placed on the back loom bar (*jawan*). Antonio Loja's loom bar is at least ten centimeters (four inches) in diameter and highly polished by time and use. It is the same loom bar used for weaving wider fabrics and is lashed between two roof-support posts. The weaver then places the front loom bar and roller bar (both *pilludor*) in the warp and places the backstrap (*chapirichij*) around his back. The weaver either sits on the ground or on a small stool. He may also use a foot brace (*pateador* S.) to increase the warp tension.

At this stage, the warp consists of double strands of red and white separated by the cross. Ultimately, however, there will be two heddle rods (*illuwa* Q.) governing the white threads (numbered 1 and 2 in Fig. 7.9 and the following text), and one heddle rod (numbered 3) and a shed rod (numbered 4), located between the two cross sticks, governing the red threads. The process of separating the paired threads is called *el cambio* (S., the change) or *cambiando* (S., changing).

To "change" the threads, the weaver begins by placing the weaving sword (*kallwa* Q.) under the white threads, which are nearest to him. Then, working from left to right, he painstakingly separates each double strand, placing one strand over the index finger and the other over the middle finger of the left hand (Fig. 7.23). He places sticks in the new sheds to hold them until he has made the heddles. After he separates the white threads, he treats the red ones in the same way. An experienced weaver needs at least two or three hours to complete the division of both colors, due to the large number of fine warp yarns used. After the division of each set, he installs the heddles, as described in Chapter 1, which takes about an hour for each heddle rod. He ties the shed rod (4) with half of the red yarns over it between the two cross sticks.

The selvedge of the belt is called *orilla* (S., edge) or *ñawi* (Q., eye) and is in plain weave, for which only two sheds are needed. For one shed, all the yarns to be lifted have heddles on both the first and the second heddle rods (and they pass over the back cross stick). The yarns for the alternate shed have

7.21 Warp for a 3/1 alternating complementary-warp weave belt on the warping stakes. Antonio Loja Loja, Gullandel, Suscal parish Cañar province. Slide by Laura M. Miller, 1985.

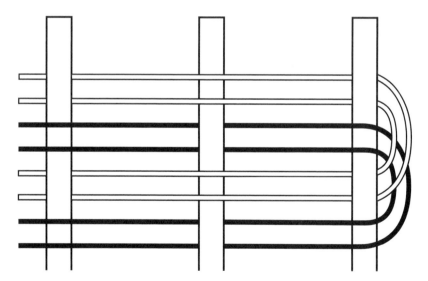

7.22 Diagram showing the linking of the two colors at the dovetail stake, for warping a Cañari 3/1 alternating complementary-warp weave belt. Drawing by Arts and Letters Ltd., based on a drawing by Ann P. Rowe.

7.23 Picking the cross of white yarns for a 3/1 alternating complementary-warp weave belt. Antonio Loja Loja, Gullandel, Cañar province. Slide by Laura M. Miller, 1985.

heddles on the third heddle rod and pass over the front cross stick. The selvedge warp yarns all pass under shed rod 4. The weft (*mini* Q.) is an acrylic yarn that has been overtwisted and wound on a stick shuttle (*jisanchi*).

Other weavers use a slightly different way of setting up the *cruzera* or cross sticks. A weaver photographed by Lynn Meisch (Fig. 7.11) has the dark yarns controlled by the third heddle rod passing over the front cross stick and under the back one, while the dark yarns that make the fourth shed pass over both cross sticks. All the light yarns pass under the front cross stick and over the back one. A loom in The Textile Museum collection (The Textile Museum 1984.46.2) is similar but has a third cross stick tied between the other two, with the yarns of the fourth shed above it and the rest below. The setup recorded by Laura Miller is similar to the preceding, but the yarns of the fourth shed pass under the farthest cross stick instead of over it.

To create the horizontal bars that separate the design motifs, two shedding devices are needed to lift the warp for each weft pass. To create a red bar on the front (white on the back), the sequence would be 3 and 4, 2 and 3, 3 and 4, 1 and 4, 3 and 4. Then, to create a white bar on the front (red on the back), the sequence would be 1 and 2, 2 and 4, 1 and 2, 1 and 3, 1 and 2. A pickup stick is inserted in one shed and left in place while the other is opened.

Placing the pickup stick only under the complementary-warp yarns, and not the selvedges, allows the plain-weave selvedges to be created automatically.

The pickup sticks, called *pallador* (*pallay* Q., pickup, with S. suffix), are smooth, flat, and pointed at one end. Two are used for making patterns, identical in dimensions, called A and B in the following text. It is important to note that the numbers and letters used to describe the sheds and pickup sticks are designations that we have applied. Cañari weavers do not think in these terms. The sequence of shedding is second nature to them after they have been weaving a while, and they concentrate on picking the design.

For pattern weaving, all of the yarns controlled by one shedding device (including the selvedges) and handpicked groups from two other shedding devices (one of each color, excluding selvedges), a total of half the warp, are lifted for each weft pass. One of the handpicked groups is carried over from the previous weft pass, and the other is newly picked. The sequence for lifting the shedding devices is as follows (see Figure 7.9): pick 4 (red) with all 1 (white); pick 1 (white) with all 3 (red); pick 3 (red) with all 2 (white); pick 2 (white) with all 4 (red). Begin repeat: pick 4 (red) with all 1 (white).

To begin a new design against a solid ground, the weaver lifts the yarns that pass over shed stick 4 (red) and places the weaving sword beneath them. With pickup stick A, he picks the background, letting the yarns for the design areas drop. With pickup stick A left in place beneath the picked yarns, he takes out the weaving sword, lifts heddle rod 1 (white), and uses the sword to open this shed. He then places pickup stick B under the complementary-warp yarns of heddle rod 1 in order to keep them separate. He removes the sword again and replaces it under all the lifted yarns. The weaver beats the shed, passes the weft, and beats again.

The white threads of heddle rod 1 had been separated by pickup stick B. Now the weaving sword is inserted under these and the pickup stick taken out. Pickup stick A is still in place and holds the picked yarns of shed stick 4. With the sword under heddle rod 1, pickup stick A with the picked red yarns is pushed up a little toward the weaving sword and away from the weaver. Since the next pick is based on the previous one, this action helps the weaver see which yarns raised by heddle rod 1 to pick up, using pickup stick B (Fig. 7.24). Working just above pickup stick A, and using pickup stick B, the weaver picks up the white yarns to fill in the design spaces where the red yarns from shed stick 4 were dropped (Fig. 7.25). Leaving pickup stick B in place, the weaver removes the sword. Then he lifts all the threads of heddle rod 3 and reinserts the sword under these as well as under the picked yarns of both pickup sticks. Thus, both the red yarns picked in the previous weft pass and the white yarns of the other color picked for the new weft pass are lifted simultaneously. He

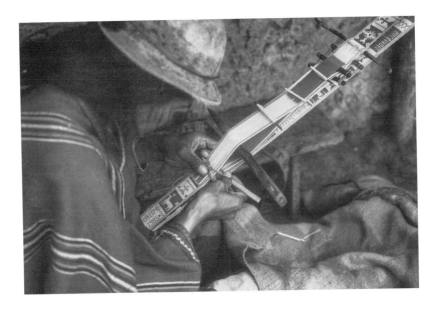

7.24 Picking up the pattern for a 3/1 alternating complementary-warp weave belt. Antonio Loja Loja, Gullandel, Cañar province. Slide by Laura M. Miller, 1985.

7.25 Both pickup sticks in place for a 3/1 alternating complementary-warp weave belt. Antonio Loja Loja, Gullandel, Cañar province. Slide by Laura M. Miller, 1985.

then takes out pickup stick A and places it under the red complementary-warp yarns of heddle rod 3. The weaver beats, passes the weft, and beats again.

The weaver photographed by Lynn Meisch in Figure 7.11 uses a slightly different procedure, leaving both pickup sticks holding their picked sheds in the warp until after he passes the weft. He can then use the shedding device and sword to reopen the shed from which the warp yarns for the next weft will be picked.

The weaving follows this sequence, picking red or white warp yarns for alternate weft passes. Since the Cañari belt is woven in fine sewing thread, very smooth gradations can be achieved and curves can be depicted. As noted in the Introduction, the horizontal color changes in the design areas of Cañari belts are clearer on one side than the other. Photographs suggest that most weavers work with the clearer face upward consistently, but The Textile Museum has one belt in which the faces are exchanged in an irregular way (see A. Rowe [ed.] 1998: 238, fig. 233). For the clearer side to face upward, the weaver must pick the background area first, and then the design.

When the sequence of the four shedding devices is maintained, a color area ends with the warp yarns interlacing over-3 and over-1 (on the clearer face), but only half of the other color begins along the same line while the rest float on the back, causing blurriness (see Fig. 7.9A). On the reverse there are three-span warp floats of each color overlapping by one or two weft yarns, which makes the transition look feathery. The overlap causes these two weft yarns to draw together, making the actual warp float span difficult to see in the finished belt.[12]

Although this type of color change is found in all six of The Textile Museum's Cañari belts, especially in smaller motifs, other configurations also occur. In one variation, found along the tops of some of the larger motifs in the belts in Figures 7.10 and 7.20, the weaver allows the threads that would form the three-span floats at the top of the motif color to drop after a two-span float (Fig. 7.9B). These yarns thus float 2/2 at the transition instead of at 3/1, but the other yarns maintain the same interlacing order as in the previous method. The elaborate belt referred to above (A. Rowe [ed.] 1998: 238, fig. 233) has some joins similar to this, but there is an additional row of three-span floats of the second color on the clearer face, which overlaps the row of two-span floats by one weft (Fig. 7.9C).

In a fourth configuration, which occurs on five of the six Textile Museum belts (all those illustrated) along the edges of larger motifs, the last row of floats before the change is four-span on the clearer face (Fig. 7.9D). These yarns then create a row of four-span floats as the second row of floats of the next color area on the other face. To create the four-span floats at the end of a color area on the clearer face, the weaver keeps lifted the threads picked for the previous two sheds (instead of only one) and does not pick a new shed of the color that is ending. Then, in the next shed, he drops the old color and picks the new one. Since the shedding device that would ordinarily be lifted in its entirety with this shed controls the threads of the old color being dropped, he has to pick from these threads only those that are needed in other areas of the belt. The picking and shedding sequence then resumes its usual form.

If the belt is for use by indigenous men, the last few designs are woven upside down in relation to the other figures (Fig. 7.19) so that, when the belt is worn hanging down, these final designs are right side up. When most of the warp has been woven, the weaver removes the loom parts. If he used strong nylon thread for the heddles, he saves it for the next weaving. If regular sewing thread was used, it is discarded, since the weaving process frays it beyond usefulness. The dovetail stick is taken out with care, releasing the initial and terminal loops. A ribbon is passed through the short initial loops, and the ends of the ribbon are sewn together. The longer terminal loops form a fringe and are often corded, or braided, in a four-strand round braid. This braid is called *tucumán* and does resemble the *tucumán,* or maypole, common at celebrations in Cañar province.

CHAPTER 8

Treadle-Loom Weaving

Introduction

ANN P. ROWE   The treadle loom operates under principles quite differ-ent from those of indigenous Andean looms (Figs. 8.1 and 8.2). The use of foot treadles to operate the shed-changing mechanism probably originated in China, spreading first to the Middle East, and then to Europe around the eleventh or twelfth centuries (Hoffman 1979). As introduced into Europe, treadle looms were used for production weaving on a commercial basis by professional male weavers, and the same is true of its introduction into the Americas.

The treadle loom is associated with professional production weaving be-cause it is much faster to operate than a loom with heddle rods and shed rods. The treadles are connected with cords to a series of rectangular frames, called *shafts* (*harnesses* in North American handweaving terminology) containing the heddles (Figs. 8.1 and 8.2). Each heddle has an eye in the middle through which a warp yarn passes. For plain weave, one shaft controls the odd warp yarns, another, the evens. To open the shed it is necessary only to press one or more treadles, without any need to scrape the warp or insert a sword.

Beating is done using a rectangular framework with closely spaced slats through which the warp yarns pass. This framework, called a *reed*, is in front of the heddles and connected to the loom supports with bars that pivot. A single jerk with the reed against the cloth suffices to beat in the weft (shown in Fig. 8.16).

The weft is wound on a tube (the *bobbin*), set on a pin in a smooth, hollow, wooden carrier (called a *boat shuttle*) so the bobbin can rotate, releasing the weft as it moves across the warp. The weaver can thus send the shuttle through the shed with a quick flick of the wrist.

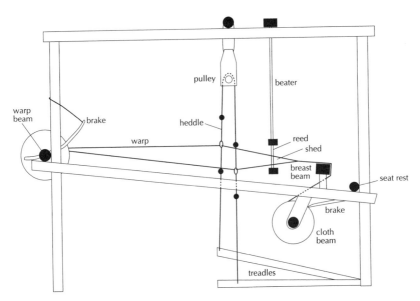

8.1 Profile diagram of a treadle loom, based on the most conservative type found in Ecuador. Solid black elements are bars that go across the full width of the loom. Dotted lines indicate elements passing behind the loom framework. Drawing by Laurie McCarriar based on a drawing by Ann P. Rowe.

The weaving motion therefore consists of (1) depressing the treadle(s), (2) throwing the shuttle, and (3) pulling once on the reed. Each of these actions can take less than a second.

Further speed is attained by using a very long warp, enough for multiple garments. The bars on which the unwoven warp and finished cloth are wound may be set underneath the plane of the weaving. These bars, called the *warp beam* and the *cloth beam*, respectively, can be rotated and secured. The working plane of the warp is supported by the breast beam and the back beam. Figures 8.1 and 8.2 show looms with a breast beam but no back beam, a common configuration in Ecuador, but looms with back beams also occur. A back beam also may allow the warp to feed more smoothly through the heddles.

European treadle looms have all these parts built into a single construction that may even include a weaver's bench, thus making them a substantial piece of furniture.

The warp tension on treadle looms is fixed, so it is easier to weave balanced and weft-faced fabrics than on the backstrap loom. Clothing fabrics woven on treadle looms in Ecuador usually have a balanced weave, with warp and

8.2 Colonial-style treadle loom. Cuicuno, Cotopaxi province. Photo by Laura M. Miller, 1988.

weft yarns similar in size and spacing. The tapestries woven for sale in the Otavalo and Salasaca areas, which are weft-faced, are also woven on treadle looms. Also, because the warp on a treadle loom is so long and the end of each yarn is cut to be put through the heddles and reed, the ends of the fabrics are necessarily cut. Therefore, it is usually easy to distinguish a backstrap-loom woven fabric, with its looped ends, from a treadle-loom woven one, with cut ends (as in Fig. 8.27) (also A. Rowe [ed.] 1998: 36–37, figs. 24–25).

Although plain weave is often woven on treadle looms, for which two shafts are sufficient, four shafts are necessary to weave twill (Fig. 8.2). In twill weaves, the weft yarn interlaces over or under more than one warp yarn at regular intervals, and these longer skips, called floats, are diagonally aligned from one shot of weft to the next. The most common twill weave in Ecuador interlaces over two, under two (Figs. 8.3 and 8.4). It is possible to produce twill on indigenous Andean looms, using additional or modified heddle rods, but in practice it is rare (except in the belts and ponchos described in Chapters 5 and 6), and most contemporary twill fabrics are produced on treadle looms.

Although the colonial *obrajes* are gone, some production weaving of old-style cloth was still being done by individual families, and some treadle-loom weaving was also being done for domestic use during the late 1980s. Some of these looms have old-fashioned features and are likely to be similar to those used in the colonial period. We also encountered some more modern types of looms, for example, with a countermarch shedding mechanism, usually to produce newer kinds of cloth.[1] These had been recently introduced or acquired as an economic development effort.

This chapter, however, will focus primarily on the older style of weaving, both because it is revealing of *obraje* production techniques, for which we have little other documentation, and because the cloth so produced is more likely to be used for traditional purposes such as indigenous clothing. Our information is incomplete, but there is enough to provide a general idea of this technology.

Context

An example of old-style production weaving and one of the most conservative treadle looms encountered by our Earthwatch teams in 1988 was in Cuicuno in Cotopaxi province (Fig. 8.2), known as a center of weaving coarse, striped, twill fabrics (*jerga* S.). We visited Reynaldo Almachi, his wife, Blanca Tipán, and their children.[2] They have some land and plant corn, potatoes, and barley for their own use, in addition to weaving. Señora Tipán said that her father

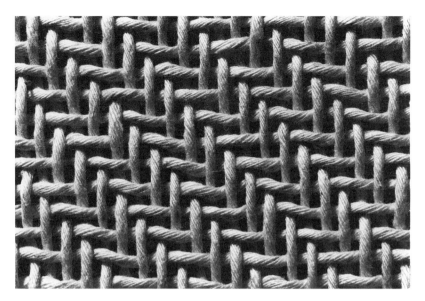

8.3 Diagrammatic construction of 2/2 twill weave. From Emery 1980, fig. 116.

8.4 Detail of 2/2 twill-weave fabric, in handspun cotton yarns, the weft with added goat hair. Woven in Cuicuno, Cotopaxi province. The Textile Museum 1988.19.57, Latin American Research Fund.

used to sell cloth to Manabí on the coast for use as saddle blankets. Señor Almachi's father is also a *jerga* weaver.

The warp consists of white and navy machine-spun cotton as well as of handspun cotton yarn (S-spun) brought down from Patutan (Macas, Cotopaxi province [Map 3]) and sold in the Saquisilí market (Fig. 8.4). There is also a single red acrylic stripe on one side selvedge. The weft is a thicker handspun cotton yarn, sometimes with goat hair mixed in, spun in La Calera, near Saquisilí (see Meisch, Miller, and Rowe 2005: 83). The cloth is warp striped in 2/2 twill and is woven in 125–130 vara (105–109 meter, or 114½–119 yard) lengths and is about 48 centimeters (19 inches) wide. We observed warping on a Wednesday, and señor Almachi said that he would finish the weaving on Saturday. The cloth is sold in Latacunga or Ambato for 150 sucres per vara or 200 sucres per meter (61 cents, or 82 cents at 1988 exchange rates). The huge rolls of fabric are trucked to Guayaquil, where they are cut into squares, edged with an overlock stitch on commercial sewing machines, and sold in the major supermarket chains as dust cloths or mop covers.

Production weaving of *chawar* (the leaf fiber from *Furcraea andina*) for produce sacks is described in the section on Santa Teresita in northern Chimborazo province below. We found similar sacks being woven in San Roque and Natabuela in Imbabura province in 1989.[3] Lynn Meisch was told in San Roque that the warp was about 150 meters (164 yards) long. The material is sent to Guayaquil to be made into sacks.

Some weavers are able to build their own looms, while others purchase a loom. A weaver recorded by our Earthwatch team in 1989 in Pulucate, Chimborazo province, Pedro Yupanqui built his own loom and set it up in a shallow cave near his house. He says he spends about half of his time weaving and the other half on agricultural tasks (Fig. 8.5).[4] He says he weaves for his family because such fabrics cost less, last longer, and are warmer than purchased fabrics. He also takes special orders and weaves for a local cooperative. He weaves shawls (*baita* Q., pronunciation of S. *bayeta*), striped carrying cloths (seldom used by 1989), and twill ponchos with dark stripes at intervals, all traditional costume items in this area. He weaves up to 40 meters (43¾ yards) at a time.

A weaver recorded by an Earthwatch team in 1988 in Pasa, Tungurahua province, Luis Martínez, who had migrated there from Simiátug in Bolivar province, weaves on both a treadle loom and a backstrap loom, depending on what item his clients want (Fig. 8.6; compare Fig. 1.14).[5] His repertoire of treadle-loom woven fabrics includes *pañolón* (S.), a heavy-weight wool shoulder cloth; *bayeta* (S.), a lighter-weight wool shoulder cloth in 2/2 twill; and *chalina* (S.), a shoulder wrap with fringe. As with backstrap-loom commis-

8.5 Treadle loom. Pedro Yupanqui, Pulucate, central Chimborazo province. Slide by William I. Mead, 1989.

sions, people bring him the yarn to be woven. If needed, his wife plies the yarn and dyes it. He had bought the treadle loom twenty-five years earlier. Another weaver, Gerardo Chuto, who uses both a backstrap loom (for ponchos) and a treadle loom (for shawls), was encountered in Cebadas, Chimborazo province in 1989.[6] The weaver and his father had built the two-shaft treadle loom, on which was an undyed dark-brown wool warp.

Our 1989 Earthwatch teams also recorded treadle-loom weavers in San Juan, Chimborazo province. They were told that most people wove for their own use but that there were four men in the community who also wove on commission. The teams visited two weavers, one from a *mestizo* family and the other indigenous.[7] The *mestizo* weaver, Gregorio Manuel Tenenuela, makes blankets and *bayetas* (shawls) (Fig. 8.7). His hand-built loom had two shafts and a white warp. He also had a new purchased loom but was waiting for someone to show him how to use it. The indigenous weaver, José Manuel Tajuana Paca, was warping his handmade loom with a white warp, which would later be commercially dyed in Riobamba. These large looms usually reside in small, dark rooms and were therefore difficult to photograph.

8.6 Treadle loom. Luis Martínez, Pasa, Tungurahua province. Slide by Betty Davenport, 1988.

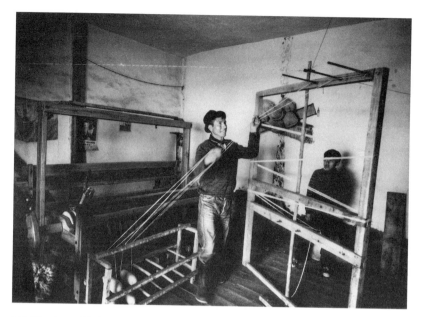

8.7 Warping with four yarns at a time on a rotating warping frame. Gregorio Manuel Tenenuela, San Juan, central Chimborazo province. Slide by Mary C. Shook, 1989.

Warping

Because the warp is so long and is not dovetailed, warping differs from that for a backstrap loom. One way to speed the process is to warp multiple yarns together. For this purpose, yarns are first wound on large spools (20–25 centimeters, or 8–10 inches long in Cuicuno), which are then set on wires in a frame (called *follidor* [S.] in Cuicuno). Yarn from all the spools can thus be warped at once. For example, the San Juan *mestizo* weaver was using four spools on a rack that would accommodate twelve (Fig. 8.7), while the Cuicuno weaver uses nine spools. More elaborate spool racks have an eye through which the yarn passes (Fig. 8.5), while simpler ones do not (see Fig. 8.19, below). Most often, the spool rack is a separate item, but some older Otavalo looms have spool supports mounted on an upper crossbeam of the loom (Collier and Buitrón 1949: 175; less clear in Parsons 1945: pl. 14).

The spools are wound in the same way as bobbins for boat shuttles, but the spools are larger than bobbins. The skein of yarn is put on a swift, which automatically rotates as the yarn unwinds, and the spools are rotated on a spindle connected with a drive cord to a hand-operated wheel (see Fig. 8.17, below). These simple wheels are often locally made of wood, though a bicycle wheel may be used instead. The worker turns the wheel with the right hand and guides the yarn onto the spool with the left hand. The type of swift and wheel is similar in all cases we observed. Winding bobbins and warping spools is often one of the first textile tasks taught to children, or it is done by the weaver's wife.

The warping frame (*urdidora* S.) is upright, as tall as a person, and rotates on a pivot at the bottom (Fig. 8.7). It may also be secured to the ceiling, for example, with ropes. For shorter warps, the frame is planar, as in Figure 8.7 (also recorded in the Salasaca [see Fig. 8.18, below] and Otavalo areas), but for longer ones, the frame consists of two rectangles set at right angles to form an X (recorded in Cuicuno and Santa Teresita; see Fig. 8.12, below). There are two or three pegs at the top (and sometimes also on the bottom) on which to make warp crosses. The warping begins at the cross pegs. The Cuicuno weaver makes the cross with his fingers and then transfers it to the pegs, but the yarns from the different spools are not always separated in this manner. The purpose of these crosses is more to keep the warp in order than to make a weaving cross.

Then the weaver rotates the warping frame in order to wind the warp. He can easily tell the length of the warp by the number of rotations he uses. For example, in Cuicuno, the warp makes twenty-three turns around the frame to create a warp of 130 varas (119 yards or 109 meters). Once the artisan reaches the other end of the frame, he reverses the yarns and winds back in the opposite direction, again making a cross. To remove the warp from the frame, he chains it on itself.

Since the new warp is often exactly like the old one, the end of the previous warp (called a *dummy warp*) is usually left passing through the reed and heddles to facilitate transfer of the new one (Fig. 8.8). In front of the reed, to secure the yarns, a bit of fabric may be left attached, or the cut ends may be knotted together. On the warp-beam end, the loops may be left passing around the loom bar, or, if the loom bar is removed, the loops are chained through each other. The reed and shafts are removable and can be stored separately (Fig. 8.8). The weaver may have two or three sets, one for each type of cloth that he weaves.

To install the new warp, the weaver cuts the rear loops of the dummy warp behind the heddles and ties the ends of the new warp to the cut ends of the old warp (see Figs. 8.13, 8.15, 8.23). Although there is a special weaver's knot named after this purpose, a square knot (as is used in Santa Teresita) or an overhand knot (as in Salasaca) may be used instead. We observed the indigenous weaver in San Juan threading heddles by hand from back to front, using

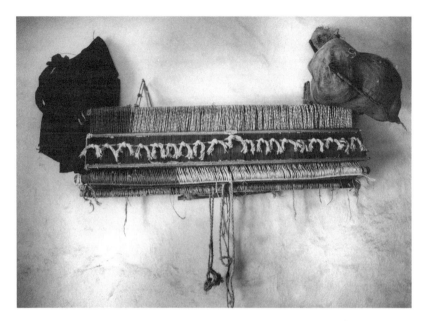

8.8 Heddles and reed with dummy warp. The warp yarns have been cut and tied in bunches in front of the reed. Gregorio Manuel Tenenuela, San Juan, central Chimborazo province. Slide by Mary C. Shook, 1989.

only his fingers. He also had a dummy warp, however, so it was clear that he did not thread the heddles for each warp.

Loom Styles

Treadle looms can differ in many ways, and Ecuadorian examples are variable in a number of respects. To begin with, the loom framework can take several forms. Many older Ecuadorian looms have vertical uprights extending to maximum height at each corner, connected by horizontal bars, forming a box frame (see Figs. 8.1 and 8.2). Alternatively, the corner uprights are only warp height, with separate uprights in the center to support the shafts or the shafts and beater, for example, a loom in Natabuela for *chawar* sacks (Fig. 8.9). Some old Otavalo-area looms for weaving the suit fabrics and shawls that were formerly the main commercial products are similar (see, e.g., Collier and Buitrón 1949: 172, 177, only the shafts; or Parsons 1945: pls. 14–15, the shafts and the beater).

A more modern style, introduced in the 1950s by the Dutch designer Jan Schreuder for tapestry weaving in both Otavalo and Salasaca (*Handweaver*

8.9 Treadle loom for weaving *chawar* fabric (*Furcraea* fiber). Natabuela, Imbabura province. Slide by Barbara Borders, 1989.

and Craftsman 1959: 20), has tall uprights at or near the back with cantilevered horizontals supporting the shafts and forming a cantilevered frame (Fig. 8.10). The cantilevered frame on the Pulucate loom was likely influenced by the dimensions of the cave in which it is set (see Fig. 8.5). We did not encounter front-to-back cantilevered frames in Ecuador.

In most Ecuadorian looms, the warp is horizontal. The looms in Cuicuno and Pasa, however, have it slanted up toward the back, which seems to correlate with the lack of a back beam.

On looms for production weaving of especially long warps, the warp beam has a large disk on either side, which helps keep the warp in place (Fig. 8.9; for Cuicuno, see Fig. 8.2; for Santa Teresita, see Fig. 8.14). The warp beam commonly also rests on supports behind the back loom posts so that it is easily detachable (as is the case with the San Juan indigenous weaver and in Pasa,

Cuicuno, and Santa Teresita). In other cases, it is supported by brackets, probably a newer style (see Fig. 8.5, and San Juan *mestizo* weaver).

The warp is not tied directly to the warp beam but passes around a smaller loom bar, which is, in turn, tied to the warp beam. Often, the warp beam has a horizontal groove into which the back loom bar fits. When the weaver approaches the end of the warp, he unties the loom bar and reties it with extensions so it can move forward until it touches the back of the heddles, so as to waste as little of the warp as possible (Fig. 8.6). The looms recorded in Natabuela, Santa Teresita, Pulucate, and San Juan (the *mestizo* weaver) had a back beam, but others did not, for example, in Cuicuno, Pasa, and San Juan (the indigenous weaver).

In most cases, the cloth simply passes around the breast beam, but the loom in Cuicuno has a slit in the breast beam through which the warp passes

8.10 Modern treadle loom for tapestry weaving. Some finished tapestries adorn the wall behind. Julio Chicaiza, a Salasaca man who maintains a workshop in Otavalo, Imbabura province. Photo by Lynn A. Meisch, 1984.

8.11 Treadle loom, with both warp and cloth beam tied with rope. Letrapungu, southern Chimborazo province. Slide by Laura M. Miller, 1989.

(Fig. 8.2). Probably, the warp yarns are tied to a loom bar that then is tied to the cloth beam, although we were not able to record this feature.

Methods of preventing the warp and cloth beams from unrolling vary, and the system may be different on the warp and cloth beams. The usual method of securing the warp beam in old-style looms is to put a rod of wood or metal through a hole near the end of the beam and to tie this rod to the loom frame, using a leather strap or *chawar* rope (Fig. 8.11). The exact configuration varies from one loom to another. Sometimes, this style of brake is also used on the cloth beam. In the loom from southern Chimborazo in Figure 8.11, it is clear that the cloth beam is tied to the frame with rope but unclear how the rope is secured to the cloth beam.

One must go back to the eighteenth century to find such a brake as typical on a north European or North American loom. For example, this type of brake is illustrated in Diderot's late-eighteenth-century encyclopedia as being the *ancienne manière* of securing both beams on a Gobelin low-warp tapestry loom.[8]

An apparently more modern device is a ratchet, and we recorded wooden ratchets on the cloth beams of looms in Pulucate and San Juan (the indigenous weaver), and Cuicuno (see Fig. 8.2). A wheel on one side of the cloth beam has holes in its circumference into which a pointed wooden bar (a pawl) tied to the loom frame fits. Modern treadle looms usually use metal ratchets.

Many Ecuadorian looms have a weaver's bench or seat rest built in, but some do not. The old looms with a seat rest built in, for example, in Santa Teresita (Fig. 8.16, below), often support the weaver in a position intermediate between sitting and standing, allowing him to place greater weight on the treadles. If a separate bench is used, the weaver works seated.

The beater usually rests on the top framework of the loom and pivots from the top, which is probably the old style (Fig. 8.2). A few old Otavalo-area looms (including the *chawar* loom in Natabuela) and some newer styles of loom have the beater pivoting from the bottom (Fig. 8.9). In locally built looms, the slats of the reed are often pieces of split bamboo held together by wrapping with twine, but we also saw modern-style reeds of metal. The reed itself is detachable from the framework of the beater so that different reeds and dummy warps may be exchanged (Fig. 8.8).

In many old North American looms, the heddles are made of cotton or linen string with an eye in the center through which a warp yarn passes. Commonly, each heddle is a separate unit with knots delineating the eye, and with the heddle bars passing through the loops above and below the eye to form the shaft. This style also occurs in Ecuador (for instance, in San Juan, Chimborazo province), but the heddles are often made of cabuya.

Another type of heddle is made of two threads looped through each other in an interlocked join with one of them also knotted to form an eye (as appears to be the case in Santa Teresita and Pasa), or with only an interlocked join through which the warp yarn passes. The heddles may either pass around the heddle bars above and below (as in Santa Teresita), or they may be bound to the heddle bars in some way (as in Pasa). The Pasa weaver uses cabuya heddles for making finer fabric and nylon for heavier fabric.

In the Salasaca loom described below, the heddles appear to be made of a thick re-plied cabuya yarn, with the warp yarns splitting the ply of the heddles (Fig. 8.23, below). The heddles on the looms for weaving *chawar* in Natabuela and San Roque are of metal wire, twisted together but with the twist open in the middle to make an eye. These heddles are kept an even distance apart by a row of twining next to the heddle bars.

In a two-shaft loom, each shaft is attached to a treadle by a cord. The two shafts are connected to each other at the top by cords that pass over pulleys or a rod or that are suspended from short horizontal bars called *horses*. Thus, when one treadle is depressed, the shaft to which it is attached is lowered and the other is simultaneously raised. A loom with this mechanism is called a *counterbalance loom*. All of the locally built treadle looms we saw were counter-balanced, with the shafts suspended over pulleys.

Four shafts are suspended in a similar way to two. In the four-shaft looms we saw, in Pasa and Cuicuno, the pulley housing has two wheels in it, one for the front two shafts and one for the back two (Fig. 8.2).

The treadles are usually simply suspended from the shafts individually in the looms we recorded (not fixed to the loom frame or to each other) and they usually pivot at the front (Fig. 8.6). An extra stick is frequently tied parallel to the lower heddle bar at both ends, to which the treadle is tied, in order to make the pull on the shafts more even (as in the Pasa, Cuicuno, and San Juan looms). Alternatively, the tie is Y-shaped instead of straight. More elaborate tie-ups are possible, for example, with extra treadles, but were not encountered in these simple looms.

Finishing Techniques

Because treadle-loom woven cloth has cut ends, the ends usually have to be treated so that they do not unravel. Most shawls and carrying cloths have a simple hem, sometimes sewn with a contrasting color of thread (for example, in central Chimborazo province), but in Salasaca a more elaborate embroidered end finish is used, as described below. Alternatively, the warp ends may be used as fringe. The striped twill ponchos of central Chimborazo province have a short fringe, secured at the weft edge with a line of hand stitching.

Sometimes, the cloth is treated further after weaving. Wool fabric may be brushed with teasels, as described in Chapter 1 for Pualó. Or it may be fulled, as described for Salasaca below. Dyeing is also often done at this stage (see Chapter 9).

In the past, handspun and handwoven cotton cloth, called *lienzo* (if coarser) or *liencillo* (if finer), was used for women's blouses and men's shirts and pants in Imbabura province and elsewhere. We talked to a few people who had formerly woven such cloth or remembered its being woven, but we saw no one producing it in the 1980s.

After weaving, this cloth was cleaned. In Otavalo, Humberto Muenala Maldonado of Quinchuquí, who helped us obtain old-style garments, told us that each evening for a week the newly woven fabric was covered with wet horse or cow manure and soaked overnight, then washed well the next morning. The family we met in Ovalos (Natabuela) described a similar process using horse manure, although they also described beating the wet fabric, which probably helped the manure penetrate the fibers. Although this was described to us as a bleaching process, in fact, the alkali in the dung acts as a scouring agent (which removes impurities) rather than as a bleach (which oxidizes or reduces coloring matter). The use of camel dung is traditional in India (Bilgrami 1990: 60, 80), and cow dung was also used in early industrial Europe to prepare cotton cloth for printing (Brédif 1989: 58, 62, 73). On the other hand, Meier (1985: 134, 137) reports that weaving *lienzo* was a specialty of the community of San Juan near Otavalo and that there the fabric was cleaned using local mineral water.

Santa Teresita, Northern Chimborazo Province

ANN P. ROWE AND LAURA M. MILLER   Santa Teresita is a suburb of Guano, in northern Chimborazo province, where in 1989 we recorded the weaving of coarse fabric made from *chawar* (see Miller et al. 2005).[9] The fabric is sold in Riobamba to people who cut it and sew it into sacks used for shipping produce. The sacks vary in the tightness of the weave, with smaller products in more closely woven sacks.

The workshop we visited, run by Enrique Samaniego Pilco, has three looms, operated by the owner and two hired workers. The owner had learned the work from his father. His wife, Lucila Vilema, and adult daughter, Lupa Samaniego Vilema, also assist with warping, and a hired woman winds weft yarn onto bobbins. He and his hired men weave from 6:00 AM to 6:00 PM and can weave 208 meters (227 yards) in four days. Each warp is 200–250 meters (219–273 yards) long.

For warping, a huge X-shaped frame (*urde*) is used, about 2 meters (6½ feet) high and about 4 meters (13 feet) across (Fig. 8.12). A cinder block at one corner gives it weight. Two nails project from one of the crossbeams for the cross. Warping is done from six bamboo spools (*rolas* S.), about 50 centimeters (20 inches) long, mounted on a rack (*cajón*). The warp is removed from the frame starting at the top, chaining it on itself (*obra*) (Fig. 8.12).

Because the warp is so long, the looms have breast and back beams and the warp beam has disks. The warp beam rests in a socket formed by the loom uprights and heavy blocks of wood with a slanting top that are tied behind the uprights (Fig. 8.13). The ends of the cloth beam pass through holes in a pair of uprights under the middle of the loom. The looms are set up over holes fifteen to twenty centimeters (six to eight inches) deep in the soil, to accommodate the huge roll of cloth.

The loom that was to be warped had a roll of finished cloth on the cloth beam that first was removed (Fig. 8.13). The cloth is simply pulled out through

8.12 Chaining a *chawar* warp from the warping frame for bag fabric. Lucila Vilema, Santa Teresita, northern Chimborazo province. Photo by Lynn A. Meisch, 1989.

8.13 Loom with completely woven cloth ready to be taken off. Santa Teresita, northern Chimborazo province. Photo by Laura M. Miller, 1989.

8.14 Winding the warp onto the warp beam of the loom through the raddle. Enrique Samaniego Pilco, Santa Teresita, northern Chimborazo province. Photo by Lynn A. Meisch, 1989.

the back of the loom into a loose pile. The back beam is removed, and the warp beam is then lifted up and placed where the back beam normally rests (Fig. 8.14). The heddles and reed are removed and the beater framework is tied to the breast beam to keep it out of the way. Another rod, over which the warp passes as it is wound on, is tied to the front of the loom just below the breast beam.

The weaver next ties a raddle (*rastrillo* S.) onto the loom between the beater and the back (Fig. 8.14). The raddle is a board with a row of nails pounded into it and used to space out the warp. The end loops of the new warp are slipped over the loom bar, a bamboo rod that fits into a groove in the warp beam. The weaver then separates the warp yarns so that they are evenly spaced on the raddle and along the loom bar. Then he ties the loom bar to the warp beam. The warp runs from below the loom, up and over the front rod, through the raddle and onto the warp beam (Fig. 8.14). The weaver inserts another bamboo rod into a hole in one side of the warp beam to use as leverage to roll the warp. One of the hired workers holds the warp and provides tension as the owner rolls the warp onto the warp beam.

When the end cross in the warp is reached, the weaver inserts a pair of bamboo cross sticks (*cruzeras*) through it and ties the ends of the sticks together.

8.15 Tying the new warp ends to the dummy warp. Lucila Vilema and Lupa Samaniego Vilema, Santa Teresita, northern Chimborazo province. Photo by Lynn A. Meisch, 1989.

8.16 Weaving *chawar* fabric. Most of the warp has been woven and is on the cloth beam. Samaniego workshop, Santa Teresita, northern Chimborazo province. Photo by Lynn A. Meisch, 1989.

8.17 Bobbin winding. Enrique Samaniego Pilco, Santa Teresita, northern Chimborazo province. Photo by Laura M. Miller, 1989.

He then divides the end loops into three groups and twists them, slipping these loops onto another bamboo stick.

The next step is to move the warp beam back down about sixty centimeters (two feet) to its normal position. The back beam is then put back on. To lift it high enough over the huge roll of warp, it actually rests on a pair of rocks placed on the horizontal braces of the loom just behind the uprights. Then the weaver is ready to add back the heddles (*lisos* S.) and the reed, which have the end of the previous warp passing through them, with the end loops chained through each other in groups behind the heddles. The weaver cuts the end loops of the old and the new warps and his wife and daughter tie the ends together, using a square knot (Fig. 8.15). The weavers work in a nearly standing position (Fig. 8.16).

The owner also demonstrated for us how they wind the bobbins (*canillande* S.) with weft yarn, though normally this is women's work (Fig. 8.17). The bobbins are pieces of bamboo, around twenty-three centimeters (nine inches) long. The worker holds two other pieces of bamboo so as not to cut or burn his or her hands as the yarn passes from the swift (*bailadera* S.) to the bobbin.

Salasaca, Tungurahua Province

LAURA M. MILLER AND ANN P. ROWE   In the 1980s the treadle loom was used in Salasaca for weaving many items of clothing, including women's wrapped skirts (*anaku*) and shawls (*bayeta*), and men's ponchos, as well as tapestries for sale. These items are plain weave, except the ponchos, which are 2/2 twill. Some ponchos on the loom are all white, some have white warp and brown weft, and others are all brown. Since cloth is dyed after weaving, the colors do not matter at this stage.

Many families have looms but may rent heddles from someone else for a specific period of time. The rent on heddles for someone who knows how to weave is less than for a novice, since an experienced weaver works faster. The weaver we recorded, Margarita Masaquiza Chango, had rented her heddles. It is unusual in Salasaca for a woman to weave on the treadle loom.

Señora Masaquiza's loom, on which she was preparing to weave skirt fabric (enough for five skirts), has a cantilevered framework with both back and breast beams. It is made from varnished boards, so may have been purchased rather than locally built.[10] Unlike the other Ecuadorian counterbalance looms we recorded, the two shafts are connected to each other by cords passing around a roller bar instead of over pulleys (see Fig. 8.22, below).

Warping and Dressing the Loom

These processes are similar to those in Santa Teresita, except for details relating to the shorter warp and minor differences in the looms. The rotating warping frame is a flat rectangle with two pegs for the cross on the top crossbar and two more farther down for the other end of the warp (Fig. 8.18). The warp is wound with six threads carried together, from spools on a rack (Fig. 8.19). A cross is made at each end, but the six threads are not separated. Both crosses are secured with string before the warp is chained and removed from the frame.

A dummy warp had the black wool warp ends tied together in front of the reed (visible in Fig. 8.22, below) and the loom bar still passing through the end loops behind the heddles. Señora Masaquiza removes the loom bar and chains the loops from left to right. She removes the beater and shafts from the loom and leans them against the wall. She then moves the loom from the corner of the room to the front door with the front facing out.

She places the loom bar from the dummy warp through the warp loops of the new warp and attaches it to extension cords of the warp beam. She ties a raddle with nails set into it every centimeter (⅜ inch) on the back beam with rope (visible in Fig. 8.21, below). She places one warp cross bundle, or twelve ends, in each space of the raddle.

She then stretches the warp out through the open doorway and across the yard. She inserts a stick into the far end loops. Her husband holds the warp taut while she makes sure that the warp yarns are not sticking or tangled (Fig. 8.20). Then she uses a finished skirt fabric to measure off the length for each of the five skirts, marking the divisions with white thread.

Next, señora Masaquiza winds the warp onto the warp beam, with the helper providing tension and the weaver turning the beam, which has a handle projecting from each of its four sides (Fig. 8.21). This process is halted to repair broken warp yarns and straighten out any remaining tangles. As the warp builds up on the beam, señora Masaquiza makes the edges angle in narrower. Once the warp is all wound on, she moves the loom back into the corner of the room, remounts the beater and shafts (Fig. 8.22), and reattaches the treadles.

The next step is to tie the warp ends to the dummy warp (Fig. 8.23). After cutting an eight- to ten-centimeter (three- to four-inch) section of the warp loops with a knife, señora Masaquiza separates the first group of six from the others with her right hand and then ties them. She matches up the two ends so they are parallel, twists them slightly, and ties them with an overhand knot.

8.18 Warping frame. Salasaca, Tungurahua province. Slide by Laura M. Miller, 1984.

8.19 Spool rack for warping. Salasaca, Tungurahua province. Slide by Laura M. Miller, 1984.

8.20 Spacing the far end of the warp. Margarita Masaquiza Chango and her husband, Salasaca, Tungurahua province. Slide by Betty Davenport, 1988.

8.21 Winding the warp onto the warp beam. Margarita Masaquiza Chango, Salasaca, Tungurahua province. Slide by Betty Davenport, 1988.

8.22 Attaching the beater and shafts to the loom. Margarita Masaquiza Chango, Salasaca, Tungurahua province. Slide by Betty Davenport, 1988.

8.23 Tying the new warp ends to the dummy warp. Margarita Masaquiza Chango, Salasaca, Tungurahua province. Slide by Betty Davenport, 1988.

Finishing the Raw Ends

The cut ends are sewn to keep them from raveling. While ponchos and skirts are often just coarsely overcast, shawls have a carefully sewn finish, using fine handspun wool and cotton in alternating blocks (Fig. 8.24). On acrylic shawls, colored acrylic thread may be used. For this fine finish, the sewing is done first, and the shawls are cut apart afterward (Fig. 8.25). The stitches are worked parallel to the warp, like a double running stitch. Each stitch passes over or under one weft yarn; the last three weft yarns are covered in this manner. The stitches are very closely spaced, and only with close inspection can one tell that the edges have been sewn. On some skirts, a similar but less closely spaced edging is done entirely in matching black wool that is invisible in the finished piece.

8.24 Detail of a Salasaca shawl showing the embroidered finish. Plain-weave wool with white cotton stripes. The Textile Museum 1987.9.10, Latin American Research Fund.

8.25 Embroidering the ends of several shawls on the same warp. Salasaca, Tungurahua province. Slide by Laura M. Miller, 1989.

8.26 Fulling ponchos. At right men roll up a poncho, while at left they full another one with their feet. Salasaca, Tungurahua province. Slide by Laura M. Miller, 1984.

Fulling Woven Cloth

After weaving, a poncho is fulled, or *batanado* (S., beaten). In this process, hot water and friction are applied to a wool fabric in order to cause the scaly fibers to catch on each other and become felted. The fabric shrinks and becomes denser.

Fulling with only human muscle power is hard physical labor requiring several participants and is used as an occasion for feasting in Salasaca. The session has a festival atmosphere. A great deal of food and maize beer (chicha) are consumed. One person remarked: "Pork must be served for two days [when ponchos are fulled]." Usually, more than one poncho is fulled at a time. At one session I attended, five families participated, each contributing one poncho to the occasion.

Each poncho is rolled (the length of the roll is warp-parallel) and then wrapped and tied very tightly with a cord (Fig. 8.26, *right*). The roll is then tied into a coil and soaked in a huge pot of hot water. While men do most of the fulling, women cook, making soup to feed the party and stoking the fire to keep the coiled ponchos hot.

After the rolled poncho has been in the hot water some time, the men take it out, uncoil it, and place it on a long wooden slab. Then five men begin to step on the roll with one foot and roll it back and forth in unison (Fig. 8.26, *left*). They keep their balance by hanging onto a rope hung between two posts or roof supports.

After a half hour rolling the poncho with their feet, they unroll the poncho in the open patio and reroll it in a different position. Three men work side by side to reroll it. Then it is secured in four places along its length and tightly rewrapped with a plastic rope. It is again placed in the hot water and, after a period of soaking, returned to the five men for more rolling.

The process usually takes several hours for one poncho, and if more ponchos are done, the work (and feasting) continues for up to two days.

Belt Weaving in Ariasucu, Otavalo Area, Imbabura Province

LYNN A. MEISCH AND RUDI COLLOREDO-MANSFIELD   Ariasucu is a small community of 130 families located outside Otavalo between Agato and La Compañía. These communities traditionally have been known for weaving supplementary-warp patterned belts on the backstrap loom. Sometime around 1977, several weavers in Ariasucu decided that they could increase their belt production and sales if they wove belts on the treadle loom. By 1994 there were twenty main households in the community that were producing belts in this manner. The designs are necessarily standardized, and three basic motifs are woven (Fig. 8.27): a simple bar pattern (called *yanga chumbi*, Q., "humble belt"), a diamond grid design (called *coco chumbi*), and a more elaborate diamond design (called *rumbu chumbi*). The weavers use the same white cotton ground warp and colored acrylic supplementary warp as those who weave on the backstrap loom, but the treadle-loom woven belts have cut rather than looped ends. Women and girls, as well as men and boys, weave these belts.

We documented the weaving in two households, more extensively in the home of Antonio Castañeda Camuendo, where Colloredo-Mansfield was living while doing his dissertation research in 1994 (Colloredo-Mansfield 1999). Señor Castañeda and his sons mainly weave belts with the *coco* design; *coco* means the pit or seed of a fruit (Fig. 8.27, *center*). Señor Castañeda says he can weave at least six belts a day on the treadle loom, as opposed to two per day maximum on the backstrap loom. The belts produced in Ariasucu are sold in the Otavalo market, but the weavers also travel to markets in the central highlands. Señor Castañeda, for example, goes to the markets in Riobamba and Latacunga where he sells his belts for 1,800 sucres apiece (approximately U.S. $1.20 at the 1994 exchange rate).

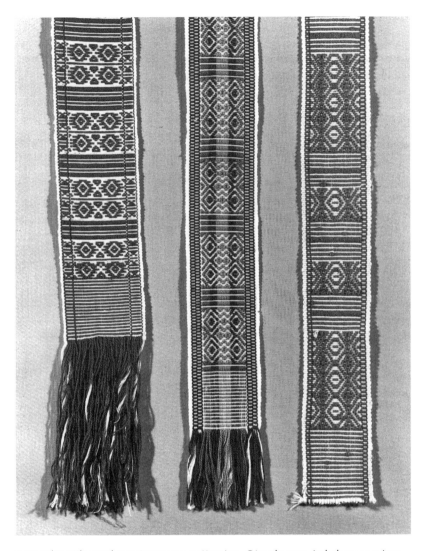

8.27 Belts with supplementary-warp patterning, Otavalo area, Imbabura province. The right-hand belt is backstrap-loom woven while the center and left ones are treadle-loom woven in Ariasucu. Plain-weave cotton with acrylic supplementary warp. Widths (left to right): 5.7, 5, and 5 centimeters (2¼, 2, and 2 inches). The Textile Museum 1989.22.18, 1994.18.3, and 1986.19.7, Latin American Research Fund.

The two shafts for the plain-weave ground are counterbalanced over pulleys, as are the looms described above (Fig. 8.28). The pattern shafts, however, are suspended from a separate beam at the top of the loom with strips of rubber cut from the inner tubes of tires. The rubber stretches when the treadle is depressed and springs back when the weaver takes his or her foot off the treadle.[11] The looms first used in Ariasucu were purchased in Otavalo or Agato. Now many of the weavers make their own.

The supplementary-warp diamond design is based on a balanced twill weave. Antonio's loom has six shafts (*marcos*, S.) and six treadles (*pedales*, S.). The two shafts controlling the ground warp are at the front of the loom, near the weaver, followed by the four for the supplementary warp. From the weaver's point of view, the leftmost treadle is tied to pattern shafts 1 and 2, the next treadle is tied to ground shaft 1, the next to pattern shafts 3 and 4, the next to pattern shafts 2 and 3, the next to ground shaft 2, and the rightmost treadle is tied to pattern shafts 4 and 1. This seemed like a strange tie-up until we realized that the weaver has only two feet but needs to be able to treadle both ground-warp and supplementary-warp shafts at the same time. The weaver can depress the two leftmost treadles with the left foot, or the two treadles just inside the leftmost treadle, and, in each case, a pattern shaft and ground shaft will be affected. To make the bars between the diamond motifs, the weaver depresses all three left treadles alternately with all three right ones.

To center the pull of the treadles on each shaft, the center of each shaft is tied first to an intermediate stick (a *lamm*), which pivots from one side of the loom (Fig. 8.29). Cords then connect the lamms with the treadles.

We also visited the family of Rafael Chiza, one of the first two weavers to switch to treadle looms. Up to five boys and girls as young as twelve years of age were weaving the more complicated *rumbu* (S. *rombo*, diamond) *chumbi*. These belts are similar to those woven by José Manuel Bautista of Agato on the backstrap loom, described in Chapter 4, using eleven heddle rods. The treadle loom setup consists of nineteen shafts, two ground shafts, and seventeen pattern shafts, all connected to eight treadles.

Another, similar, loom in the home of a family visited during the Earthwatch project in 1989 had its ground-weave shafts behind the pattern shafts instead of in front (Fig. 8.30). The two plain-weave treadles are both at left in the photograph.

One of our Earthwatch teams encountered a similar loom in Mancheno, south of Cajabamba in central Chimborazo province, in 1989. It was being used to weave hatbands, with a design of supplementary-warp floats lined up diagonally (Fig. 8.31).[12] This loom has a pair of counterbalanced shafts at the back for the plain-weave ground, four additional shafts in front of these for

8.28 Treadle loom for weaving supplementary-warp patterned belts. The pattern shafts are suspended with dark rubber strips, while the plain-weave shafts are suspended with white rope over pulleys. Ariasucu, Otavalo area, Imbabura province. Photo by Lynn A. Meisch, 1994.

8.29 Side view of the treadle loom for weaving supplementary-warp patterned belts. The bottoms of the heddle frames are tied to lamms that pivot from the side of the loom. These, in turn, are tied to the treadles. Ariasucu, Otavalo area, Imbabura province. Photo by Lynn A. Meisch, 1994.

8.30 Treadle loom for weaving supplementary-warp patterned belts, with the plain-weave shafts behind the pattern ones (used to weave the belt at left in Fig. 8.27). Ariasucu, Otavalo area, Imbabura province. Slide by Ann P. Rowe, 1989.

8.31 Supplementary-warp patterned hatbands woven on a treadle loom. Mancheno, central Chimborazo province. Photo by Ken Henisey, 1989.

8.32 Treadle loom used to weave supplementary-warp patterned bands. The plain-weave shafts are at the back. A comb-shaped framework separates the treadles. Mancheno, central Chimborazo province. Photo by Ken Henisey, 1989.

the pattern, and six treadles (Fig. 8.32). The loom construction includes di-agonally set slats to separate the treadles and limit their motion to up and down. The front ends of the treadles are tied with cord to a board along the bottom of the front of the frame. The back plain-weave shaft is tied to the treadle second from the left, while the front one is tied to the treadle second from the right. Again, one foot can depress two treadles at a time, one for the ground and one for the pattern.

CHAPTER 9

Natural Dyeing Techniques

Introduction

ANN P. ROWE   Brightly colored textiles have a nearly universal appeal, and the lore of dyeing, with its often sophisticated chemistry, has therefore been important throughout history to both art and commerce. Until the mid-nineteenth century, dyes were derived from natural materials, primarily plants, but also certain animals and minerals.

It is much easier to dye protein (animal) fibers, such as wool, camelid hair, and silk, with natural materials than it is to dye cellulose (plant) fibers such as cotton, linen, or the leaf fibers. Consequently, if a society has access to both, usually the animal fibers are dyed while the plant fibers are frequently undyed. Exceptional dyes that can be employed for cellulose with methods similar to those for protein include indigo for blue, shellfish for purple, and tannic acid from plants for brown. In pre-Hispanic Peruvian textiles, for example, blue and brown are the only commonly used colors of cotton, while camelid hair yarns are dyed in a rainbow of colors.

Certain colors are easier to obtain from natural materials, and some are more resistant to fading than others. For example, many plants produce yellow, but no yellow is as colorfast as blue from indigo or red from one of the root or insect dyes.

Some materials, such as plants containing tannic acid, will dye a fabric without any other treatment, but most natural dyes require a more elaborate procedure. Most commonly, the material to be dyed is first treated with a metallic salt such as alum, iron, or copperas, called a *mordant*, which helps the dye form a chemical bond with the fiber. Use of an aluminum, iron, or copper pot aids in this process as well. Some indigenous American recipes, however, employ plant materials instead of minerals as mordants, and such recipes (and their associated plants) bear closer scrutiny than has heretofore

9.1 Selling synthetic dyes and teasels in the Ambato market, Tungurahua province. Slide by Laura M. Miller, 1988.

been the case (see the section on cochineal below). Indigo requires a different type of preparation, as described below.

Despite the ready availability of synthetic dyes, some natural dyeing persisted in highland Ecuador through the 1980s, although it appeared to be endangered. We did not make an exhaustive study of this subject (see Jaramillo 1984, 1988a for additional dye plants and recipes) but include here such information as we have gathered, chiefly on indigo and cochineal. Our focus is on indigenous materials and procedures, not on practical modern methods, for which other books are available.

The unspun fiber, the yarn, or the finished fabric can be dyed. In highland Ecuador, cloth dyeing is perhaps the most common, but fiber and yarn dyeing are also done. In the Otavalo area, most dyers prefer to work with unspun fiber, in the belief that the color is taken up more evenly and yarns tend to get tangled in the bath.

Most dyeing in Ecuador is done with synthetic dyes, since they are much easier to use than natural dyes. They require no preparation and significantly less firewood. Synthetic dyes may also be used in the same bath as natural dyes, to modify the color. Synthetic dyes are locally referred to as *anilina* (S.), or "aniline," after the first synthetic dyes developed in the 1850s and 1860s. Since then, however, many other types of synthetic dyes have become available. Those used by Ecuadorian weavers in the 1980s were probably acid dyes (Jaramillo 1990: 29), which work best on protein fibers, or union dyes, which also include a direct dye suitable for cellulose. The powders are sold from tins, which the seller extracts and folds in a piece of paper for the customer

(Fig. 9.1). He or she may combine powders from different tins to create the desired color. The dyes are imported from Germany, Japan, Peru, and Colombia.

The procedure for synthetic dyes involves simply boiling the material to be dyed in water in a metal or ceramic pot to which the dye powder and an assistant such as salt, lemon juice, or sulfuric acid has been added. Examples of such procedures are described in the sections on Segundo Mena's poncho weaving workshop in Pualó in Chapter 1, and on the warp-resist dyed ponchos of Abel Rodas of Chordeleg in Chapter 2.

Walnut

ANN P. ROWE A common natural dye we recorded in Imbabura and Azuay provinces is the bark, nut hulls, or leaves of the South American walnut tree (*Juglans neotropica*, called *nogal* in Spanish and *tukti* in Quichua), which produce a rich brown color (Fig. 9.2). The dye is predominantly a naphthoquinone (juglone), but tannic acid is also present and so no mordant is required (Cardon 2003: 75–76). The use of the bark by Abel Rodas of Chordeleg is described in Chapter 2.

9.2 The South American walnut tree, *Juglans neotropica.* Daniel de la Torre, San Luis de Agualongo, Otavalo area, Imbabura province. Photo by Lynn A. Meisch, 1984.

Carlos Conterón, of Ilumán, in the Otavalo area, explained to me in 1999 how he uses the nut hulls. He says that the leaves produce an inferior dye. It is best to pick the nuts off the tree. If one gathers them after they are ripe, it is harder to control the color. The nut hulls yield the same quality of dye no matter how many or how few nuts the tree has at any given time of year. The hulls are ground between stones. The nuts are, of course, eaten. The hulls are counted in pairs, with four pairs the minimum for one kilo (2.2 pounds) of wool and 10–12 liters (10½–12¾ quarts) of water. Deeper colors are obtained with 8 or 16 pairs; 30–40 pairs is the maximum. Wool is steeped in clean water (preferably rainwater) for one or two hours if unspun or overnight if spun. Then it is boiled with the dye for an hour. The dye bath is stirred every five minutes or so. When the wool is removed from the water, it changes color (darkens) in the first ten minutes, from oxidation. It is best to dry the yarns in the shade, since the color will not be as good if dried in the bright sun. If the color is not dark enough, more hulls can be added and the yarn boiled for another hour, and so on. A more brilliant (*brilloso* S.) color can be obtained by using lye (ash water) in the last dye bath.

To alter the color, yellow, orange, or green synthetic dye can be added. Since walnut is cheaper than synthetic dye, walnut is sometimes combined with black synthetic dye to produce black.

In comparison, Lynn Meisch reports that Abel Rodas boils the ground-up bark for three hours, while Jaramillo's recipe (1988a: 167), for which he gives no precise source, suggests boiling the bark for five minutes, removing it for oxidation for two minutes, and repeating this operation until the desired color is obtained. Don Carlos's procedure is thus somewhere between these extremes.

Indigo

ANN P. ROWE AND LYNN A. MEISCH   Indigo is prized in many parts of the world for the deep, rich blues and blacks it imparts to both cotton and wool fabric. The same dye chemical, indigotin, is found in a number of different plants, though in varying amounts. There is a species native to tropical America, *Indigofera suffruticosa* Mill. (formerly known as *I. anil*) (family Fabaceae, formerly Leguminosae) that is as productive of the dye as the most productive Asian species, *Indigofera tinctoria* L. Another species, *Indigofera micheliana* Rose (also called *I. guatimalensis* or *I. guatemalensis*) is indigenous to Central America but now grows in South America as well. Old World species were introduced after the conquest. Indigo cultivation and processing was a major industry in Central America during the colonial period (see, e.g., Rubio Sánchez 1974; Mariano Moziño 1976).

The *Indigofera* species are tropical plants and were presumably extensively grown at lower elevations in South America before the Spanish conquest. In modern Peru, *Indigofera suffruticosa* grows in areas below 1,500 meters (4,920 feet) on both sides of the Andes (Macbride 1943: 379). Indigo is, however, mentioned in only a few early post-conquest written sources and only by its Spanish name, *añil*.[1] For example, there are late-sixteenth-century reports of *añil* in the Coange (modern Mira) River valley in northern Ecuador (Paz Ponce de León [1582], last paragraph; idem 1897: 119) and the Tucumán area of Argentina (Sotelo Narváez [1583] 1885: 145). The names for indigo we recorded in Ecuador are Spanish: *añil* (indigo), *tinte* (dye), *baño* (dye bath), or *tinaco* (vat, pronounced *tinaku* by Quichua speakers).

The leaves of another tropical plant, cultivated in the department of San Martín in eastern Peru, *Cybistax antisyphilitica* (family Bignoniaceae), locally called *achiwa-achiwa* (*achiwa* Q., parasol) or *llangwa*, contain indigotin in lesser amounts (Antúnez de Mayolo Ms: 28–29; 1989: 182, 187).

A highland Peruvian plant said to yield a blue dye, *Mühlenbeckia volcanica* (family Polygonaceae), locally called *mullaka* (Cobo [1653] 1956, lib. 5, cap. 45; Antúnez de Mayolo Ms: 85–86), is in the same family as the Oriental indigotin-producing species *Polygonum tinctorium*.[2] The most commonly mentioned source of blue dye in early documents is another highland plant, an inedible (bitter-tasting) species of potato, *Solanum stenotomum* (family Solanaceae), locally called *ch'apina papa* (Q.) or *papa negra* (Q., S.) (Monzón [1586] 1881: 193, 213; González Holguín 1608, 1952: 96; Murúa [1613] 1964: [vol. 2] 154; Antúnez de Mayolo Ms: 102; 1989: 189). A source on Bolivia says that a mordant of alum or copper sulfate was used (Cárdenas 1969: 293, citing Haenke 1798, 1909). The dye from these highland plants may be anthocyanin (Rodriguez-Saona et al. 1998; Cardon 2003: 197).

In Peru, indigotin (from whatever source) has been identified in both cotton and camelid hair textiles from both Ocucaje and Paracas on the south coast, dating to around 350–50 BC (Fester 1954: 239; King 1965: 97–98). A few earlier cotton textiles with blue exist, but analysis is not available. Although evidence is so far unavailable, it would be strange if indigo was not used in pre-Hispanic Ecuador as well.

In the eighteenth century, Juan and Ulloa reported that most indigo used in South American Spanish weaving workshops (*obrajes*) came from the coast of New Spain, that is, Mexico (1748 [vol. I]: 403, para. 713; 1964: 153). A document from 1765 notes that two voyages per year were permitted from Guayaquil to Guatemala (Zelaya 1994: 362). The boats carried wine and distilled liquor from Peru and brought back indigo and brazilwood, another dye, among other cargo. A document from 1766 reports that cochineal and indigo from Guatemala also came into the ports of Santa María del Puerto, Tumaco, Palma Real, and Buenaventura in the province of Los Pastos (modern Colombia) to meet the demand in the *obrajes* to the south (Alsedo y Herrera 1994: 431).

A document written in 1774 reports, in terms that confirm that it was a new venture, an attempt to cultivate and process indigo in Babahoyo, near Guayaquil, on the coast (Requena y Herrera 1994: 541–542). The author notes: "On many occasions the *obrajes* of this realm are halted because the boat that brings dyes from the coasts of Guatemala does not arrive, even though the profit is 100 percent" (Meisch translation). Two species were grown, one as tall as a man and the other only two feet high. Different classes of dye used different parts of the plant: *tinta flor* was made from the most delicate leaves, *tinta de color y corte* from the leaves and sprouts, and *tinturrón* from the stalks, leaves, and sprouts of the plant.

Indigo "of various species" is noted as growing on the Ecuadorian coast in at least one late-nineteenth-century source (Wolf 1892, 1976: 467, cited in Klumpp 1983: 84), and an Ecuadorian botanist mentions many relicts growing on the Esmeraldas coast (Acosta Solís 1961: 265, cited in Klumpp 1983: 85). In the highlands it would have been a trade item.

Cloth can be dyed directly from the leaves, and such a process was recorded using *Cybistax antisyphilitica* in northeastern Peru, in what seems to be an indigenous recipe (Antúnez de Mayolo 1989: 182). Frequently, however, indigo dyeing involves two steps: first, the dye from the leaves is concentrated; second, the dye vat is prepared (see Gerber 1977, 1983). The first process is obviously done only where the plant grows. Cakes are formed, which can be transported easily to other areas for sale. It is possible, however, that this two-part process was not utilized in pre-Hispanic South America.

The process of concentrating the dye described in the 1774 document in Requena y Herrera is the same as in Central America and in India.[3] Indeed, it was probably introduced to the Americas by the Spanish, since the large brick or masonry tanks typical of this process in colonial Central America are not found in pre-Hispanic sites. The leaves are steeped in an open tank of water for twelve to eighteen hours, after which the water is drained off into a second tank and the leaves discarded. The water is beaten in order to incorporate atmospheric oxygen, and form the insoluble dye, which then coagulates and precipitates out of the water (see Liles 1990: 54, for an explanation of the chemistry). The sludge is then gathered, dried, and formed into blocks.

Little information on indigenous South American methods is available, but some evidence suggests that the steeping was done in clay pots for a longer period of time.[4] Kathleen Klumpp (1983: 83–84) talked to some old people in Manabí province on the Ecuadorian coast who said they had observed (but not performed) the process of indigo dyeing in their youth, though their information was incomplete. The leaves were placed in cold, fresh water for thirty days, during which time they were kept covered. Covering the pot would have promoted fermentation. Before dipping the yarns alum was added, which the informant said facilitated coagulation.[5]

In recent times, as in the colonial period, the major plant growing and processing areas have been in Central America (see Clara de Guevara 1975, 1976). The indigo formerly found in Ecuadorian highland markets such as Ambato and Cuenca consisted of cakes imported from El Salvador. This trade ceased around 1980, presumably due to disruptions from the civil war.

Indigo was first synthesized in 1880 in Germany, but a method for producing it cheaply enough to market it competitively with natural indigo was not perfected until 1897 (Liles 1990: 56, 100). In South America, however, the price of synthetic indigo imported from Germany apparently remained high enough not to provide serious competition for the natural product from El Salvador until the supply of the latter ceased.

In the highlands, as one would expect, only the dyeing process itself has been recorded. The dye is insoluble in water so the process requires something as a reducing agent (to remove oxygen atoms from the molecule) as well as an alkali in which the reduced indigo can be dissolved (Gerber 1977, 1983). The color develops only after the fiber or yarn is removed from the bath and is exposed to atmospheric oxygen. In one type of indigo vat, referred to as a urea vat, stale urine provides both bacteria that reduce the indigo and ammonia compounds that are an effective alkali. This most basic technique is used in Saraguro. However, less-noxious dye baths are possible, and elsewhere in Ecuador the alkali is generally provided by lye made with wood ashes (potassium hydroxide), and the reducing agent is provided by bacteria found on other plant material added to the bath. This type of indigo bath is referred to as a fermentation vat. Some plant material may serve as food for rather than carriers of the bacteria. The favored plant additive in Ecuador seems to be mashed up *Furcraea* or maguey leaves, but the use of various other plants has also been recorded. Urine is also sometimes added to the vat for good measure.

There is a document written in 1703, evidently by a Jesuit administrator of the *obraje* in Cajamarca in the province of Vilcashuaman, Huamanga, in what is now Peru, that details how indigo dyeing was to be done in this establishment (Anonymous 1923). A fermentation vat was used, and it seems likely that this was the normal procedure in the Ecuadorian *obrajes* as well. The recorded procedure employs some European elements (a kettle for cooking the lye) and some American elements (the addition of "maguey" leaves and other native plants to the lye). It involves several steps: making the lye; cooking the lye with plant materials; fermenting the dye; and, finally, dyeing the cloth. The process is similar to procedures we recorded in Otavalo, although some Otavalo dyers omit the step of cooking the lye. Ecuadorian dyers also use a simpler lye-making method.

The dye substance (indigotin) in synthetic indigo is the same as in natural indigo, but natural indigo usually also contains some additional plant residue, so is less concentrated. Some experts have noted that a fermentation vat does not always work with synthetic indigo, perhaps due to chemical impurities (Gerber 1983: 26; Liles 1990: 56). Ecuadorian dyers do not adjust their recipes for the type of indigo, however.

Wool

The contrast between the process of dyeing wool with indigo in Saraguro and that used in Otavalo is fascinating. It seems likely that they have a different history.

SARAGURO, LOJA PROVINCE

Carmen Chalán of Las Lagunas in the Saraguro area explained to Lynn Meisch in 1994 the process of dyeing with indigo (*tinaku* S. with Q. suffix). Although she has never dyed with indigo alone, she has helped her mother, Nati Guamán, do so many times. After the supply of indigo from El Salvador was cut off around 1980, the Saraguros begged anyone they knew who was traveling to the United States (e.g., anthropologists, Peace Corps volunteers, and other development workers) to please return with indigo to sell.

The dye is ground up and put in a large pottery vessel (*balde* or *olla* S.). Water is added, the jar is covered, and the mixture is left for three or four months to steep (*remojar* S.). Toward the end of this period, the dyer collects her urine in another ceramic jar and lets it ferment for two or three weeks. The urine is then added to the dye and water mixture and a wood fire is built around the pot. Nothing else is added. Carmen emphasized, first, that the pot must be close to but not in the fire, and, second, that it must be tightly covered, often with another ceramic pot turned upside down, so that no dirt or ashes enter, because any foreign matter "damages the dye."

When the dye comes to a boil, the textile is put into the pot and left for about six hours as the pot cools down. For example, a textile put in the pot in the morning is taken out sometime in the afternoon of the same day. The cloth is retrieved with a wooden pole and allowed to drip as the dye oxidizes.

This is called the "first opening" (*la primera boca* S.). The textile is reimmersed and steeped in the dye again for up to two *bocas* in two days, resulting in the dark blue-black color so prized in Saraguro.

Next, the textile is washed. Carmen stressed that it was extremely important that the newly dyed piece not touch or be mixed with grease in any way. For example, it should not be washed in the same pan used to wash dishes. Saraguros have a saying that "the dye is very jealous of other things." Then the textile is buried in "clean," loose (meaning untrampled) mud for two to four days. By "clean" mud, Carmen meant it was free of foreign objects and rotting organic matter. The purpose of this latter step is both to remove the strong smell of urine and to make the color fast. Finally, the cloth is washed thoroughly in water and dried.

It is difficult to comment on the practice of burying the fabric in mud without knowing the chemical composition of the mud, but it is possible that this practice has its origin in dyeing with mordant dyes, since some mud contains iron, a common mordant, which also tends to darken the resulting color. While indigo has a different chemistry from other dyes and does not require a mordant, the Saraguros do like their cloth as dark as possible, and the removal of the smell of the urea vat is surely a plus as well. This recipe shows no obvious European influence. The use of indigo is not necessarily of great antiquity in Saraguro, however, since before the 1940s Saraguro clothing is said to have been undyed (Meisch in A. Rowe [ed.] 1998: 266).

OTAVALO AREA, IMBABURA PROVINCE

In the Otavalo area, those few indigenous people whom we encountered dyeing with indigo use synthetic indigo imported from Germany. Cotton bound-warp-resist dyeing, although formerly practiced, has not been done in recent memory, and the indigo dyeing we recorded is with wool for ponchos.

Indigo dyers have become few, mainly men who weave ponchos on the backstrap loom. The process is complex and takes place over several days, so it is not easy to record, nor are the dyers necessarily willing to share all their secrets. Thus, although we have information from several dyers, we do not have complete information from any of them. A general sense of the typical process nevertheless emerges, despite evident variations.

Lynn Meisch recorded indigo dyeing by Rafael de la Torre of San Luis de Agualongo (Meisch 1987: 44–45). First, a ceramic pot with a hole in the bottom is stuffed with grass and set over a plastic bucket (Fig. 9.3). Next, the pot is filled with wood ashes. Water is poured over the ashes and drips into the bucket, forming a weak lye. The lye is poured into another ceramic pot that is covered with a lid and set over a clay oven with a fire built under the pot (Fig. 9.4). This oven was built especially for dyeing and is not used for baking bread.

Next, some chopped *Furcraea* leaves are added to the dye water and stirred vigorously. The dye-jar lid, about 9 centimeters (3½ inches) in diameter, is filled with synthetic indigo, which comes in the form of small, glittery, blue gold crystals. This lidful is dumped into the dye pot and stirred. A wood fire is lit under the dye pot, and the mixture is heated, but not boiled, for twelve hours. The mixture is allowed to cool for twelve more hours, after which the dye bath is considered "ripe" (*maduro* S.). Washed wool fleece is put into the cold dye bath for six to eight hours and stirred occasionally. It is removed, rinsed in the stream, dried, and then carded and spun.

In 1989 we interviewed two other dyers, Carlos de la Torre of Carabuela,[6] and Alejandro Quinatoa Santillán of Agato, although we did not observe their procedures. The information don Alejandro gave Laura Miller differs slightly from that in a publication about him (Quinatoa 1982). Jaramillo also provides a description of indigo dyeing.[7] He says that 12 pounds (5.5 kilograms) of fleece are needed for the double-sided poncho in two shades of blue (see Chapter 6), so this is the quantity dyed at one time.

Jaramillo notes that *chilka* (Q., see possible identification below) ash is preferred for the lye, which makes sense, since it contains soda and potash, which are alkaline (Gade 1975: 218; Antúnez de Mayolo 1976: 41). Don Carlos told us he uses eucalyptus ash from his cooking oven, however, while don Alejandro said he uses ash from walnut wood, *chilka*, corn leaves, a type of cherrywood (*capulí* S.), or alfalfa roots, or, indeed, anything except eucalyptus. All these dyers use a lye-making setup like that described above, except that the publication on Quinatoa says a basket lined with coarse cabuya fabric set on three large stones is used as a strainer. Also, the lye may be caught in a clay pot. Jaramillo notes that the lye is considered ready if it tastes salty or if it floats a fresh egg, mentioned also in the Peruvian colonial document cited above (Anonymous 1923).

The most distinctive part of the procedure, however, is that these dyers said they cook twelve plants picked fresh on Mt. Imbabura in the lye. The list of plants given by each dyer is different, although there is some overlap and all the lists are incomplete, presumably the result of the dyer's wishing to protect his secrets. Don Alejandro crushes the plants. Don Carlos and don Alejandro said they use a *paila* (S.), a large metal pot, to cook the lye, although the Quinatoa publication says the lye is cooked in a clay pot. Don Carlos boils the plants for three hours.

Don Carlos uses *arrayán* (S., myrtle), walnut, *chilka blanca* (Q., S.), *wallwa*

9.3 Lye-making setup. Rafael de la Torre, San Luis de Agualongo, Otavalo area, Imbabura province. Photo by Lynn A. Meisch, 1985.

9.4 Indigo dye pot set in the fermenting oven. Rafael de la Torre, San Luis de Agualongo, Otavalo area, Imbabura province. Photo by Lynn A. Meisch, 1985.

(Q., pronounced "*wazhwa*"), *oraleto tierno* (*tierno*, S., young, unripe), *all-nallwa* (Q., pronounced "*azhnazhwa*"), *marku* (Q.), *fili muyu* (Q.), *payku* (Q.), *killu yuyu* (*killu* Q., pronounced "*kizhu*," yellow; *yuyu*, wild plant), and *Furcraea* leaf.[8] He said that none is added in greater quantity than the others, although *Furcraea* is particularly important. The published list for don Alejandro includes *retama* (S., broom), *capulí*, alfalfa, *ortiga* (S., nettles), *marku*, *izo* (*aliso*[?] S., alder tree), "and others." The list given to Miller includes, besides *capulí* and *marku*, *payku*, verbena, *nogal*, *moras* (S., blackberries), romerillo, *ashnak yura* (Q., stink plant), *murtiñoz* (S.), *muku chajcha* (Q.), *alpatzisera* (*allpa* Q., earth), and *jaritzisera* (*jari* Q., male). Jaramillo's partial list includes *ñacha* (Q.), eucalyptus, *marku*, *trinitaria* (S., pansy), *kulkas* (Q.), and *yerba mora* (S., blackberry).

Some of the plants mentioned in these recipes can be identified with more or less confidence from the available literature. It needs to be emphasized, however, that we did not actually collect specimens and have them identified by a qualified botanist.

According to the literature, then, some of the plants yield yellow to brown dyes, including myrtle (*Eugenia halli*), walnut (*Juglans neotropica*), *chilka* (*Baccharis* spp.), broom (*Spartium junceum*), *capulí* (*Prunus serotina*), eucalyptus (*Eucalyptus globulus*), blackberry (*Solanum interandinum*), *killu yuyu* (*Miconia coelata*), *kulkas* (*Miconia* spp.), and *ñacha* (*Bidens humilis*).[9] *Marku* (*Ambrosia peruviana*, often called *altamisa* or *artemisa* in Spanish), a type of ragweed, and romerillo (possibly *Hypericum laricifolium*), as well as *chilka* yield a green dye.[10] Some of these plants are native (e.g., *chilka* and *ñacha*), while others were introduced after the Spanish conquest (e.g., broom, *capulí*, and eucalyptus). The leaves of *wallwa*, or scurf pea (*Psoralea* spp.), were "formerly used in the dye industry" (Yacovleff and Herrera 1935: [vol. 4] 87). Alfalfa (*Medicago sativa*) and *killu yuyu* are used as mordants for other natural dyes in Saraguro (information from Meisch). *Payku* (*Chenopodium ambrosioides*) is a medicinal plant (Yacovleff and Herrera 1935: [vol. 4] 39–40; Gade 1975: 156), as is verbena (Yacovleff and Herrera 1934: [vol. 3] 280). *Marku* and *chilka* also have medicinal uses. *Ashnak yura* (*Cassia hirsuta*, so identified by Soukup 1971) obviously has a potent smell but no other known purpose.

The other plants listed cannot at present be identified, and the transcriptions may contain errors, but we include them for future reference. It is not really necessary to have a lot of different plants to produce the bacterial action. Nevertheless, adding these ingredients does not inhibit the dyeing process, and people naturally tend to repeat whatever works.

All the dyers add *Furcraea* or maguey leaves. Don Alejandro cooks both *Furcraea* and maguey in his lye together with the other plants. Don Alejandro's daughter told us he might also add fermented urine. Don Carlos boils six very ripe leaves ("pencas muy maduras") until soft after the other plants have cooked for three hours. Jaramillo's recipe adds the juice of three large maguey leaves after cooking the other plants.

After the lye is cooked, the plants are removed and the liquid is transferred back to a clay pot. The dye is added and allowed to ferment for two (don Carlos), three (Jaramillo; Quinatoa 1982), or eight (don Alejandro interview, 1989) days. Don Alejandro heats the bath when the dye is added (interview) and may fire the oven each night (Quinatoa 1982).

Don Alejandro heats the dye before submerging the wool. The wool is left in for a half hour before being hung up to dry (interview). Alternatively, the hot liquid is beaten with thin sticks, then the yarns or fibers are dipped briefly (Quinatoa 1982). Don Alejandro's daughter said that the bath was heated the night before but the dye was used cold. These variations are all plausible and may represent experimentation on the dyer's part. He innovated as a weaver, too (see Chapter 6). Jaramillo notes that the dye bath is heated to no more than 70 degrees Celsius (158 degrees Fahrenheit) and the fleece is immersed for ten minutes. If the color is not satisfactory, more indigo is added and the process is repeated. He also notes the terminology of *bocar* for each dipping, as in Saraguro. Don Carlos dips his fleece or yarn only briefly ("un momento"). After dyeing, the fleece is washed in cold water and dried.

Cotton

As noted, indigo is one of the few natural dyes that will dye cotton using the same procedures as wool, but it requires more dippings to obtain a good color (Liles 1990: 79).

RUMIPAMBA, COTOPAXI PROVINCE

In Rumipamba, near Salcedo, as recorded by Laura Miller in 1988, the indigo used for bound-warp-resist dyed shawls (see Chapter 3) is purchased in Ambato. The method of making lye is similar to that already described. The indigo pot is inside a small shed with an adobe oven-like structure built around it — presumably to keep the dye pot insulated and at a constant temperature for fermentation (Fig. 9.5). This setup is very similar to that used in Otavalo.

The dye is stirred before dipping the skeins. The woman dips the warp while the man squeezes the excess dye back into the pot. After each dipping, the warp is aired to oxidize the dye, and the couple continues opening the untied portions with their thumbs so that the dye will penetrate. The dipping is done six times.

9.5 Indigo dye pot set in the fermenting oven. Rumipamba, Cotopaxi province. Photo by Lynn A. Meisch, 1988.

BULCAY, AZUAY PROVINCE

Indigo was traditionally used to dye the cotton bound-warp-resist patterned shawls made in the Cuenca area (see Chapter 3), and was still being used when Lynn Meisch and Dennis Penley were recording this production in the late 1970s. By 1985–1986, when Laura Miller was there, however, most people were using black synthetic dye instead.

Arcelia Pérez of Bulcay demonstrated the process for Meisch in 1981. Lye is made by pouring water through a mixture of earth and ashes in a pot with a hole in the bottom (Fig. 9.6). In a separate pot, some chopped-up *altamisa* (for possible identification, see note 9) is soaked in urine. *Altamisa* is also used with indigo, as reported in the Peruvian *obraje* document (Anonymous 1923). The crumbled indigo is put in the dye pot, the lye is added, then the *altamisa* and urine, and, finally, some chopped *Furcraea*. The mixture is beaten, covered, and left to ferment for eight to fifteen days and yields enough dye for four shawls. The knee-high pot sits on the ground; no special structure is used, and the dye is not heated (Fig. 9.6).

Dennis Penley's account provides some quantities (1988: 5–6, 67–69, 107–108, 141–143). For each shawl, 22 grams (less than an ounce) of indigo are needed. The bath is made from seven liters of water filtered through an almud (4.625 liters) of ash, forming lye, plus one liter of urine and foam from two maguey leaves.[11] The ash is soaked in a clay pot for three days, and ash from bread bakers' ovens is preferred. After soaking, the ashes are put in a pot with two holes in the bottom and placed over the mouth of a larger clay pot. The top pot is then filled with the water, which filters through the ashes, forming lye.

The indigo cakes are broken up in a stone mortar and added to the lye along with the urine and maguey foam. The mixture is beaten and then left

9.6 Pot with ash (*left*) and cold indigo dye bath (*right*). Fajardo-Pérez family, Bulcay, Azuay province. Slide by Lynn A. Meisch, 1979.

to ferment for two weeks until a butterlike substance forms on the surface. The bath is beaten again before dyeing the shawl warp. The warp is wetted in hot water and beaten with a stick before being immersed in the cold dye for a minute or so as the dyer continues to stir the bath. The warp is removed and wrung out, then returned to the dye and stirred again, a process that may be repeated up to twelve times if a dark color is wanted. The dye can be reused by adding two more cups of urine and letting it ferment some more. The recipe is similar to that recorded by Meisch, except for the additives.

Cochineal in Salasaca, Tungurahua Province

Introduction

ANN P. ROWE Cochineal is one of the best red natural dyes known. It is a scale insect (*Dactylopius* spp., family Coccidae) parasitic on the prickly-pear cactus (*Opuntia* and *Nopalea* spp., family Cactaceae) and is native to the Americas (Fig. 9.7). The females, which spend most of their lives with their mouthparts embedded in the cactus and eating, produce the dye, carminic acid. Insects yielding carminic acid exist both in the wild and under cultivation. The most commonly cultivated species (*Dactylopius coccus*) is larger and produces a higher concentration of dye than the others.

Cochineal was extensively cultivated in southern Mexico, both in the pre-Hispanic and the colonial periods. Mexican cochineal was a major export to Spain during the colonial period, since it produces considerably more color by weight than the insect dyes previously used in Europe (Gerber 1978: 14, 21). In the nineteenth century, the main producing area was Guatemala. Attempts to export cochineal production to the Old World were made after the collapse of the Spanish empire, and some cochineal dye is still produced in the Canary Islands.

Because of the relatively elaborate cultivation techniques used in Central America, some authors have assumed that domestication has taken place (Donkin 1977: 14).[12] Nevertheless, no genetic alteration seems to have occurred, since botanist and dye researcher Kay Antúnez de Mayolo collected *Dactylopius coccus* both under cultivation and in the wild in eight departments of highland Peru at elevations ranging from 1,300 to 2,910 meters (4,264–9,545 feet) (Pérez and Kosztarab 1992: 48). *D. coccus* has also been identified in Loja province, Ecuador (Pérez and Kosztarab 1992: 47). Less elaborate methods of cultivation were and are used in South America, perhaps because of more suitable environmental conditions, but the Spanish did not develop a

9.7 *Opuntia* cactus infested with cochineal insects. Salasaca, Tungurahua province. Slide by Laura M. Miller, 1984.

major industry there. Interestingly, *D. coccus* is considered, evolutionarily, the most primitive of the *Dactylopius* species (Pérez and Kosztarab 1992: 78–79).

Among the other species, *Dactylopius confusus* has also been reported from Peru (Yacovleff and Muelle 1934: 158; Fester 1954: 241; Pérez and Kosztarab 1992: 56) and *Dactylopius ceylonicus* from the Cochabamba area of Bolivia (Pérez and Kosztarab 1992: 43). The others have so far been identified only in lowland South America. Of the eight currently accepted wild species of cochineal, three (including *D. confusus*) are common in Mexico and North America, but the others have been identified mainly in South America, three only in Argentina.

The location of the largest cochineal production in Peru, as described in early colonial sources and today, is the Ayacucho area (Rivera and Chaves [1557], para. 26; 1881: 124; Gade 1972). At least one species of *Opuntia* cactus

(*Opuntia subulata*, formerly *Opuntia exaltata*) existed in South America before the Spanish conquest, although Mexican species have been introduced since (Yacovleff and Herrera 1934: [vol. 3] 317–318; Madsen 1989: 60). Although in the past the dye was exported from South America to a much lesser extent than from Central America, Peru has been exporting cochineal increasingly since 1918 for use in food, pharmaceutical, and cosmetic products, for which it is suited, since it is less toxic than synthetic red dyes (Gade 1972, 1979). The Inca term for the dye was *maknu* (Monzón [1586]: para. 28; 1881: 193; González Holguín 1608, 1952: 224).

In Peruvian textiles, however, the earliest red yarns that have been analyzed, dating to the cotton preceramic stage (ca. 2000 BC) at La Galgada, were found to have been dyed with the roots of *Relbunium* sp., from the same family, Rubiaceae, as madder (Grieder et al. 1988: 180–181). The genus name comes from the Mapuche word for the plant, *relbun*. The same dye was used on painted cotton textiles from Ocucaje and for red camelid hair in Ocucaje, Paracas, and early Nasca textiles, dating circa 350–50 BC.[13] The dye produces a stronger red on camelid hair than on cotton, and, indeed, the Paracas textiles have the brightest and fastest reds in pre-Hispanic Peru. Several species of *Relbunium* exist, some found in the highlands while others apparently were available on the coast.

Cochineal, however, is much easier to use than *relbun*. You just scrape the bugs off the cactus lobes instead of having to dig up long, narrow roots. Therefore, it is the usual source of red in the majority of later Peruvian pre-Hispanic camelid hair textiles. Among the earliest cochineal-dyed yarns with known archaeological context are those from the Nasca 7 burial excavated by Lothrop and Mahler at Chaviña on the south coast dating to around AD 450–650 (Young 1957: 53–54). It may not be coincidental that the beginning of widespread use of cochineal appears to coincide with the expansion of the Huari empire, beginning around AD 750, since Huari is in the Ayacucho area, where the insect is known to have been cultivated in later times. Some contacts with the Ayacucho area are also attested by aspects of Nasca 7 iconography on ceramics (Menzel 1964: 29).

Cochineal was sometimes also used on cotton in pre-Hispanic Peru, but these yarns are usually pinkish or brownish rather than red (Young 1957: 53; Wouters and Verhecken 1989: 196). Early colonial sources suggest that cochineal may have been used to dye cotton in ancient Mesoamerica, where animal fibers were absent (Donkin 1977: 20). Since preservation is poor, however, it is difficult to confirm this, and historical examples have so far not been identified either. Although purple can be obtained with cochineal alone on animal fibers, it is usually not considered to be a particularly fast color, and most of the purples analyzed to date from pre-Hispanic Peruvian textiles contain both a red dye and indigo (Fester 1954; Saltzman 1978). In any event, purple is not a common color in surviving Peruvian fabrics.

Evidence of cochineal in Ecuador exists for the colonial period. In the governor's report for Cuenca in 1582, cochineal is mentioned as produced in small quantities in the warm valley of Cañaribamba (Pablos [1582]: para. 25; 1897: 160). Cochineal is also mentioned in the governor's report for Loja (Salinas Loyola [1571-1572]: para. 37; 1897: 200). During the eighteenth century, cochineal was produced in Loja as well as, to a lesser extent, in the Ambato area (Juan and Ulloa 1748 [vol. 1], lib. VI, cap. II, para. 787, pp. 441-442; other sources cited in Donkin 1977: 59-60). Some cochineal production is also documented in the nineteenth century in Ambato (Stevenson 1825 [vol. 2]: 272-273; Hassaurek 1867: 69-70; 1967: 39; other sources cited in Jaramillo 1988a: 49-50). The historical importance of cochineal in the Ambato area may account for the Salasacas' continuing use of this dye in modern times.

Both Juan and Ulloa and the nineteenth-century accounts state that in Ecuador little care is taken for the cultivation of the cactus or the insect, in contrast to the Oaxaca area of Mexico. Stevenson also notes that in the Ambato area the insects were killed by crushing, the procedure still used in Salasaca, whereas in Mexico they were exposed to heat. Stevenson gives a local name for the dye, *pilcay* (his spelling), a term also recorded in the Tarma area of Peru in the eighteenth century (Donkin 1977: 33).

Unfortunately, neither the insect cultivated in Salasaca nor the cactus has been scientifically identified as to species. The white material secreted by the insects is cottony rather than powdery, however, so a normally wild species such as *D. confusus* is likely (Cardon 2003: 494). The most recent literature on Ecuadorian cacti indicates that the indigenous *Opuntia subulata* as well as some other *Opuntia* species occur in the highlands (Madsen 1989: 52-60). Definite identification would therefore be of considerable interest. Edward and Christine Franquemont, who recorded cochineal dyeing in Salasaca in 1983, report that the cochineal cacti are said never to flower. Similar cacti less heavily infested with cochineal are also found in Salasaca, and these plants attain greater stature, flower, and make fruit. The question remains whether these two are the same species.

The Salasaca recipes for cochineal dyeing are interesting in providing possible clues to the use of this dye in pre-Hispanic times. Most modern recipes are based on European dye technology and depend on metallic salt mordants. It appears that the Salasacas have adopted some European techniques, such as the use of an aluminum pot and lemon juice (the citrus fruits are a Spanish import). However, they also continue to use a variety of indigenous plants that appear to contribute to the dyeing process, and it is possible that the European techniques are an addition to rather than a substitution for native technology.

Cochineal will yield different shades, depending on the mordant and the pH of the dye bath. For example, it will give a lilac color on wool without any mordant (Gerber 1978: 45). An alkali treatment (such as stale urine and ashes) or an iron mordant will further modify the color toward purple (Gerber 1978: 3, 32, 34).[14] Contrarily, an acid bath will modify the color toward red, with different acids yielding slightly different shades (Gerber 1978: 45). A tin mordant (discovered in Europe about 1630) and an acid bath will give the most orangey reds.

A mordant is considered necessary to obtain a really bright red and to increase color fastness. Therefore, modern dye manuals advise treating the wool with a mordant before placing it in the dye bath. Alum and iron are known to have been used for this purpose with pre-Hispanic Peruvian textiles and are also common in European dyeing. Although alum in mineral form is known in Salasaca, it is not readily available or used in most of the dye recipes recorded. Instead, the Salasacas use a variety of plant materials. These plants were collected and identified by Christine Franquemont in 1983, and she has generously shared her information with us. Her plants are deposited in the herbarium of the Field Museum of Natural History in Chicago. Unfortunately, however, they have not yet been analyzed for their chemical composition, so we can only guess what they are contributing to the process.

The recipes suggest that some of the plants may contain enough tannin, aluminum, or iron to act as a mordant.[15] Others probably contain alkalis or acids. Still others are dyes in their own right. For example, *puma maki* (Q., puma hand), identified as *Oreopanax mucronulatus* Harms. (family Araliaceae), used for purple dyeing, may contain a mineral and/or alkali.[16] *Chanjilwa*, not collected by Franquemont but identified by Jaramillo (1988a: 54) as *Cassia tomentosa* (family Leguminosae), used for both purple and red, may contain tannins, since other species of *Cassia* do.

Kulkas (Q.) (Fig. 9.8), identified as *Miconia crocea* (Desv.) Naud (family Melastomataceae), and used in red dyeing, is a yellow dye and may also contain acid.[17] Other plants of the same family contain oxalic acid, and another member of the genus is used in cochineal dyeing in Mexico (Ross 1986: 67, 70). *Ñacha* (Fig. 9.9), identified as *Bidens andicola* H.B.K. (family Asteraceae), used in red dyeing, is also a yellow dye (as noted above), which would obviously brighten the red.[18] Some species of *Bidens* also contain tannins.

Although Franquemont did not record a native name for it, she did collect a plant with a red root in Salasaca, identified as *Relbunium croceum* (Ruiz & Pavon) K. Schum, family Rubiaceae, which, as noted, is a red dye com-

9.8 Putting *kulkas* leaves into a gourd bowl for dyeing cochineal red. Salasaca, Tungurahua province. Slide by Laura M. Miller, 1983.

9.9 *Ñachaj* flowers used in dyeing red with cochineal. They produce a yellow dye. Salasaca, Tungurahua province. Slide by Laura M. Miller, 1984.

parable in quality to cochineal. Shown Laura Miller's slide of *puka angu* (Q., red root), Franquemont agreed that it looked like *Relbunium* (personal communication 1999).[19] It is indeed interesting that the Salasacas use *relbun* and cochineal together, for both red and purple dyeing, although knowledge of using *relbun* alone seems to have been lost.

Dyeing Procedures

LAURA M. MILLER   Salasaca is the only place known in Ecuador where cochineal was used for dyeing in the 1980s. Rich reds and purples, characteristic colors of Salasaca shawls (*bayetas*), come from this ancient source (Pl. 6). Cochineal use is declining with the increasing availability of synthetic dyes. It is considered pesky and difficult to use, and the ease of dyeing with synthetics is appealing. People cite the increasing cost of cochineal as another reason for the decline. In 1984 one cake of dye cost 1,200 sucres, or the equivalent of $12.00. Many Salasacas know how to dye using cochineal, however, and garments dyed with it are highly prized. Both the plant and the insect are called *cochinillo*. Salasacas refer to the insect as a worm, *kuru* (Q.) or *gusano* (S.).

A great deal of cochineal dyeing takes place before the Capitán festival in October as well as before Difuntos (the Day of the Dead) and in May and June, before Corpus Christi, in part because people want to have freshly dyed pieces to wear to these festivals. Dyeing is done after the cloth has been woven. Salasaca shawls are woven on the treadle loom with wool yarns (see Chapter 8) but have a few stripes of cotton yarn. These cotton yarns do not absorb the dye and remain a contrasting white color in the finished shawl (Pl. 6).

Families that dye usually have a small plot, some ten to twenty meters (yards) square, near the house, with cacti on which the cochineal live. The plants are fertilized but not watered.[20] They are propagated by taking an infected lobe from the base of a cactus and planting it in a hole about one-fourth as deep as the lobe is long.

Cochineal is harvested from the plants at least every four months, but people are careful never to clean off the cactus completely. They wait to harvest until a sufficient number of insects will be left to ensure further crops. They use a stick or pampas grass stem spindle to scrape the insects off the plant into a bowl and then mash them with a rock. People are always careful with cochineal for fear of the cactus thorns that are often mixed in. The red mash is formed into a cake, called a *tanda* (Q., bread) (Cardon 2003: 487, fig. 16). If the cakes are not used immediately, they may be stored.

I found that interview accounts of dyeing differed slightly from my observations during dye sessions, and also that the dye sessions I recorded differed from each other. It appears that the exact methods differ from one dyer to another. Although in Salasaca women are dyers, I also interviewed a fifty-year-old man, Narciso Jérez Comasanta, who explained to me his wife's procedures. In addition, some information collected by Christine and Edward Franquemont in 1983 is included here.

DYEING PURPLE

Señor Jérez said that the first step in dyeing a *bayeta* purple is to boil the piece with *puma maki* leaves for some twenty minutes, after which the leaves are taken out and discarded. *Puma maki* can be used fresh or dried. Señor Jérez said that "*puma maki* makes it so that the dye will come out strong, like a pharmaceutical liquid; it makes the dye faster." It thus is considered to act like a mordant. The method described by Jaramillo (1988a: 53–54; 1989) also calls for a pretreatment of *puma maki* leaves, and one of the Franquemonts' informants, Rudy Masaquiza, mentioned this usage as well.[21] Usually an aluminum pot is used, which would also contribute to mordanting.

Next, the cochineal is added to the dye bath. Dyers believe that it is best to let the cochineal cakes soak overnight. The cake is broken up and allowed to dissolve. Many dyers who do not have their own cochineal lament that those who prepare the cochineal put dirt in the cake to make it larger and heavier. The juice of twenty lemons is added along with the dye. In several sessions I attended, slightly rotten lemons were used. These lemons are cheaper, and rotting may increase the efficacy of the acid.

After the cochineal is added, the cloth is put back in and kept moving. Señor Jérez said that it should be kept moving so that the cloth will not burn (Jaramillo says the reason is so that the dye will be evenly distributed). Señor Jérez said that the piece should be left in the simmering dye bath for six or seven hours, until there is no color left in the bath.

When the dye bath is exhausted, the cloth is removed and rubbed with a mixture of ashes and a man's stale urine. Señor Jérez said that the urine of a woman would not be effective. Two pounds of ashes and a liter and a half of urine (*miado* S.) should be used. The urine must be allowed to sit for at least eight days, or up to half a year. The cloth is rubbed in this mixture for five to ten minutes and then washed with water but no soap. After two or three months, the textile can be washed with soap, but until then it is still considered *tierna* (S.), tender or young. Another woman stated that if she were displeased with a dye job, she would take it to someone who had urine and ashes and that this treatment would fix the color.

I later attended a dye session in which a shawl was dyed purple by Manuel Pilla and Francisca Colquis Chango. They did not use *puma maki* but, rather, a reddish-colored root, *puka angu* (*relbun*, as noted above), and a yellow flower, *chanjilwa*. Two cakes of cochineal were dissolved in water while the *chanjilwa* and *puka angu* were put in a large pot to boil. Five roots of *puka angu* were used, and several handfuls of flowers were added.

Señora Colquis mashed the cochineal with her hands, sometimes adding warm water from the dye bath to hasten the dissolving. The cochineal was their own and had been saved for two years. Señor Pilla said that six months is the minimum time that cochineal should be dried and stored, since it improves with aging.

The plants boiled for twenty minutes, and then the wetted cloth was placed in the dye bath. After ten minutes, the cloth was lifted out and the bowl of dissolved cochineal was added. None of the other plants were removed. The couple both began to squeeze twenty slightly rotten lemons. After the lemon juice and cochineal were added to the dye bath, the cloth was replaced and the fire stoked. The bath was kept boiling for an hour and then the pot was removed from the fire. The cloth was rinsed twice in water. By the third rinse, very little color came out. The fabric was a deep, dark purple.

I attended another dye session in 1988, with Margarita Masaquiza Chango, in which none of the above-mentioned plants were used (Fig. 9.10). Only cochineal and lemon were used, yielding a rich, dark purple (Pl. 6); this shawl has not been worn. One man, identified only as Luis, also told the Franquemonts that purple was achieved only by adding lemon.

The depth of the purple color obtained can fade with time and multiple washings, as suggested by the lavender-colored rebozo also illustrated in Plate 6. Perhaps this piece was dyed without using native plants.

DYEING RED

Red is considered more complex and requires more mordanting plants. According to Señor Jérez, the cloth is first boiled with *ñacha* flowers (Fig. 9.9), *kulkas* leaves (Fig. 9.8), and the root *puka angu*. *Ñacha* or *ñachaj* (the Salasaca pronunciation) is a small bright yellow flower that grows in many places in Salasaca and is common in the highlands. *Kulkas* leaves are collected on Cerro Teligote, a prominent nearby hill. They have a pleasant citrusy smell.

I observed a session in which Dominga Sailema dyed a shawl red, using a method similar to that described by Señor Jérez. Her son stripped *kulkas* leaves from the branches. She boiled these leaves, *ñachaj* flowers, and the cloth in a large pot. Her daughter stirred this solution at all times. I squeezed slightly rotten lemons for the dye bath.

After an hour in the initial bath of plants, the cloth was lifted out and the plants discarded. The cloth had turned yellow from the dye in the plants.

9.10 Dyeing with cochineal. Margarita Masaquiza Chango, Salasaca, Tungurahua province. Photo by Laura M. Miller, 1988.

She then added dissolved cochineal along with lemon juice and a thumb-sized chunk of alum. The cloth was allowed to simmer in this dye bath for an hour. She was not entirely satisfied with the resulting color, however, and added some synthetic dye as well.

She stated that she uses lemon only to dye red. If she did not use lemon, there would be no color. When she wants purple, she uses the treatment described above with ashes and urine.

The dye session recorded by the Franquemonts, with María Dolores Sailema as the dyer, was similar to the one I observed, but no alum was used. The procedure Jaramillo describes (1988a: 54–55) is, again, similar, but *chanjilwa* and *puka angu* were used in addition to *kulkas* and *ñachaj* as mordants.

DYEING BLACK

Synthetic dyes are currently used for ponchos. One woman told me that it was best to use the exhausted dye liquor from a cochineal dyeing session as a base and then add black synthetic dye to dye ponchos. Before the advent of synthetic dyes, ponchos were made of dark-colored wool. Señor Jérez told me of a substance called *tinta morocho* that his father used in dyeing ponchos. It came from overseas and was purchased in Quito, either as a powder or in cakes, and was expensive. Ponchos were first boiled with *puma maki* and *kulkas* and then with *tinta morocho*. Afterward, they were treated with ashes and urine, as in the cochineal process described above. *Tinta morocho* is identified as alum by Costales and Costales (1959: 43), but alum is a mordant and not a dye, so either the identification is incorrect for the substance used in Salasaca or the dye itself is missing from this recipe.

DYEING LORE

Dyeing is surrounded by mystery and many beliefs. Both *puma maki* and *kulkas* leaves are collected on Cerro Teligote every year before the Capitán festival in October. Salasacas say that young people go up to Teligote with the pretext of getting the plants for dyeing but actually go up there to make love. Teligote is a forbidding and magical place for Salasacas. It is supposed to have an enchanted lake. It is believed that if one falls asleep on Teligote, one will awaken crazy, mute, or crippled.

Cochineal insects are thought to have a capricious nature. One woman told me, when beginning the dye session, "We don't know what color will come out; only they, the cochineal bugs, know." The insects are also thought to be jealous. During one of my visits, a Salasaca woman had washed some purple and red cochineal-dyed shawls. These pieces had been drying outside, and when it started to rain she moved them inside the house. She was careful to hang the purple pieces on one side of the room and the red ones on the other side. She explained: "The cochineal bugs will fight among themselves if they are not separated."

Dyers believe it is very important to keep strangers out of the way when dyeing, since the cochineal will become jealous and the stranger's footprints will appear on the shawl as spots. Even a stray chicken can cause footprint spots. To protect against these spots, nettles (*ortiga*) are sometimes hung in the doorway. Salasacas also believe that all those who are to be present during a dye session must be there from the very beginning or the piece will be ruined.

The phase of the moon is very important when gathering cochineal. One woman stated that one must harvest when the moon appears very early in the day. Señor Jérez said that it is best to collect cochineal when there is a new moon, so that the plant will not be damaged. Likewise, he said, a tree should be cut for timber when there is a new moon or the beams will quickly become termite ridden. His nineteen-year-old son said that he would harvest at any time, without regard for the phase of the moon.

Dyeing is a guarded art. It is difficult to get people to teach the skill. One Salasaca woman brought a lunch of roast guinea pig to persuade a dyer to teach her. Another person told me that one had to take a guinea pig, bananas, and oranges to persuade someone to teach dyeing, as well as supply the cloth and the cochineal.

Conclusions

ANN P. ROWE

Of course, one of the fascinations of studying the surviving technological tradition of the indigenous people of the Andes is its inherent conservatism. Basic techniques such as hand-supported spinning and backstrap-loom weaving have survived largely intact from pre-Hispanic times and are therefore a window on the past. Although, regrettably, few pre-Hispanic textiles have survived in the Ecuadorian highlands, so that fewer links can be securely made than would otherwise be the case, some technologies we recorded are unquestionably indigenous. To those noted above can presumably be added looping with *chawar*, dyeing cochineal with the help of local plants, and baskets of 2/2 twill interlacing. There are undoubtedly others.

One of the most prestigious techniques found in pre-Hispanic Peruvian textiles is the use of discontinuous warp as well as weft yarns to form designs. That is, the warp yarns do not pass from one end of the cloth to the other but, instead, turn back at the edge of each color area. This technique seems to have died out at a relatively early date in the colonial period, except for simple fabrics with a single horizontal join still woven in the Cuzco area (although in one community more elaborate designs have been revived). These joins are usually dovetailed, although in the ancient cloths they are sometimes interlocked. The various methods of handling the dovetailed join in Ecuadorian backstrap-loom weaving nevertheless provide possible clues as to how these ancient fabrics may have been woven.

While there appears to be significant Inca influence in indigenous Ecuadorian costume, it is interesting that, except in the area of complementary-warp weave belts and hair bands, there seems to be relatively little Inca influence technologically. Evidence of Inca textile structures and techniques, from both early colonial written records and archaeological finds (A. Rowe 1997), enables us to conclude confidently that the basic aboriginal Ecuadorian spinning and weaving techniques persisted through the Inca occupation.

The exception, of complementary-warp weave belts brought by both Inca and provincial Inca migrating peoples, is, however, very interesting indeed.

The Spanish conquest had a greater impact, although, in many cases, the new technologies only supplemented and did not replace aboriginal methods. Treadle-loom weaving, tailoring, raising nap with teasels, fulling, and felt hat making are the obvious additions, along with carding wool and the walking wheel in certain areas. More surprising, as well as more interesting, is the degree to which aboriginal and Spanish textile ideas seem to have become integrated. In techniques like *chawar* processing and indigo dyeing, it can be difficult to determine which aspects are aboriginal and which are the result of Spanish influence. Here, not having more archaeological or colonial-period evidence is a major handicap. Nevertheless, some speculations are possible.

The textile forms that occur in several areas, including bound-warp-resist dyed blankets and ponchos with chevron or stepped-diamond designs, bound-warp-resist dyed shawls with knotted warp fringe, and supplementary-warp patterned belts in particular, seem likely to postdate the extreme political fragmentation characteristic of the period before the Inca conquest. Again, neither these forms nor the techniques used to produce them are Inca. The fact that these textiles are woven on indigenous looms does not prove that they are pre-Hispanic in other details. The knotted warp fringe on the shawls and the hole-and-slot heddle used to make poncho fringe can be identified as European influence, but the source of the other features is obscure. Presumably, we have here something akin to the spread of the poncho itself, a development primarily within the indigenous tradition but taking place in a colonial context.

The many diverse methods recorded to produce the same finished effect in these cases suggest that weavers were not learning from each other but were independently working out how to produce a given effect. Rather than being the result of migration, as seems to be the case with the complementary-warp patterned belts, the finished products seem to have been transported from one area to another, perhaps by trade, and then copied. Laura Miller (1986 [with Proyecto Juvenil de Historia Oral], 1989, 1991) has documented such a scenario for the elaborate warp-resist-dyed shawls of Azuay, and something similar seems likely to be true of some of the other forms as well.

The variety in the methods used to weave a simple structure like plain weave with supplementary-warp patterning or plain weave with bound-warp-resist dyeing also cautions us that there is a limit to what one can assume about the technique of producing something without field documentation. Without such field documentation, the kind of historical reconstruction we are making here would not be possible.

Apart from any particular historical interest, however, one factor that emerges from the data presented here is the amount of technical innovation and variety. This technical variety is far beyond what one might expect from the amount of plain fabric used in indigenous costumes and the similarity of both structures and designs in the patterned textiles of different areas. Technical innovation is apparent not only in the tradition as a whole, for example, as represented by all the different ways of weaving patterns with a supplementary warp, but also in the work of individual weavers we recorded. Although many of these consciously innovating weavers are from the Otavalo area, as one might expect from the general Otavalo adaptability to textile markets, we found creative weavers elsewhere as well, such as Santiago Sula Sisa in Nitiluisa. Such technical innovation is a common characteristic of artists within the European definition, and one can begin to see how textiles attained the status of a major art form in many places and times within the Andean world.

Notes

Introduction: The Land and the People

1. A convenient English summary of the various Spanish-language sources on Andean geography is provided by Salomon (1986: chap. 1).

2. This historical account of the Incas in Ecuador is based on J. Rowe Ms.

1: Plain Weave on the Backstrap Loom

1. The information includes not only my own observations but also those of Earthwatch volunteers. The information on weaving in Chicticay, Azuay province (as practiced by Celina Calle), and in the Saraguro area is from films taken by Lynn Meisch in 1977–1979. A complete published description of poncho weaving in the Otavalo area (village unspecified) was also consulted (Redwood 1973).

2. Recorded by an Earthwatch team consisting of Maritza Mosquera, Helen Daly, Roberta Siegal, and Leonard Evelev, together with María Aguí and Gail Felzein.

3. The other weaver was reported by Earthwatch volunteers Kathleen Jahnke and Louise Taylor in Riobamba. He said he was originally from Latacunga but had lived in Riobamba for fifty years.

4. This weaver, Luis Martínez, was recorded by Breenan Conterón and Earthwatch teams consisting of Maritza Mosquera, Betty Davenport, Carol Mitz, and Norma Jean Nelson.

5. An Earthwatch team also recorded the use of two needles to finish a poncho half in Guasuntos, on the Pan-American Highway southeast of Alausí, in southern Chimborazo, in 1989. The team consisted of Julio Chérrez S., Jacquelyn Engle, Sandra Baker, and Patricia Meloy.

6. The orthography follows Harrison 1989. Cordero's dictionary of Ecuadorian Quichua (1967) was also consulted. It should perhaps also be noted that the terms were collected by a variety of people, most of whom are not professional linguists.

7. The following information is taken from reports by Breenan Conterón and Earthwatch volunteers Darby C. Raiser and Carol Holmes, and the accompanying photographs of William H. Holmes.

8. This text is based on the Earthwatch team report and photographs made by volunteers Eileen Hallman, Liz Drey, and Jennifer Lantz, July 6, 1989. The team was led by Lynn Meisch.

2: Warp-Resist-Patterned Wool Ponchos and Blankets

1. This section was written by Ann Rowe, based on notes and photographs by Laura Miller.

3: Warp-Resist-Patterned Cotton Shawls and Ponchos

1. Pfyffer (2002: 206) reports that only two families were left in 1997, in Rumipamba de Navas and Cuatro Esquinas.

2. According to the English cotton yarn numbering system, 30 is the number of 840 yard lengths of unplied yarn per pound and 2 means a 2-ply yarn.

3. When asked why she wove, she said that she could earn more as a weaver. She had a partnership with her sister up the road to supply the warps. Her husband had left and she liked being different.

4. This section combines field observations by Laura Miller with information from a videotape taken by Earthwatch volunteer Judith Kelly.

4: Belts with Supplementary-Warp Patterning

1. This section was written by Ann Rowe based on films made by Lynn Meisch.

2. This section was written by Ann Rowe, based on photographs by Lynn Meisch, notes by Earthwatch volunteers Lorraine O'Neal and Emily Marsland, and a loom collected by Meisch for The Textile Museum (The Textile Museum 1988.22.13).

3. This section is based on a report for July 14, 1988, by Breenan Conterón and photographs by Earthwatch volunteers Carol Mitz and Leonard Evelev. Unfortunately, there is no description or photograph of the operation of the underneath heddle rod.

4. Initial reconnaissance of the area was by Mrill Ingram and Ellen Hanley on June 8, 1988. The reports for June 10 were written by Pam Lipscomb and Sara Laas, and the photographs were taken by Bonnie O'Connor. The report on June 13 was written by Breenan Conterón, and the photographs were taken by George Crockett. The town visited on the tenth is identified as Collana and on the thirteenth identified by different project members as Collage, Pilaló, or Quilajaló. However, these places are all in the same general area. The weavers are identified consistently as the Toapanta family.

5. We were introduced to Antonio Cando Camuendo through the courtesy of Humberto Muenala Maldonaldo of Quinchuquí, a friend of Lynn Meisch's.

6. Earthwatch teams to Ovalos were led by Leslie Grace. I recorded the weaving, but a videotape made by Earthwatch volunteer Elizabeth Drey was also helpful.

7. Jaramillo (1988a) reports that weaving had practically died out in the com-

munity and that people from Cotopaxi and Tungurahua provinces were brought in as teachers. No influence from these areas was apparent to us, however, either in the techniques used or in the finished belts.

8. Ramón Paucar was recorded by Earthwatch teams consisting of Louise Taylor, Jean Fuley, Jean Hayden, and Kathleen Jahnke, and of Helen Healy, Edward Healy, Jean Hayden, and Robyn Potter.

9. The astute reader will notice that, because of the temporary shed stick, the plain-weave sheds of the borders do not match those of the central section. Also, my notes do not indicate the purpose of the last shed before the temporary shed stick is removed. I regret this incomplete information but I feel confident that I have correctly deduced how the central patterned area is produced.

10. Angélica Asqui Janita was recorded in 1988 by Earthwatch volunteer Judith Kelly.

5: Turn-Banded 2/1 Twill Belts

1. The Earthwatch team reporting on the Guaranda market in July 1988 consisted of Betty Davenport, Carol Mitz, Helen Daly, and Norma Jean Nelson.

2. Edward Franquemont (personal communication, September 2001) suggested considering this weave as a warp-faced plain weave with warp substitution (see A. Rowe 1977: 50–52). But the regularity of the floats is not accounted for if the weave is described in this way, and the color use differs. In fact, there are some other interesting related 2/1 twills, for example, the one called "bound rosepath" in handweavers' jargon, which is a weft-faced, symmetrical, vertical herringbone woven with alternating colors (Larson 2001: 86–93).

3. I am grateful for the help of Breenan Conterón, who found the weaver, acted as intermediary and interpreter, and elicited additional weaving information.

4. This section was written by Ann Rowe, based mainly on Laura Miller's field notes and photographs. Some details were also derived from an example of the belt collected at the session for the Textile Museum (Pl. 2) and from Lynn Meisch's photographs.

6: 2/1 Herringbone Complementary-Warp Weave Ponchos of the Otavalo Area, Imbabura Province

1. In an earlier article (A. Rowe 1985: 64–65), I suggested using the word *reciprocal* instead of *complementary* to describe weaves of this kind. Although the reasons for this suggestion are still good, this revised terminology has not been taken up by others, while *complementary-warp* is now well understood. Also, the term *reciprocal* has, reasonably, been suggested as a term for the automatic mirror-image interworking of threads that occurs in sprang and some braiding techniques (Speiser 1983: 117). Therefore, I have gone back to the terminology I proposed in *Warp-patterned Weaves of the Andes* (1977: chap. 10).

2. In an earlier article (A. Rowe 1985: 67) I did not recognize the relationship of this weave to a 2/1 herringbone. According to Emery (1980: 102–103), the word *stag-*

gered, which I previously used, is thus not appropriate for this structure. It may also be noted that the alignment of the two warp colors to each other differs slightly from that in the diagram in A. Rowe 1985: 66, fig. 18, which was derived from a related weft-faced structure.

3. My notes are not completely clear on whether the initial weft insertion was from the same or opposite sides of the warp. But if you start on opposite sides of the warp, the second shedding sequence starts on the same side of the warp and vice versa, so this is not a critical point.

7: 3/1 Alternating Complementary-Warp Weave Belts

1. I am grateful to Mattiebelle Gittinger for reading an earlier version of this introduction.

2. See A. Rowe 1977, chap. 10, pp. 67ff. (based on Emery 1966: 150).

3. The variation common in southern Peru and Bolivia in which the three-span floats are aligned in alternate pairs (A. Rowe 1977: 83, construction 7) can be called "3/1 alternate-pair complementary-warp weave."

4. In Tarabuco, pickup is done above a temporary "picking cross" formed by inserting a cord under one color near the fell and a stick under the other color that is pushed up toward the heddles. When the pickup stick gets too full, another, temporary, stick is inserted to hold the picked shed. These details, although of cultural interest in a different context, are undetectable in the finished product and so do not affect the general principles of the technique under discussion. There are other ways of creating such a picking cross, for example, using multiple swords, as in Chinchero, Peru (A. Rowe 1975: 44–45), and it is possible that the Incas might have used such a method rather than that used in Tarabuco.

5. Coastal examples are shown in A. Rowe 1977: 72, fig. 83; 103, fig. 122. This style is found between Acarí and Arequipa (see further discussion in A. Rowe 1992).

6. Examples of such areas include the Vila Vila area of Tarabuco (A. Rowe 1977: 77, fig. 94; Meisch 1986: 273, fig. 23) and Calcha (Medlin 1986: 285, fig. 8). It is likely that in these areas two different methods of weaving complementary warps coexist, as has been documented in the Cuzco area and is apparent in Cacha as well. It is also possible that the dual-lease technique is found in the northern Peruvian highlands. Schjellerup (1980: 29; 1988: 69, fig. 16) has photographed a loom in the highland village of Cochabamba in the department of Amazonas in which the textile being woven has 2/2 horizontal color change, and three heddle rods plus a shed rod are visible.

7. The other examples are University Museum numbers 31527 (which resembles the Inca pattern of zigzags with eyes); 31536a and b, and 31528 (with fretted diamond designs separated by horizontal bars; similar designs, but with 3/1 horizontal color change, occur on other belts in this collection); and 31531 (a triangle and fret design).

8. The poncho (lacking side seams) has four loom panels, with the center two solid red and the side ones patterned as shown. There is a short corded fringe on each end, but the area across the shoulders is broken.

9. See also J. H. Rowe 1946: 190 and map 3, for location and additional references. Garcilaso de la Vega (1609: lib. I, cap. XX; 1966 [vol. I]: 52) also mentions this group. It was in a conversation with John Rowe in which he was telling me about some

research he was doing and mentioned the Kawiñas that I realized the likely source of the name of the belts in Chimborazo.

10. Unfortunately, the description of the color change in Cañari belts given in A. Rowe 1977: 73 and fig. 86 there, is in error. Knowing the technique is a definite advantage in analyzing this structure.

11. Miller recorded the basic weaving technique, while Rowe is responsible for the descriptions of the technical variations, the way the selvedges are set up and woven, and the horizontal color changes, as well as editing Miller's text.

12. Rowe set up and wove a very coarse warp in order to verify what she was seeing.

8: Treadle-Loom Weaving

1. For a detailed explanation of the countermarch loom mechanism, see, e.g., Fannin 1979, pp. 76–84.

2. Information on Cuicuno is from notes by Laura Miller and Earthwatch volunteers Pam Lipscomb and Carol Holmes, as well as photographs by Lynn Meisch.

3. Photographs of the San Roque loom were taken by Earthwatch volunteer Gayle Bauer and of the Natabuela loom by Barbara Borders. The teams were led by Leslie Grace.

4. Information on Pedro Yupanqui and his loom is drawn from photographs taken by Earthwatch volunteer William I. Mead and a report written by Nancy Tucker. The team was led by Carlos Moreno.

5. Information on Luis Martínez is taken from reports written by Breenan Conterón and Earthwatch volunteer Betty Davenport, as well as photographs by Betty Davenport. The teams were led by Maritza Mosquera.

6. Information on Gerardo Chuto is from a report written by Earthwatch volunteer Kirby Hall.

7. The information on the *mestizo* weaving equipment is drawn from photographs taken by Earthwatch volunteer Mary C. Shook and notes written by Cynthia M. Ferguson. The information on the indigenous loom is from notes and sketches by Lari Drendell and photographs by Mary C. Shook.

8. See pl. 8 in the section on Tapisserie de Basse-Lisse des Gobelins in Diderot and d'Alembert (eds.) (plate vol. IX, published 1771), as well as in the later revised edition, *Encyclopédie méthodique ou par ordre de matières*, plate vol. VI (text in *Manufactures, arts et métiers*, vol. II). The more modern low-warp tapestry looms illustrated use a screw. Other treadle looms shown in Diderot have a pair of weights on the warp beam and a ratchet on the cloth beam. Some eighteenth-century North American looms with a tied brake also exist. Norman Kennedy's loom at Colonial Williamsburg has this style of brake on the warp beam and a wooden ratchet on the cloth beam (Slater 1972: cover photo). The loom differs from Ecuadorian examples in other respects, however.

9. This section was written by Ann Rowe, based on field notes by Laura Miller as well as photographs by both Laura Miller and Lynn Meisch. A brief report by Earthwatch volunteer Kirby Hall was also utilized.

10. The following description of the loom and warping process was written by Ann Rowe, based on reports and photographs by 1988 Earthwatch volunteers Betty Davenport and Roberta Siegel, led by Laura Miller. Some photographs by Laura Miller were

also used. The introductory paragraphs and the sections on finishing techniques were written by Laura Miller.

11. *Editor's note:* This method of creating a sinking shed obviously depends on the availability of rubber bands, a comparatively recent invention. Although sinking sheds have been used for patterning on Old World looms for centuries, it is unfortunately unclear where the Ariasucu weavers got this idea.

12. The information on this loom is from notes by Earthwatch volunteer Bee Henisey and photographs by Ken Henisey. The team was led by Kevin O'Brien and also included Jack DeLong. This paragraph and the preceding were written by Ann Rowe.

9: Natural Dyeing Techniques

1. Cobo ([1653] 1956: lib. 5, cap. 31) describes *Indigofera* sp. under its Aztec name, *xiquilitli*. The modern name for *Indigofera suffruticosa* in Peru is *mutuy*, which seems to have been borrowed from the Quechua name of a similar plant in the same family, *Cassia* sp. (Soukup 1971).

2. Cobo (quoted in Yacovleff and Herrera 1935: [vol. 4] 75) describes the dye as coming from the mature (blackened) flowers, while Antúnez de Mayolo says it comes from the fruits. Herrera (1940: 105) says that the flowers are very small and the fruits are black. Antúnez de Mayolo collected the plant but used the stems and flowers to try out the dye. She did not handle it like indigo.

3. Another eighteenth-century document preserved in the Archivo Histórico del Banco Central, Quito, explains indigo processing "in the manner used in Guatemala" (Jaramillo 1984: 47–54; 1988a: 154–163).

4. See also Antúnez de Mayolo 1976: 29, citing procedures recorded by Pedro Weiss and Barbara Mullins for *Cybistax quinquefolia*.

5. Alum is commonly used with other dyes but is not necessary for indigo, but Liles (1990: 83–84) includes alum among ingredients that speed up fermentation.

6. Both Breenan Conterón and Ann Rowe were present at this interview and the text draws from their notes.

7. Jaramillo's first account (1988a: 21; 1991: 83–85) is contradicted in a few particulars by his second account (1990: 28). In these cases, we have assumed that the second account is more accurate.

8. What don Carlos said was "arave," which is a believable Quichua-speaking variant of "agave." This is not, as noted, the usual local term, but don Carlos frequently demonstrates for tourists and might have picked up the word from them. It is also possible he was referring to maguey leaf.

9. These identifications are from Jaramillo 1984, 1988a. He provides no information about the source of his identifications, but he is not a botanist.

10. *Marku* (*altamisa* or *artemisia* in Spanish) is often identified as *Franseria artemisioides* (Yacovleff and Herrera 1934: [vol. 3] 280; Ríos and Borgtoft Pedersen 1991). The identification as *Ambrosia peruviana* is from Antúnez de Mayolo (1976: 38), who is a botanist and who based her identification on specimens collected. It is possible, however, that more than one plant is subsumed under the indigenous name. The identification of *romerillo* is from Jaramillo 1984: 96, and idem, 1988a, citing Spier and

Biederbick 1980. This Spanish word is used for other plants in other countries in Latin America.

11. Penley, unfortunately, gives contradictory amounts of water and ash in different parts of his text: on p. 6 he indicates seven gallons of water and one almud of ash; on pp. 67–68, he indicates two almuds of ash ("[10 *galones*]") and seven liters of water. Since two almuds is equivalent to ten quarts or liters, and not to ten gallons, the seven liters of water seems likely to be correct, but no similar logic can be brought to bear on the question of the amount of ash. The amount of urine is given as "1 *galón*," here translated as one liter, as above. The amount of maguey foam is also given as four cups.

12. I am grateful for discussions with Mary Ballard, of the Smithsonian Institution's Conservation Analytical Laboratory, and with David McJunkin, of the University of Wisconsin, Madison, on this topic. Donkin's otherwise deservedly influential monograph (1977) does not cite the more up-to-date entomological literature (e.g., De Lotto 1974).

13. Although Saltzman (1978, 1986) has reported cochineal in 3 of his 141 samples from Paracas, this finding is so aberrant that the possibility exists that the samples were contaminated with dust from later textiles. For Ocucaje, see also King 1965: 98. Dye analysis of early Nasca textiles has been published by Schweppe (1992: 47, Abb. 6) and De Bolle (1994: 100–101). Although all these authors focus on *Relbunium* spp., some species of the closely related genus *Galium* (also Rubiaceae) evidently also produce a similar dye (Wallert and Boytner 1996: 857; Cardon 2003: 100).

14. Pre-Hispanic Chiribaya-style (far south coast of Peru) examples of purple made with cochineal and an iron mordant are cited in Wallert and Boytner 1996: 857.

15. See, for example, Kajitani 1980: 312. She notes that some plants do contain aluminum compounds and that plants with smaller quantities of aluminum can be used as mordants after being burned into ash. The recipe given by Irmgard Johnson for dyeing wool with cochineal in Mitla, Mexico, includes boiling the yarn in lye (water seeped through wood ash) before dyeing, and unidentified leaves and limes are added to the dye (1977: 242–243).

16. Franquemont specimen #126. Jaramillo (1988a: 52) gives *Oreopanax heterophyllus* or *Oreopanax ecuadorensis* (p. 203). It is not clear if the difference is a matter of botanical disagreement or if more than one species is subsumed under the indigenous name.

17. Franquemont #176. Jaramillo (1988a: 54) gives *Miconia quitensis* Benth.

18. Franquemont #184. Jaramillo (1988a: 54, 127) identifies it as *Bidens humilis* H.B.K. Again, it is possible that both plants are subsumed under the indigenous name.

19. Jaramillo's identification (1988a: 54) of *puka angu*, however, is *Phenax hirtus*, family Urticaceae. Jaramillo does not indicate on what his identification is based. Franquemont's specimen number is 185. Unfortunately, Miller's slide of this plant was lost in the process of commercial duplication, so cannot be reproduced here. The Franquemonts collected another native name for a root used, *chisaj* (Q.). This plant is apparently also of the Rubiaceae family but no definite identification was possible (Franquemont specimen #167).

20. This and the following cultivation information was collected by Christine and Edward Franquemont in 1983.

21. Editor's note: Roquero (2006: 148–149) describes dye recipes from the Caisabanda family in Salasaca. To get purple they use "tiri (*Miconia* sp.), culquis (sin identificar), paja-sijsi (*Poa* sp.), maqui-maqui (*Oreopanax* sp.), y un helecho sin identificar de la familia de las Polipodiáceas." It seems likely that "maqui-maqui" is the same as *puma maki* here. "Culquis" is the same as *kulkas* here. She says *tiri* (leaves are pictured) contains tannins and aluminum. Roquero's book came out after this book was in press, so I was not able to incorporate her information into the text except for this note. She also presents data on indigo dyeing in Otavalo (pp. 180–181).

Glossary

acrylic. Synthetic fiber that mimics the appearance of wool.

alforja (S., from Arabic). Double bag or saddlebags, made by folding each end of a rectangle toward the center. Form introduced by the Spanish during the colonial period but often backstrap-loom woven. *See also* **backstrap loom.**

anaku (Q.). Originally referred to the Inca-style woman's full-length rectangular dress, pinned at the shoulders and belted, but by 1980 the term usually referred to a wrapped skirt (half length) made of a rectangle and secured with a belt. The length and width vary regionally (*see* A. Rowe [ed.] 1998).

back beam. A beam at the back of a treadle loom over which the warp passes on its way from the warp beam to the heddles. Not all looms have a back beam, but it helps the warp feed into the heddles more smoothly. *See* Figs. 8.5, 8.9. *See also* **heddle; treadle loom; warp; warp beam.**

backstrap loom. Indigenous loom in which tension is maintained by a strap passing around the weaver's back or hips. The variable tension created by the weaver leaning forward and backward tends to draw the warp yarns closer together. *See also* **warp.**

bayeta (S.). 1. Coarse treadle-loom woven wool fabric. The equivalent English fabric name is *baize. See also* **treadle loom.** 2. Woman's rectangular shawl pinned on the chest, made from *bayeta* fabric.

boat shuttle. A type of shuttle used in treadle-loom weaving, in which the weft is wound on a spool or bobbin, which is set into a smooth wooden frame such that it can rotate freely. The yarn passes through a hole in the shuttle. As the shuttle skims across the warp, the weft yarn unwinds automatically. *See* Chap. 8. *See also* **shuttle; treadle loom; warp.**

bobbin. A spool on which yarn is wound to prepare it for use in making textiles. In treadle-loom weaving, the bobbin is the spool with weft yarn wound on it that is set into the shuttle. *See also* **shuttle; treadle loom; weft.**

bolsicón (S.). Spanish-style skirt gathered into a waistband, with a series of horizontal pleats near the lower edge.

bound-warp resist dyed. A technique in which groups of selected warp yarns have been partially wrapped and bound and then dyed before weaving, in order to create designs in the finished fabric. *See* Chaps. 2, 3.

braiding.   Technique of interworking a set of elements fixed at one end by deflecting the free ends.

breast beam.   A beam at the front of a treadle loom over which the woven fabric passes on its way to the cloth beam. In this way the cloth beam can be placed out of the weaver's way under the plane of the weaving. *See* Figs. 8.1, 8.2. *See also* **cloth beam; treadle loom.**

camelid.   A member of the camel family. There are four Andean camelids, the domesticated alpaca and llama, and the wild vicuña and guanaco. In pre-Hispanic Peru the hair of all these animals was used, but only a few llamas were present in central Ecuador in the 1980s.

chawar.   Fiber from the leaves of *Furcraea andina*, a plant indigenous to the Andean area. The fiber, which is similar to maguey, is used for binding resist for dyeing, woven food sacks, rope, braided sandal soles, looped bags, etc. The word is of Inca origin. *See also* Miller et al. 2005.

cholo (S.).   Term used in Cañar and Azuay provinces for a group of people intermediate between *mestizos* and whites on the one hand and indigenous people on the other in the social-economic hierarchy, who are distinguishable by their costume. *See also* **mestizo.**

chumbi (Q.).   Cloth belt, usually handwoven. *See* Chaps. 4, 5, 7.

cloth beam.   A beam at the front of a treadle loom on which the woven cloth is wound. It is set underneath the plane of the weaving, out of the way of the weaver's knees. *See* Figs. 8.1, 8.2. *See also* **treadle loom.**

cochineal.   Red or purple dye from an insect (*Dactylopius* spp.), indigenous to the Americas, that is parasitic on the prickly-pear cactus. *See* Chap. 9.

coil rod.   On a backstrap loom, a rod behind the heddle rod around which the warp yarns take a full turn before reaching the back loom bar. It helps keep the warp yarns in alignment when the warp is not tied to the loom bars. In Ecuador it is used in weaving the warp-resist dyed shawls in Azuay province. *See* Chap. 3. *See also* **backstrap loom; heddle rod; warp.**

complementary-warp weave.   A weave with two sets of warp, each of a different color, that are co-equal in the fabric. One set floats regularly on one face of the fabric while the other set floats regularly on the opposite face. *See* Chaps. 6, 7. *See also* **float; warp.**

cross.   *See* **warp cross.**

cross sticks.   Two (or more) sticks located near the back of either a backstrap or a treadle loom that are placed into the same sheds created by the main shedding devices, so they simply hold the main weaving cross and help keep the warp yarns in alignment. *See also* **backstrap loom; shed; shedding device; treadle loom; warp; warp cross.**

counterbalance loom.   Type of treadle loom most common in Ecuador, in which shafts are connected to each other at the top of the loom, in Ecuador usually by cords passing over pulleys. Thus, depressing a treadle causes that shaft to sink, and the connecting shaft to rise, which opens a shed for passage of the weft. *See* Figs. 8.1, 8.10. *See also* **shaft; shed; treadle loom; weft.**

cruzera (S.).   On an Ecuadorian belt loom, a group of two or three cross sticks whose ends are tied together and that are located behind the heddles. It holds one or more warp crosses. Often, the front stick functions as a shed rod. *See also* **heddle; warp; warp cross.**

dovetail cord. A cord around which both ends of the warp pass during weaving, the warp yarns from each direction alternating (*see* Fig. 1.3E; *see also* **warp**). The cord is removed when weaving is complete so that the fabric can be opened out flat.

dovetail stake. Warping stake around which both ends of the warp pass, the warp yarns from each direction alternating. *See* Fig. 1.16. *See also* **warp.**

dual-lease weaving. Term suggested by Franquemont (1991: 285) for the Andean technique of having the same warp yarns controlled by two different shedding devices (or leases), instead of the usual one. It is used particularly for weaving complementary warps. *See* Chap. 7. *See also* **complementary-warp weave; warp.**

dummy warp. The tail end of a treadle-loom woven warp from which the cloth has been cut, but still passing through the heddles and reed. When a new warp is put on the loom, the ends of the dummy warp are tied to it, eliminating the need to thread the new warp through the heddles and reed. *See* Chap. 8, Figs. 8.8, 8.13. *See also* **heddle; reed; treadle loom; warp.**

dye. A liquid containing a color-producing compound capable of being chemically bonded to fibers.

fell. The working edge of a fabric as it is being woven. Each new weft pass is beaten down against the fell. *See also* **weft.**

float. Any portion of a warp or weft element that extends unbound over two or more units of the opposite set on either face of a fabric (Emery 1980: 75). *See also* **warp; weft.**

fulling. Subjecting woven wool cloth to agitation and moisture, causing the fibers to catch on each other so that the cloth shrinks and becomes denser. Technique introduced to Ecuador by the Spanish. *See* Chap. 8.

heading. The weft yarns placed at the beginning of the weaving that are different from the rest of the textile. *See* **weft.**

heddle. On a loom, a loop of thread passing around a warp yarn. A group of heddles is lifted (or lowered) together to open a space (shed) for the weft to be passed in weaving. For plain weave on the backstrap loom, every other warp yarn (those under the shed rod) is enclosed by a heddle, which is usually affixed to a heddle rod. On a simple treadle loom, the heddles are mounted in two or more frames called shafts and all the warp yarns pass through heddles on one or another shaft. *See also* **backstrap loom; heddle rod; shaft; shed; treadle loom; warp; weft.**

heddle rod. On the backstrap loom, a rod holding the heddles, used to lift the warp yarns passing through the heddles. *See also* **backstrap loom; heddle; warp.**

herringbone twill weave. A twill weave in which the direction of the diagonal alignment of the floats changes regularly. The changes may be on either a vertical or a horizontal axis. *See* Chaps. 5 and 6. *See also* **float; twill weave.**

indigo. Blue dye. The dye compound (indigotin) is produced by various plants, of which the most important one native to the Americas is *Indigofera suffruticosa*. The same compound is now also produced synthetically. *See* Chap. 9.

interlacing. A fabric structure in which each element simply passes over or under elements that cross its path (Emery 1980: 62).

interlocked join. A join formed by linking the elements of adjacent areas with each other each time they meet (Emery 1980: 80).

jerga (S.).   Coarse twill-weave wool cloth, woven on the treadle loom. *See also* **treadle loom; twill weave.**

kawiña chumbi (Q.).   Belt woven of wool or acrylic yarns in a complementary-warp weave, mainly in central Chimborazo province, but worn all over the province and in Bolívar province. *See* Pl. 4; Chap. 7.

kushma (Q.).   Man's tunic, sometimes sewn up the sides (as in Saraguro) and sometimes not (as in Cañar).

lease rod.   An alternate term for cross stick. It can be used instead of cross stick if there is only one such rod, instead of the two or more usually implied by cross stick. *See also* **cross sticks.**

liencillo (S.).   Fine plain cotton cloth, handwoven on the treadle loom. *See also* **treadle loom.**

lienzo (S.).   Plain-weave cotton cloth handwoven on the treadle loom.

lliglla (Q.).   Woman's rectangular shawl, worn pinned on the chest. The term is Inca, but is used in only a few areas of Ecuador, including Saraguro and the indigenous parts of Azuay province.

loom.   A device for weaving that contains a means of lifting selected warp yarns above other warp yarns, forming a space called a shed through which the weft is passed. Such devices cannot function unless the warp is under tension, so looms also include a means for stretching the warp. *See also* **shed; warp; weft.**

loom bars.   The end bars of a loom around which the warp yarns pass or to which the warp ends are bound. *See also* **warp.**

macana (S.).   Shawl patterned with bound-warp resist and with knotted fringe on the ends. Term commonly used for the shawls made in Rumipamba in Cotopaxi province, occasionally, for the shawls in Azuay province. *See* Chap. 3.

maguey.   A plant of the genus *Agave* originating in Mexico. In Mexico several closely related species of *Agave* are usually included under this name, but in Ecuador *Agave americana* is generally meant. This species was introduced into Ecuador during the later colonial period. It has long, fleshy leaves from which fibers are extracted for use in bound-warp-resist dyeing, looped bags, etc. *See also* Miller et al. 2005.

mestizo (S.).   Literally, a person of mixed indigenous and European ancestry, but in Ecuador the name implies a social class somewhere between the top and the bottom, rather than race.

mitima (Spanish spelling of the Inca word *mitma*).   People moved by the Incas from previously conquered areas to newly conquered ones as part of the pacification process.

mordant.   A substance (frequently a metallic oxide) that helps create a chemical bond between the dye and the fiber in the dyeing process.

obraje (S.).   Spanish-run factories common during the colonial period that produced textile yardage on Spanish-style equipment.

paño (S.).   1. Wool treadle-loom or machine-woven fabric, finer than *bayeta. See also* **bayeta; treadle loom.** 2. Rectangular shawl with bound-warp-resist patterning and fringed ends made and worn in Azuay province. *See also* **bound-warp resist dyed.**

pick.   Short pointed tool used to strum the warp on a backstrap loom in order to help separate the even and odd warp yarns in order to open a shed for the passage of the weft. *See also* **backstrap loom; shed; warp; weft.**

pickup stick. Short, flat pointed stick used to aid in selecting warp yarns for patterning purposes. *See also* **warp.**

plain weave. The simplest possible interlacing of warp and weft elements in which each weft element passes alternately over and under successive elements (over one, under one), and each reverses the procedure of the one before it (Emery 1980: 76). *See* Fig. 1.1. *See also* **warp; weft.**

pollera (S.). Spanish-style gathered skirt sewn into a waistband. The lower edge may be embroidered, usually by machine.

poncho (S.). Man's overgarment consisting of a square or rectangle with a neck slit in the center. In Ecuador, ponchos are usually made of two loom panels sewn together, except in Salasaca, where they are a single panel.

raddle. A device with a row of spikes set into a wooden base that is used for spacing the warp while winding it onto a treadle loom. *See* Chap. 8, Fig. 8.14. *See also* **treadle loom; warp.**

reed. A rectangular framework with closely spaced slats, originally made of split reeds, but now often made of metal, through which the warp yarns pass on a treadle loom. The reed is mounted in the beater on the loom, but is detachable so that reeds with different spacing of the slats can be exchanged. The reed keeps the warp yarns evenly spaced as well as serving to beat in each new weft pass. *See* Chap. 8. *See also* **treadle loom; warp; weft.**

resist dyeing. A method of patterning yarns or cloth by protecting selected areas so that they are able to "resist" the dye when the material is immersed and remain undyed. *See* Chaps. 2, 3.

roller bar. A bar on a backstrap loom usually similar to the front loom bar, and placed next to it on top of the warp or woven fabric. The two bars are jointly rotated clockwise in order to shorten the warp and, on Ecuadorian looms, to secure it for weaving. Attaching the backstrap around the ends of the farther of the two bars and underneath the nearer one prevents the warp from unrolling. *See also* **backstrap loom; loom bars; warp.**

S-spun, S-plied. A way of describing the lie of the fibers in a spun or plied yarn. The slant is parallel to the slant of the midpoint of the letter *S* when the yarn is viewed vertically. *Compare* **Z-spun; Z-plied.**

selvedge. The edge of a fabric where the elements of one set reverse direction around the elements of the opposite set. Most woven fabrics have weft (side) selvedges parallel to the warp direction. Many Andean textiles woven on indigenous looms have warp (end) selvedges as well.

shaft. On a treadle loom, a rectangular frame containing the heddles ("harness" in North American handweaving terminology). *See also* **heddle; treadle loom.**

shed. In weaving, the opening created when selected warp yarns are lifted above others for the passage of the weft. *See also* **warp; weft.**

shedding device. Any device for raising or lowering groups of warp yarns to make a shed in weaving, including both heddles and shed rods or shafts. *See also* **heddle; shaft; shed rod; warp.**

shed rod. On the backstrap loom, a rod carrying the warp yarns not controlled by the heddles. For plain weave, every other warp yarn (those not controlled by heddles) passes over the shed rod. *See also* **backstrap loom; heddle; shed; warp.**

shuttle.   A stick or other device on which yarn to be used for weft is wound in order to make it easier to pass it through the shed during weaving. *See also* **shed; weft.**

stick shuttle.   Type of shuttle indigenous to the Americas, consisting of a slender straight stick around which the weft yarn is wound. *See* Fig. 1.27. *See also* **shuttle; weft.**

supplementary warp.   Extra set of warp yarns added between the ground-warp yarns. In Ecuador, it is floated either on the front of a fabric to create patterns or on the back between pattern areas. *See* Chap. 4. *See also* **float; warp.**

swift.   A rotating device, of European origin, for winding yarn from a skein into a ball or onto bobbins or warping spools, etc. *See* Fig. 8.17. *See also* **warping.**

sword.   In weaving, *sword* refers to a blade-shaped wooden implement that is used to help open the shed, to hold the shed open while the weft is inserted, and to beat in the weft. See Chap. 1. *See also* **shed; weft.**

synthetic dye.   Dye in which the coloring agent is chemically manufactured.

synthetic fiber.   Fiber manufactured from coal-tar derivatives. Examples include polyester, nylon, and acrylic.

tapestry.   Woven pictorial panel, usually made in tapestry weave, that is, weft-faced plain weave with the patterns created by reversing the direction of the weft yarns at the edges of each color area. *See also* **weft.** Tapestries are woven on treadle looms by both Otavalos and Salasacas for sale to tourists. *See* Fig. 8.10. *See also* **treadle loom.**

teasel.   The flower head of a thistle-related plant, *Dipsacus fullonum*, which is covered with stiff, hooked bracts. Usually a number of teasels are set into a wooden frame for use. Used to raise the nap on wool cloth. It is a European plant, introduced into Ecuador by the Spanish. *See* Figs. 1.31, 9.1.

tenter.   Stick pointed or with hooks on both ends that pierces the cloth at the side selvedges just below the working edge in order to maintain the width of the fabric being woven on a loom. *See also* **selvedge.**

treadle loom.   European-style loom in which the warp yarns are separated for the passage of the weft by depressing foot pedals or treadles. *See* Chap. 8. *See also* **weft.**

turn-banded 2/1 twill.   A warp-faced twill weave with a weft interlacing order of over two, under one (or vice versa), with the direction of the diagonal changing after every second weft, on a horizontal axis (horizontal herringbone), and with the face of the weave turned after every third (or fifth) weft yarn, creating a design of horizontal bands. *See* Chap. 5. *See also* **twill weave; weft.**

twill weave.   A weave with floats of consistent length in diagonal alignment. *See also* **float.**

vara (S.).   Old Spanish unit of measurement, equivalent to about 84 centimeters (33 inches).

walking wheel.   A type of simple spinning wheel, that is, a spindle wheel, in which a spindle is rotated by a drive band passing around the wheel. The size of the apparatus is such that it is operated by a person standing up. The spinner walks backwards as the yarn lengthens, and then forward as it is wound onto the spindle. It was introduced to Ecuador by the Spanish after the conquest, and in the 1980s, it was still being used in Imbabura province. *See* Meisch, Miller, and Rowe 2005: 91, fig. 24.

warp.   On a loom, the warp is the set of yarns stretched in place before the actual weaving process can begin. In a finished fabric, the warp is the longitudinal set of elements. *Compare* **weft.**

warp beam.   Beam at the back of a treadle loom around which the unwoven warp is wound. *See* Fig. 8.1. *See also* **treadle loom; warp.**

warp cross.   Alternation of warp yarns above or below each other in order to create sheds for weaving. *See also* **shed; warp.**

warp-faced.   In weaving, when the warp elements outnumber and hide the weft elements. *See also* **warp; weft.**

warping.   Process of winding yarn into a configuration where it is ready to be put on a loom for weaving. *See* Chaps. 1, 8. *See also* **warp.**

warp loops.   Open loops created by the turning of the warp yarns at the ends of a fabric. *See also* **warp.**

warp resist.   A patterning technique in which portions of the warp yarns are protected from the dye bath before weaving. A liquid may be applied or the yarns may be compressed by binding or clamping. In Ecuador, bound-warp resist is the usual technique. *See also* **warp.**

weaver's knot.   A special knot traditionally used by European weavers to tie warp ends together. In finished form it is like the sheet bend, but the method of tying it is different. We did not encounter this knot in Ecuador. *See* Ashley 1944: 78.

weft.   On a loom, the weft is inserted over and under the warp during the weaving process. In a finished fabric, the weft is the transverse set of elements. *Compare* **warp.**

weft-faced.   In weaving, when the weft elements outnumber and hide the warp elements. *See also* **tapestry; warp; weft.**

Z-spun, Z-plied.   A way of describing the lie of the fibers in a spun or plied yarn. The slant is parallel to the slant of the midpoint of the letter *Z* when the yarn is viewed vertically. *Compare* **S-spun, S-plied.**

zamarro or *zamarros* (S.).   Chaps, usually made of sheepskin with the fleece left on (e.g., in Chimborazo and Cañar provinces), but in Saraguro made of cloth.

References Cited

Acosta Solís, Misael
    1961   *Los bosques del Ecuador y sus productos.* Editorial Ecuador, Quito.

Alchon, Suzanne Austin
    1991   *Native Society and Disease in Colonial Ecuador.* Cambridge University Press, Cambridge.

Alsedo y Herrera, Dionisio
    1994   "Plano geográfico y hidrográfico del distrito de la Real Audiencia de Quito [y] de las provincias, gobiernos y corregimientos que se comprenden en su jurisdicción y las ciudades y villas, asientos y pueblos que ocupan sus territorios." *Relaciones histórico-geográficas de la Audiencia de Quito (siglo XVI–XIX),* ed. Pilar Ponce Leiva, vol. 2, pp. 418–464. Instituto de Historia y Antropología Andina and Abya-Yala, Quito. Written 1766.

Álvarez, Silvia G.
    1987   "Artesanías y tradición étnica en la Península de Santa Elena." *Artesanías de América,* no. 25, pp. 45–119. Centro Interamericano de Artesanías y Artes Populares (CIDAP), Cuenca.

Anonymous
    1923   "Tecnología indígena." *Inca,* vol. 1, no. 2, pp. 455–474. Museo de Arqueología de la Universidad Mayor de San Marcos, Lima. Written 1703.

Antúnez de Mayolo, Kay
    1989   "Peruvian Natural Dye Plants." *Economic Botany,* vol. 43, no. 2, pp. 181–191. New York Botanical Garden, Bronx.
    Ms   "Peruvian Natural Dyes and Coloring Sources: An Ethnobotanical Study." MS thesis, biological sciences, California Polytechnic State University, San Luis Obispo, 1976.

Ashley, Clifford W.
    1944   *The Ashley Book of Knots.* Doubleday and Company, Garden City, N.Y.

Barrett, Samuel A.
    1925   *The Cayapa Indians of Ecuador.* 2 vols. Indian Notes and Monographs, no. 40. Museum of the American Indian, Heye Foundation, New York.

Beals, Ralph L.
1966   *Community in Transition: Nayón, Ecuador.* Latin American Studies, vol. 2. Latin American Center, University of California, Los Angeles.

Bianchi, César
1982   *Artesanías y técnicas shuar.* Ediciones Mundo Shuar, Quito, Ecuador.

Bilgrami, Noorjehan
1990   *Sindh jo Ajrak.* Department of Culture and Tourism, Government of Sindh [Karachi?], Pakistan.

Blomberg, Rolf (ed.)
1952   *Ecuador: Andean Mosaic.* Hugo Gebers Förlag, Stockholm.

Bolland, Rita
1979   "Demonstration of Three Looms." *Looms and Their Products,* Irene Emery Roundtable on Museum Textiles, 1977 Proceedings, ed. Irene Emery and Patricia Fiske, pp. 69–75. The Textile Museum, Washington, DC.

Brédif, Josette
1989   *Printed French Fabrics: Toiles de Jouy.* Rizzoli, New York.

Bruhns, Karen Olsen
1990   "Prehispanic Weaving and Spinning Implements from Southern Ecuador." *The Textile Museum Journal,* vols. 27–28, 1988–1989, pp. 70–77. Washington, DC.

Bustos M., Gonzalo, and Magdalena Pilco J.
1987   *Chumbi: Diseños de fajas.* Ediciones Abya-Yala, Quito, Ecuador.

Cardale Schrimpff, Marianne
1977   "Weaving and Other Indigenous Textile Techniques in Colombia." *Ethnographic Textiles of the Western Hemisphere,* Irene Emery Roundtable on Museum Textiles, 1976 Proceedings, ed. Irene Emery and Patricia Fiske, pp. 44–60. The Textile Museum, Washington, DC.

Cárdenas, Martín
1969   *Manual de plantas económicas de Bolivia.* Imprenta Ichthus, Cochabamba.

Cardon, Dominique
2003   *Le monde des teintures naturelles.* Belin, Paris.

Cason, Marjorie, and Adele Cahlander
1976   *The Art of Bolivian Highland Weaving.* Watson-Guptill Publications, New York.

Català Roca, Francesc (photographs)
1981   *Arte popular de América.* Editorial Blume, Barcelona.

Cieza de León, Pedro de
1984   *Crónica del Perú, primera parte.* Pontificia Universidad Católica del Perú, Fondo Editorial; Academia Nacional de la Historia, Lima. Originally published by Martín de Montesdoca, 1553.

Clara de Guevara, Concepción
1975   "El añil de los indios cheles." *América Indígena,* vol. 35, no. 4, pp. 773–796. Instituto Indigenista Interamericano, Mexico City.

1976 *El añil, su artesanía actual en el departamento de Chalatenango.* Administración del Patrimonio Cultural, Sección de Investigaciones, Departamento de Etnografía, Colección Antropología, no. 4. Ministerio de Educación, San Salvador.

Cobo, Bernabé
1956 *Historia del Nuevo Mundo.* Biblioteca de Autores Españoles desde la Formación del Lenguaje hasta Nuestros Días, Continuación, vols. 91–92. Madrid. Finished 1653.

Collier Jr., John, and Aníbal Buitrón
1949 *The Awakening Valley.* University of Chicago Press, Chicago.

Colloredo-Mansfield, Rudi
1999 *The Native Leisure Class: Consumption and Cultural Creativity in the Andes.* University of Chicago Press, Chicago.

Cordero, Luis
1967 *Diccionario quichua: Quichua shimiyu panca.* 3rd ed. Proyecto de Educación Bilingüe Intercultural, Quito, Ecuador. Originally published 1895.

Cortés Moreno, Emilia
[1989] *Así éramos, así somos: Textiles y tintes de Nariño.* Banco de la República, Museo del Oro, Pasto, Colombia.

Costales, Piedad Peñaherrera de, and Alfredo Costales Samaniego
1959 *Los Salasacas.* Llacta, year IV, vol. III. Instituto Ecuatoriano de Antropología y Geografía, Quito, Ecuador.

Cushner, Nicholas P.
1982 *Farm and Factory: The Jesuits and the Development of Agrarian Capitalism in Colonial Quito, 1600–1767.* State University of New York Press, Albany.

Davis, Virginia
1991 "Resist Dyeing in Mexico: Comments on Its History, Significance, and Prevalence." *Textile Traditions of Mesoamerica and the Andes: An Anthology,* ed. Margot Blum Schevill, Janet Catherine Berlo, and Edward B. Dwyer, pp. 309–335. Garland Publishing, New York. Reprinted by the University of Texas Press, Austin, 1996.

De Bolle, Jacqueline and Marc G. De Bolle (eds.)
1994 *Rediscovery of Peruvian Textiles.* Lamandart Publishers, Ruiselede, Belgium.

De Lotto, G.
1974 "On the Status and Identity of the Cochineal Insects (Homoptera: Coccoidea: Dactylopiidae)." *Journal of the Entomological Society of Southern Africa,* vol. 37, no. 1, pp. 167–193. Pretoria.

Desrosiers, Sophie
1986 "An Interpretation of Technical Weaving Data Found in an Early 17th-century Chronicle." *The Junius B. Bird Conference on Andean Textiles,* April 7–8, 1984, ed. Ann Pollard Rowe, pp. 219–241. The Textile Museum, Washington, DC.

Diderot, Denis, and Jean le Rond d'Alembert (eds.)

1751–1772 *Encyclopédie, ou Dictionnaire raisonné de sciences, des arts et des métiers.* 28 vols. André Le Blanc and David Durand Briasson, Paris.

1782–1832 *Encyclopédie méthodique ou par ordre des matières.* 166 vols. Charles Joseph Panckoucke, Paris.

Donkin, R. A.

1977 *Spanish Red: An Ethnogeographical Study of Cochineal and the Opuntia Cactus.* Transactions of the American Philosophical Society, vol. 67, pt. 5. Philadelphia.

Emery, Irene

1980 *The Primary Structures of Fabrics: An Illustrated Classification.* The Textile Museum, Washington, DC. Originally published 1966.

Fabish, Joseph, and Lynn Meisch

2006 "A Tale of Survival: Textiles of Huamachuco, Peru," *Hali,* issue 147, July–August, pp. 55–57. Hali Publications, London.

Fannin, Allen

1979 *Handloom Weaving Technology.* Van Nostrand Reinhold Company, New York.

Fester, Gustavo A.

1954 "Some Dyes of an Ancient South American Civilization." *Dyestuffs,* vol. 40, no. 9, pp. 238–244. National Aniline Division, Allied Chemical and Dye Corporation, New York.

Franquemont, Edward M.

1991 "Dual-Lease Weaving: An Andean Loom Technology." *Textile Traditions of Mesoamerica and the Andes: An Anthology,* ed. Margot Blum Schevill, Janet Catherine Berlo, and Edward B. Dwyer, pp. 283–308. Garland Publishing, New York. Reprinted by the University of Texas Press, Austin, 1996.

Gade, Daniel W.

1972 "Red Dye from Peruvian Bugs." *The Geographical Magazine,* vol. 45, no. 1, pp. 58–62. Geographical Press, London.

1975 *Plants, Man and the Land in the Vilcanota Valley of Peru.* Biogeographica, vol. 6. Dr. W. Junk B.V., Publishers, The Hague.

1979 "Past Glory and Present Status of Cochineal." *The Geographical Review,* vol. 69, no. 3, pp. 353–354. American Geographical Society, New York.

Garcilaso de la Vega, "El Inca"

1945 *Comentarios reales de los Incas.* 2 vols. 2nd ed. Emecé Editores, Buenos Aires. Originally published 1609.

1966 *Royal Commentaries of the Incas and General History of Peru.* 2 vols. Trans. Harold V. Livermore. University of Texas Press, Austin.

Gardner, Joan S.

1979 "Pre-Columbian Textiles from Ecuador: Conservation Procedures and Preliminary Study." *Technology and Conservation,* vol. 4, no. 1, pp. 24–30. The Technology Organization, Boston.

1982 "Textiles precolombinos del Ecuador." *Miscelánea Antropológica Ecuatoriana,* no. 2, pp. 24–30. Museo del Banco Central, Cuenca, Guayaquil, Quito. Translation of Gardner 1979, but with some different illustrations.

1985 "Pre-Columbian Textiles, Los Ríos Province, Ecuador." *National Geographic Society Research Reports*, vol. 18 (grants in the year 1977), ed. Winfield Swanson, pp. 327–342. Washington, DC.

Gerber, Frederick H.

1977 *Indigo and the Antiquity of Dyeing.* Author-published, Ormond Beach, Florida.

1978 *Cochineal and the Insect Dyes.* Author-published, Ormond Beach, Florida.

1983 "The Chemistry and Use of Indigo: The Mystery Removed." *Surface Design Journal*, vol. 8, no. 2, pp. 23–27. Surface Design Association, Fayetteville, Tennessee.

González Holguín, Diego

1608 *Vocabvlario de la lengva general de todo el Perv llamada lengva qquichua, o del Inca.* Corregido y renovado conforme a la propriedad cortesana del Cuzco. Francisco del Canto, Lima. Reprinted by the Instituto de Historia, Lima, 1952.

Grieder, Terence; Alberto Bueno Mendoza; C. Earle Smith Jr.; and Robert M. Malina

1988 *La Galgada, Peru: A Preceramic Culture in Transition.* University of Texas Press, Austin.

Guaman Poma de Ayala, Felipe

1936 *Nueva corónica y buen gobierno* (Codex péruvien illustré). Facsimile, Université de Paris, Travaux et Mémoires de l'Institut d'Ethnologie, 23, Paris. Finished 1615.

Haenke, Tadeo

1909 *Introducción a la historia natural de la provincia de Cochabamba.* Sociedad Geográfica de La Paz, La Paz. Originally published 1798.

Hagino, Jane Parker, and Karen E. Stothert

1984 "Weaving a Cotton Saddlebag on the Santa Elena Peninsula of Ecuador." *The Textile Museum Journal*, vol. 22, 1983, pp. 19–32. Washington, DC.

Handweaver and Craftsman

1959 "Indian Textiles from Ecuador." *Handweaver and Craftsman*, vol. 10, no. 1, pp. 19–21, 56. New York.

Harrison, Regina

1989 *Signs, Songs, and Memory in the Andes: Translating Quechua Language and Culture.* University of Texas Press, Austin.

Harvey, Virginia I.

1972 "Pattern with the Overhand Knot I." *Threads in Action*, vol. 4, no. 1, pp. 4–7. Author-published, Freeland, Washington.

Hassaurek, Friedrich

1867 *Four Years among Spanish-Americans.* Hurd and Houghton, New York.

1967 *Four Years among the Ecuadorians.* Southern Illinois University Press, Carbondale. Condensed republication of Hassaurek 1867.

Herrera, Fortunato L.
1940 "Plantas que curan y plantas que matan de la flora del Cuzco." *Revista del Museo Nacional*, vol. 9, no. 1, pp. 73–127. Lima.

Hoffman, Marta
1979 "Old European Looms." *Looms and Their Products*, Irene Emery Roundtable on Museum Textiles, 1977 Proceedings, ed. Irene Emery and Patricia Fiske, pp. 19–24. The Textile Museum, Washington, DC.

Jaramillo Cisneros, Hernán
1981 *Inventario de diseños en tejidos indígenas de la provincia de Imbabura.* 2 vols. Colección Pendoneros 48 and 49. Instituto Otavaleño de Antropología, Otavalo.
1984 "Colorantes naturales en el Ecuador." *Artesanías de América*, no. 15. Centro Interamericano de Artesanías y Artes Populares, Cuenca.
1988a *Textiles y tintes.* Centro Interamericano de Artesanías y Artes Populares, Cuenca. Includes Jaramillo 1984.
1988b "La técnica ikat en Imbabura: Un aporte para su conocimiento," *Sarance*, no. 12, pp. 151–174. Instituto Otavaleño de Antropología, Otavalo. Also published in *Ecuador indígena: Estudios arqueológicos y etnográficos de la Sierra Norte*, pp. 151–174. Instituto Otavaleño de Antropología, Otavalo and Ediciones Abya-Yala, Quito.
1989 "El teñido de lana con cochinilla en Salasaca, Tungurahua." *Sarance*, no. 13, pp. 19–31. Instituto Otaveleño de Antropología, Otavalo. Also in Jaramillo 1988a.
1990 "Técnicas textiles artesanales en Imbabura," *Sarance*, no. 14, pp. 21–40. Instituto Otavaleño de Antropología, Otavalo. Also published in *Ecuador indígena: Antropología y relaciones interétnicas*, pp. 21–40. Ediciones Abya-Yala, Quito and Instituto Otavaleño de Antropología, Otavalo.
1991 *Artesanía textil de la sierra norte del Ecuador.* Instituto Otavaleño de Antropología, Otavalo, and Abya-Yala, Quito, Ecuador. Includes Jaramillo 1988b and 1990.

Johnson, Irmgard Weitlaner
1977 "Old Style Wrap-around skirts Woven by Zapotec Indians of Mitla, Oaxaca." *Ethnographic Textiles of the Western Hemisphere*, Irene Emery Roundtable on Museum Textiles, 1976 Proceedings, ed. Irene Emery and Patricia Fiske, pp. 238–255. The Textile Museum, Washington, DC.
1979 "The Ring-Warp Loom in Mexico." *Looms and Their Products*, Irene Emery Roundtable on Museum Textiles, 1977 Proceedings, ed. Irene Emery and Patricia Fiske, pp. 135–159. The Textile Museum, Washington, DC.

Juan, Jorge, and Antonio de Ulloa
1748 *Relación histórica del viaje a la América meridional.* 2 vols. Antonio Marín, Madrid. Facsimile: Fundación Universitaria Española, Madrid, 1978.
1964 *A Voyage to South America 1734–1744.* The 1806 John Adams translation, abridged. Alfred A. Knopf, New York.

Kajitani, Nobuko
1980 "Traditional Dyes in Indonesia." *Indonesian Textiles*, Irene Emery Round-

table on Museum Textiles, 1979 Proceedings, ed. Mattiebelle Gittinger, pp. 305–325. The Textile Museum, Washington, DC.

Kane, Joe
1996   *Savages*. Random House, New York.

King, Mary Elizabeth
1965   *Textiles and Basketry of the Paracas Period, Ica Valley, Peru*. PhD dissertation, anthropology, University of Arizona. University Microfilms, Ann Arbor, Mich.

Klumpp, Kathleen M.
1983   "Una tejedora en Manabí." *Miscelánea Antropológica Ecuatoriana*, no. 3, pp. 77–88. Museos del Banco Central del Ecuador, Cuenca, Guayaquil, Quito.

Larson, Katherine
2001   *The Woven Coverlets of Norway*. University of Washington Press, Seattle, in association with Nordic Heritage Museum, Seattle.

Liles, James N.
1990   *The Art and Craft of Natural Dyeing: Traditional Recipes for Modern Use*. University of Tennessee Press, Knoxville.

Macbride, J. Francis
1943   *Leguminosae*. Flora of Peru, Botanical Series, vol. 13, pt. 3, no. 1. Field Museum of Natural History, Chicago.

Madsen, Jens E.
1989   *Cactaceae*. Flora of Ecuador, vol. 35. Systematic Botany, Göteborg University, and the Section for Botany, Riksmuseum, Stockholm, in cooperation with Pontificia Universidad Católica del Ecuador, Quito, Ecuador.

Mariano Moziño, D. José
1976   *Tratado del xiquilite y añil de Guatemala*. Administración del Patrimonio Cultural, Colección Antropología e Historia, no. 5. Ministerio de Educación, San Salvador.

Martin, Lois
1993   "Latin American Ikats and Islamic Precedents." *Surface Design Journal*, vol. 18, no. 1, pp. 12–15, 33. Surface Design Association, Oakland, California.

Medlin, Mary Ann
1986   "Learning to Weave in Calcha, Bolivia." *The Junius B. Bird Conference on Andean Textiles*, April 7–8, 1984, ed. Ann Pollard Rowe, pp. 275–287. The Textile Museum, Washington, DC.

Meier, Peter C.
1985   "Los artesanos textiles de la región de Otavalo." *Sarance*, no. 10, pp. 127–147. Instituto Otavaleño de Antropología, Otavalo.

Meisch, Lynn A.
1980   "Spinning in Ecuador." *Spin-Off*, vol. 4, pp. 24–29. Interweave Press, Loveland, Colorado.
1981a "Paños: Ikat Shawls of the Cuenca Valley." *Interweave White Paper*, vol. 1, no. 2. Loveland, Colorado.

1981b "Abel Rodas: The Last Ikat Poncho Weaver in Chordeleg." *El Palacio,* vol. 87, no. 4, pp. 27-32. The Museum of New Mexico, Santa Fe.
1982 "Costume and Weaving in Saraguro, Ecuador." *The Textile Museum Journal,* vols. 19-20, 1980-81, pp. 55-64. Washington, DC.
1986 "Weaving Styles in Tarabuco, Bolivia." *The Junius B. Bird Conference on Andean Textiles,* April 7-8, 1984, ed. Ann Pollard Rowe, pp. 243-274. The Textile Museum, Washington, DC.
1987 *Otavalo: Weaving, Costume and the Market.* Ediciones Libri Mundi, Quito, Ecuador.

Meisch, Lynn A.; Laura M. Miller; and Ann P. Rowe
2005 "Spinning in Highland Ecuador." *The Textile Museum Journal,* vols. 42-43, 2003-2004, pp. 76-97. Washington, DC.

Menzel, Dorothy
1964 "Style and Time in the Middle Horizon." *Ñawpa Pacha* 2, pp. 1-105. Institute of Andean Studies, Berkeley.

Miller, Laura M.
1989 "Tradiciones de los paños de ikat en el norte del Perú y el sur del Ecuador." *Artesanías de América,* no. 28, pp. 15-41. Centro Interamericano de Artesanías y Artes Populares (CIDAP), Cuenca.
1991 "The Ikat Shawl Traditions of Northern Peru and Southern Ecuador." *Textile Traditions of Mesoamerica and the Andes: An Anthology,* ed. Margot Blum Schevill, Janet Catherine Berlo, and Edward B. Dwyer, pp. 337-358. Garland Publishing, New York. Translation of Miller 1989. Reprinted by the University of Texas Press, Austin, 1996.

Miller, Laura M., and Proyecto Juvenil de Historia Oral
1986 *La caja ronca: Historia oral de los artesanos del cantón Gualaceo.* Cuadernos de Cultura Popular, no. 10. Centro Interamericano de Artesanías y Artes Populares, Cuenca.

Miller, Laura M.; Mrill Ingram; Ann P. Rowe; and Lynn A. Meisch
2005 "Leaf Fibers in Highland Ecuador." *The Textile Museum Journal,* vols. 42-43, 2003-2004, pp. 56-75. Washington, DC.

Montell, Gösta
1929 *Dress and Ornaments in Ancient Peru: Archaeological and Historical Studies.* Elanders Boktryckeri Aktiebolag, Göteborg, Sweden.

Monzón, Luis de
1881 "Descripción de la tierra del Repartimiento de los Rucanas Antamarcas de la corona real, jurisdicción de la ciudad de Guamanga, año de 1586." *Relaciones geográficas de Indias,* ed. M. Jiménez de la Espada, vol. 1, pp. 197-216. Ministerio de Fomento, Madrid.

Moreno Yánez, Segundo E.
1985 *Sublevaciones indígenas en la audiencia de Quito: Desde comienzos del siglo XVIII hasta finales de la colonia.* 3rd ed. Ediciones de la Universidad Católica, Quito, Ecuador.

Murúa, Martín de
1964 *Historia general del Perú.* Colección Joyas Bibliográficas, Biblioteca Americana Vetus, vol. 2. Instituto Gonzalo Fernández de Oviedo, Madrid. Manuscript dated 1613.

Nachtigall, Horst
1955 *Tierradentro; Archäologie und Etnographie einer kolumbianischen Landschaft.* Mainzer Studien zur Kultur und Völkerkunde, Band 2. Institutes für Völkerkunde and Johannes Gutenberg-Universität in Mainz, Rhein, Origo-Verlag, Zurich.

Nason, Marilee Schmit
2005 "Blouse Making in Mariano Acosta, Ecuador." *The Textile Museum Journal,* vols. 42–43, 2002–2004, pp. 108–113. Washington, DC.

Pablos, Hernando
1897 "Relacion que enbio a mandar su Magestad se hiziese desta ciudad de Cuenca y de toda su provincia." *Relaciones geográficas de Indias,* ed. M. Jiménez de la Espada, vol. 3, pp. 155–163. Ministerio de Fomento, Madrid. Written 1582.

Parsons, Elsie Clews
1945 *Peguche, Canton of Otavalo, Province of Imbabura, Ecuador: A Study of Andean Indians.* University of Chicago Press, Chicago.

Paz Ponce de León, Sancho de
1897 "Relación y descripción de los pueblos de partido de Otavalo." *Relaciones geográficas de Indias,* ed. M. Jiménez de la Espada, vol. 3, pp. 105–120. Ministerio de Fomento, Madrid. Written 1582. Reprinted 1965, vol. 2, pp. 233–242. Ediciones Atlas, Madrid.

Penley, Dennis
1988 *Paños de Gualaceo.* Bilingual ed. English translation by Lynn Hirschkind. Centro Interamericano de Artesanías y Artes Populares, Cuenca.

Pérez Guerra, Gema, and Michael Kosztarab
1992 *Biosystematics of the Family Dactylopiidae (Homoptera: Coccinea) with Emphasis on the Life Cycle of Dactylopius coccus Costa.* Studies on the Morphology and Systematics of Scale Insects, no. 16, Bulletin 92-1, Virginia Agricultural Experiment Station, Virginia Polytechnic Institute and State University, Blacksburg.

Pfyffer, Marguerite Gritli
2002 *Ikat Textiles of the Andes.* CD-ROM. Babyl-One, Arbre d'Or Editions, Fougères, France. www.arbredor.com.

Quinatoa Cotacachi de Ayala, Estelina
1982 *Alejandro Quinatoa S.* Museo del Banco Central del Ecuador and Oficina de la Secretaría General de la Organización de los Estados Americanos en el Ecuador, Quito.

Redwood
1973 *Backstrap Weaving of Northern Ecuador.* Author-published, Santa Cruz, California.

Requena y Herrera, Francisco
1994 "Descripción histórica y geográfica de la provincia de Guayaquil, en el Virreinato de Santa Fe." *Relaciones histórico-geográficas de la Audiencia de Quito (Siglo XVI–XIX)*, ed. Pilar Ponce Leiva, vol. 2, pp. 502–652. Instituto de Historia y Antropología Andina and Abya-Yala, Quito, Ecuador. Written 1774.

Ríos, M., and H. Borgtoft Pedersen (eds.)
1991 *Las plantas y el hombre*. Ediciones Abya-Yala, Quito, Ecuador.

Rivera, Pedro de, and Antonio de Chaves y de Guevara
1881 "Relación general de la disposición y calidad de la provincia de Guamanga, llamada San Joan de la Frontera y de la vivienda y costumbres de los naturales della, año de 1557." *Relaciones geográficas de Indias*, ed. M. Jiménez de la Espada, vol. 1, pp. 96–138. Written 1557. Ministerio de Fomento, Madrid.

Rodriguez-Saona, Luis E., M. Mónica Giusti, and Ronald E. Wrolstad
1998 "Anthocyanin Pigment Composition of Red-fleshed Potatoes," *Journal of Food Science*, vol. 63, no. 3, pp. 458–465. Institute of Food Technologists, Chicago.

Roquero, Ana
2006 *Tintes y tintoreros de América: Catálogo de materias primas y registro etnográfico de México, Centro América, Andes Centrales y Selva Amazónica*. Ministerio de Cultura, Madrid.

Ross, Gary
1986 "The Bug in the Rug." *Natural History*, March, pp. 67–73. American Museum of Natural History, New York.

Rowe, Ann Pollard
1975 "Weaving Processes in the Cuzco Area of Peru." *Textile Museum Journal*, vol. 4, no. 2, pp. 30–46. Washington, DC.
1977 *Warp-patterned Weaves of the Andes*. The Textile Museum, Washington, DC.
1985 "After Emery: Further Considerations of Fabric Classification and Terminology." *The Textile Museum Journal*, vol. 23, 1984, pp. 53–71. Washington, DC.
1992 "Provincial Inca Tunics of the South Coast of Peru." *The Textile Museum Journal*, vol. 31, pp. 5–52. Washington, DC.
1997 "Inca Weaving and Costume." *The Textile Museum Journal*, vols. 34–35, 1995–1996, pp. 4–53. Washington, DC.

Rowe, Ann Pollard (ed.)
1998 *Costume and Identity in Highland Ecuador*. Text by Lynn A. Meisch, Laura M. Miller, Ann P. Rowe, and others. The Textile Museum, Washington, DC, and University of Washington Press, Seattle.

Rowe, Ann Pollard, and Breenan Conterón
2005 "Felt Hat Making in Highland Ecuador." *The Textile Museum Journal*, vols. 42–43, 2003–2004, pp. 114–119. Washington, DC.

Rowe, Ann Pollard, and Lynn A. Meisch
2005 "Panama Hat Making in Highland Ecuador." *The Textile Museum Journal*, vols. 42–43, 2003–2004, pp. 120–128. Washington, DC.

Rowe, John Howland
  1946 "Inca Culture at the Time of the Spanish Conquest." *Handbook of South American Indians*, ed. Julian H. Steward, vol. 2, *The Andean Civilizations*, pp. 183–330. Bulletin 143, Bureau of American Ethnology, Smithsonian Institution, Washington, DC.
  Ms   "The Incas in Quito." Manuscript written for publication in *History of Indigenous Costume in Highland Ecuador*, ed. Ann P. Rowe.

Rubio Sánchez, Manuel
  1974 *Historia del añil o xiquilite en Centro-América*. 2 vols. Dirección de Publicaciones, Ministerio de Educación, San Salvador.

Salinas Loyola, Juan de
  1897 "Relación y descripción de la ciudad de Loxa." *Relaciones geográficas de Indias*, ed. M. Jiménez de la Espada, vol. 3, pp. 197–220. Ministerio de Fomento, Madrid. Written 1573. Reprinted 1965, vol. 2, pp. 291–306. Ediciones Atlas, Madrid.

Salomon, Frank
  1986 *Native Lords of Quito in the Age of the Incas: The Political Economy of North Andean Chiefdoms*. Cambridge Studies in Social Anthropology 59. Cambridge University Press, Cambridge.

Saltzman, Max
  1978 "The Identification of Dyes in Archaeological and Ethnographic Textiles." *Archaeological Chemistry 2*, ed. Giles F. Carter, pp. 172–185. American Chemical Society, Washington, DC.
  1986 "Analysis of Dyes in Museum Textiles, or, You Can't Tell a Dye by Its Color." *Textile Conservation Symposium in Honor of Pat Reeves*, February 1, 1986, ed. Catherine C. McLean and Patricia Connell, pp. 27–39. The Conservation Center, Los Angeles County Museum of Art, Los Angeles.

Schjellerup, Inge
  1980 *Inkapigens vaev: Vaevning og indianere i Peru*. Nationalmuseet, Copenhagen.
  1988 "Live continuidad de la tradición textil en Cochabamba (Amazonas)." *Revista del Museo Nacional de Antropología y Arqueología*, no. 3, pp. 58–77. Instituto Nacional de Cultura, Lima.

Schweppe, Helmut
  1992 *Handbuch der Naturfarbstoffe: Vorkommen, Verwendung, Nachweis*. Ecomed, Landsberg/Lech.

Slater, Deborah
  1972 "Norman Kennedy—Weaver at Williamsburg." *Handweaver and Craftsman*, vol. 23, no. 1, pp. 23–25. New York.

Sotelo Narváez, Pedro
  1885 "Relacion de las provincias de Tucuman." *Relaciones geográficas de Indias*, ed. M. Jiménez de Espada, vol. 2, pp. 143–153. Ministerio de Fomento, Madrid. Written 1583.

Soukup, Jaroslav
  1971 *Vocabulario de los nombres vulgares de la flora peruana*. Colegio Salesiano, Lima.

Speiser, Noémi
1983 *The Manual of Braiding*. Author-published, Basel, Switzerland.

Spier, Hans Peter, and Christian Biederbick
1980 *Árboles y leñosas para reforestar las tierras altas de la región interandina del Ecuador*. 2nd ed. Cuadernos de Capacitación Popular, no. 4. Comisión Asesora Ambiental de la Presidencia, Quito, Ecuador.

Stevenson, William Bennett
1825 *Historical and Descriptive Narrative of Twenty Years Residence in South America*. 3 vols. Hurst, Robinson, and Co., London.

Stothert, Karen
1997 "El arte de hilar en algodón: Una tradición milenaria ecuatoriana." *Cultura*, segunda época, no. 2, pp. 3–9. Ediciones del Banco Central del Ecuador, Guayaquil, Quito, Cuenca.
2005 "Shellfish Purple in Coastal Ecuador." *The Textile Museum Journal*, vols. 42–43, 2003–2004, pp. 98–107. Washington, DC.

Stothert, Karen, and Ana Maritza Freire
1997 *Sumpa: Historia de la península de Santa Elena*. Museo los Amantes de Sumpa, Banco Central del Ecuador, Plan Internacional Guayaquil, Santa Elena.

Stothert, Karen E., and Jane Parker
1984 "El tejido de una alforja en la península de Santa Elena." *Miscelánea Antropológica Ecuatoriana* 4, pp. 141–159. Museo del Banco Central, Cuenca, Guayaquil, Quito, Ecuador. Translation of Hagino and Stothert 1984.

Stübel, Alfons, and Wilhelm Reiss
1888 *Indianer-Typen aus Ecuador und Colombia*. Den mitgliedern des VII. Internationalen Amerikanisten-Kongresses, Berlin.

Sturtevant, William C.
1977 "The Hole and Slot Heddle." *Ethnographic Textiles of the Western Hemisphere*, Irene Emery Roundtable on Museum Textiles, 1976 Proceedings, ed. Irene Emery and Patricia Fiske, pp. 325–355. The Textile Museum, Washington, DC.

Tyrer, Robson Brines
1976 *The Demographic and Economic History of the Audiencia of Quito: Indian Population and the Textile Industry, 1600–1800*. PhD dissertation, history, University of California, Berkeley. University Microfilms, Ann Arbor, Mich.

Uhle, Max
1903 *Pachacamac: Report of the William Pepper, M.D., LL.D., Peruvian Expedition of 1896*. Department of Archaeology, University of Pennsylvania, Philadelphia. Reprinted by University Museum of Archaeology and Anthropology, University of Pennsylvania, Philadelphia, 1991.

Wallert, Arie, and Ran Boytner
1996 "Dyes from the Tumilaca and Chiribaya Cultures, South Coast of Peru." *Journal of Archaeological Science*, vol. 23, pp. 853–861. Academic Press, London and New York.

Wardle, H. Newell
  1936 "Belts and Girdles of the Inca's Sacrificed Women." *Revista del Museo Nacional*, vol. 5, no. 1, pp. 25–38. Lima.

Wolf, Teodoro
  1976 *Geografía y geología del Ecuador.* Casa de la Cultura Ecuatoriana, Quito. Originally published 1892.

Wouters, Jan, and André Verhecken
  1989 "The Coccid Insect Dyes: HPLC and Computerized Diode-Array Analysis of Dyed Yarns." *Studies in Conservation*, vol. 34, no. 4, pp. 189–200. International Institute for Conservation of Historic and Artistic Works, London.

Yacovleff, Eugenio, and Fortunato L. Herrera
  1934–1935 "El mundo vegetal de los antiguos peruanos." *Revista del Museo Nacional*, vol. 3, no. 3, pp. 241–322; vol. 4, no. 1, pp. 29–102, Lima.

Yacovleff, Eugenio, and Jorge C. Muelle
  1934 "Notas al trabajo 'Colorantes de Paracas.'" *Revista del Museo Nacional*, vol. 3, nos. 1–2, pp. 157–163. Lima.

Young, William J.
  1957 "Appendix III: Analysis of Textile Dyes." *Late Nazca Burials in Chaviña, Peru*, by Samuel K. Lothrop and Joy Mahler. Papers of the Peabody Museum of Archaeology and Ethnology, vol. 50, no. 1, pp. 53–54. Harvard University, Cambridge.

Zelaya, Juan Antonio
  1994 "Estado de la provincia de Guayaquil." *Relaciones histórico-geográficas de la Audiencia de Quito (siglo XVI–XIX)*, ed. Pilar Ponce Leiva, vol. 2, pp. 361–368. Instituto de Historia y Antropología Andina and Abya Yala, Quito, Ecuador. Written 1765.

Contributors

ANN POLLARD ROWE, curator of Western Hemisphere collections, The Textile Museum, Washington, DC.

LAURA MARTIN MILLER, MD, Oakland, California

LYNN ANN MEISCH, professor of anthropology, Saint Mary's College of California, Moraga

RUDI COLLOREDO-MANSFIELD, associate professor of anthropology, University of Iowa, Iowa City

Index

Page numbers in italics refer to maps and figures. Plate numbers refer to color plates.